# Issues in Economics

## An Introduction

James B. Herendeen

UNIVERSITY PRESS OF AMERICA,® INC.
*Lanham • Boulder • New York • Toronto • Plymouth, UK*

**University Press of America,® Inc.**
4501 Forbes Boulevard
Suite 200
Lanham, Maryland 20706
UPA Acquisitions Department (301) 459-3366

Estover Road
Plymouth PL6 7PY
United Kingdom


Printed in the United States of America
British Library Cataloging in Publication Information Available

Library of Congress Control Number: 2006933351
ISBN-13: 978-0-7618-3613-1 (paperback : alk. paper)
ISBN-10: 0-7618-3613-6 (paperback : alk. paper)

∞™ The paper used in this publication meets the minimum requirements of American National Standard for Information Sciences—Permanence of Paper for Printed Library Materials, ANSI Z39.48—1984

To: Jack and Ann
Best regards
Jim [illegible]

This book is dedicated to my grandchildren:
Jamie and Daniel Wojtowicz and Parker and Fiona Walther

# Contents

# List of Figures

# List of Tables

# Preface

This book is aimed at students in the one semester course in economics for non-business or non-economics majors. It could also be used as a supplement to standard two semester principles of economics textbooks. Graphs and equation have been kept to a minimum so as not to discourage introductory students, most of who will not take another economics course. Graphs and equations are a great tool in economics because they are a special language that economists use to communicate with each other. They allow a level precision, clarity, and simplification for those who know the language that could not be attained using Standard English. Unfortunately they narrow the audience to the specialist, and to students in the discipline. The challenge of doing a book like this is to be able to develop the key ideas of economics with the minimum use of graphs and equations. A few tables have been included where some numerical data seems useful.

The book is structured around major policy issues and the book has been divided into Micro Issues and Macro Issues. The first three chapters are basically an introduction into the subject matter of economics with emphasis on theory, institutions and policy. The idea being first, that you can't intelligently discuss policy issues without first having some understanding of the theory and second, you can't intelligently discuss policy without some understanding of our basic economic, financial, political and social institutions. Theory and institutions becomes the framework for policy analysis. The second part of the book gives an introduction to micro theory (supply and demand, cost of production and theory of firm and theory of markets) and then discusses several micro policy issues In the third part of the book the first chapter is "Measuring Economic Activity" and the second is "Aggregate Supply and Demand." The first develops the accounting framework on which macroeconomics is based. The second develops the concepts of aggregate supply and demand and the concept of normal output around which short-run output fluctuates with shifts in demand and short run supply. Again, the intent is to develop these concepts with a minimum of graphs or equations. The rest of part II deals with specific policy issues.

# Acknowledgments

The author would like to acknowledge the help and encouragement of several colleagues at The University of Texas at El Paso. Special thanks go to Professor Tim Roth, who offered helpful comments on Chapter 14 as well as on several Seminars that I have given over the years in the College of Business Seminar Series and also to the Rio Grande Economics Association. These seminars served as the basis for Chapters 7, 9, 12, 14, and 20. I would also like to acknowledge the helpful comments on several Chapters by Professor Tom Fullerton and the encouragement and help of Professor, Mo Adam Mahmoud. Also, I would like to thank my former colleague at Penn State, Professor Emeritus, Milton Hallberg. I would also like to acknowledge Lakshmi Narayan who did the computer work for the figures, and Jim Earley who did the index. In addition, I would like to thank my editors at University Press of America: David Chao, Brian DeRocco, and Beverly Baum. Any faults of course are all mine.

# *Part I*

# INTRODUCTION TO ECONOMIC ISSUES

# *Chapter One*

# Introduction to Economics

## WHAT IS ECONOMICS?

What is economics? Economics has been defined as the study of how society allocates scarce resources among alternative uses. For the non-specialist in economics this definition is not very useful. A better definition might be that economics studies how society organizes production, consumption, and distribution. In other words what goods and services will be produced, how will they be produced and who will produce them? Second, who gets to consume (or use) the goods and services produced and how do we provide for future consumption? Third, how is the income generated by production distributed to the various participants (and sometimes non-participants) in the production process? These are the types of questions that are asked and answered in this book.

Next we can divide economics into to two primary fields. First microeconomics. Microeconomics is the study of the theory of the firm, the theory of the household and the theory of how firms and households interact through markets. We define two broad classes of markets: Output markets where firms supply output to households or other demanders of goods or services. The interaction of the two through markets determines output prices and quantities of outputs produced. The other types of markets are called input markets. In input markets, firms hire (demand) various inputs used in the production process. These inputs include labor services, the services of capital goods, the services of land, the services of raw materials, the services of marketing and distribution, etc. The interaction of firm demanders and input suppliers through input markets determines prices and quantities of inputs hired. In addition we can classify markets for various types of industries such as the auto industry, the computer industry, the meat industry, etc. On the input side we have markets for autoworkers, for computer chips, for feed grains to produce cattle for the meat industry. Also in microeconomics we look at government policies aimed at specific industries or markets such as agriculture, banking, labor, financial securities, etc.

Second, we have macroeconomics which is concerned with the determination of aggregate (total) output for the economy (or its rate of growth), with the level of total employment (or the unemployment rate), with the general level of prices (or its rate change, the rate of inflation) and with the exchange rate (or its rate of change) between the domestic currency and with currencies of other countries with whom we trade. In macroeconomics we are also concerned with government policies that might affect the aggregate economy.

## HOW SOCIETY COORDINATES ECONOMIC ACTIVITY

Society coordinates economic activity in basically three way: through the market process; through the political process; and though the administrative process. The market process is the primary concern of economists. Markets coordinate economic activity through the invisible hand of the market. It coordinates between producers and their customers (through output markets) and between producers and their suppliers (through input markets). The wheat farmer in South Dakota decides how much wheat to grow based on how much land and equipment he has, how much it cost him for fertilizer, seed, gasoline and other inputs and what he expects the price of wheat to be when he harvests the crop. He in turn sells the wheat to (or stores it with) a grain elevator business. The grain elevator buys or stores wheat based on its storage capacity and its expected costs and on what it expects to sell the wheat for. In turn the grain elevator sells the wheat to a miller or to an exporter. The miller sells the wheat to a food processor. The food processor sells the processed foods to a food wholesaler. Eventually the wheat ends up on the shelves of grocery stores as Wheaties, as flour, as baked goods, as frozen pizza, or as macaroni or spaghetti. Or it may end in a restaurant in the form of pizza, spaghetti, bread or baked goods. Much of our wheat is exported and it may end up on the grocery shelves in China or eaten by an American tourist in a Chinese restaurant. And if markets are competitive the wheat and wheat products will be supplied at a cost to consumers that reflects the cost of production at each of the stages and allows only a normal rate of return on producers invested capital. That is the glory of the market when it works properly. The products end up with consumers with no central plan or explicit direction. We will return to the market in latter chapters.

The second primary way that society coordinates economic decisions is through the political process. The political process provides public goods such as national defense, or the legal and court system or national parks. It also determines macroeconomic policies such as monetary policy of the Federal Reserve System or income redistribution through Social Security or Medicare. In general the political system provides the rules of the game under which the market system and the administrative system operates.

The political system coordinates between political decision makers (primarily elected politicians) and their constituents. The constituents make up two broad classes. First there is the electorate who has a veto power over who gets elected or doesn't get elected. The electorate varies with the political office. For the mayor it is a city electorate; for a US Congressman it is the electorate of his congressional district. For a US Senator it is a statewide electorate. For the President and Vice President it is a national electorate. The President plays a unique role in the US system in part because he (along with the Vice President) is the only elected official who has a national electoral constituency.

The second class of constituents is made up of various interest groups that organize to get access to the political decision making process. Interest goups include both public and private interests and economic and non-economic interests. Large group interests, such as labor unions, farm interest groups, and the National Association of Retired People offer to politicians several things. First votes. In close elections they may be able to deliver enough votes to defeat or elect a candidate.

Second, there is organizational and informational support. They can help get voters to the polls and they can provide information or sometimes disinformation about the issues. Third, they can form coalitions with other interest groups to increase their political power. Last, they can furnish money. Elections are financed primarily out of contribution by organized groups, by corporate or non-profit donors, by wealthy individuals and by small contributors. Interest groups have access primarily though the committee structure of Congress. Congressional committees in both the House and the Senate are organized around policy areas: agriculture, national defense, labor, education, taxation, banking, etc. These are broken down further into subcommittees. When a Representative or Senator become a committee member he (she) gains what is basically a national constituency. The agricultural industry, the defense industry, labor unions, the public and private educational establishment, the large number of groups and businesses that are interested in tax policy, and the banking and financial services industry. Committee members get financial contributions and often voter support and organizational support from these interest groups.

This does not mean that interest groups always have their way with Congressional Committees. The reasons are several. First, there is a lot of competition between interest groups. Second, there are also public interest lobbies (such as Common Cause). Committees must reach a consensus among the major groups before they can act. Third, Committees are constrained by the public interest. If a proposed bill goes strongly against their electoral constituency, they risk not getting reelected. And, for a bill to become law, it must be adopted by both Houses of Congress and signed by the President. Interest groups also lobby the government agencies and the office of the President.

The third way society coordinates economic activity is through the administrative (or bureaucratic process). This process coordinates decisions within large organizations: public, private and non-profit. Examples would be The Department of Defense, General Motors Corporation or Harvard University. Within the organization markets are not normally used to coordinate economic decisions. The key problem within any large organization is how to insure that worker and managers at lower levels of the organization make decisions that are in the interest of the organization as articulated by the top executives or administrators.

There are several methods to do this. First, there are budgeting and accounting rules and procedures. Accounting rules ensure that, at each level of the organization, the use of funds must be accounted for to administrators at the next higher level. Budgets can be increased or decreased to reward or punish performance of any sub unit of the organization. Next, there is hiring, firing, retention and salary adjustment. Organizations have highly formalized procedures for hiring new employees, for promoting employees to higher positions and for allocating salary adjustments to the various participants. At each level the decisions are subject to review by the administrators at the next higher level. Third, there are standard operating procedures that are usually written or unwritten rules that tell administrators and workers how to proceed in all these various decisions. Last, there is the organizational culture. This is the set of shared values that have developed with the history of the organization. These shared values help ensure that members of the organization will behave in a way that is in the interest of the organization.

## TYPES OF ECONOMIC ANALYSIS

First, economists make a distinction between positive economics and normative economics. Positive economics is concerned with what is. That is, it is concerned with explaining how the economic world works. Economists develop abstract models to explain the economic world. Normative economics is concerned with what ought to be. It makes judgments about how the economic system ought to be organized. When we do economic analysis we try to be non-partisan. When we make policy recommendations we often have to rely both on our analysis but also on our own judgments on how things ought to be.

Economics also distinguishes between static analysis and dynamic analysis. Static analysis deals with an economic system at a point in time. For example we might look at supply and demand for apples for a given month. We may look at increases in supply or demand that change price and quantity. But time does not explicitly enter the model. However if we look at supply and demand over time, then price and quantity and supply and demand shifters are time dated and we can trace out an equilibrium path of price and quantity over time. This is dynamic analysis.

Economists also distinguish between short-run and long run analysis. If it is static analysis, the short-run involves some variables as fixed and some as variable. In the theory of the firm we usually assume in the short run that the firm can vary the quantity of labor and raw materials in producing output but the firm faces a given stock of capital goods. In the long run all inputs can be varied including the capital stock. Long run dynamic analysis involves tracing out an equilibrium path over time with all inputs allowed to vary.

Economists also distinguish between partial and general equilibrium. Partial equilibrium deals with equilibrium for a particular market or sector of the economy. Other things are assumed given. General equilibrium assumes equilibrium for the total economy. In other words all markets are assumed to clear simultaneously.

Another branch of economics is the analysis of economic institutions. Here economists look at how different institutional arrangements influence the way economies function. This is closely related to evolutionary economics, which treats economics as an historical science and studies how economies evolve over time.

Next we can mention econometrics. Econometrics uses the methods of statistics and economic analysis to estimate and test economic models. By estimation we can get models that put numbers to the theoretic relations. For example we can estimate demand curves and supply curves and find the equilibrium price and quantity. Also knowing supply and demand we can calculate elasticity's of each. As we will see later these can be very useful for policy purposes. Also estimation allows us a way to test the theories. If the estimated models fit the theories it gives us confidence that the theories may be correct.

Last we can mention policy analysis. Policy analysis involves the use of economic theory, economic institutions and econometrics to study policy issues. Theory and institutions gives us a framework for studying policy issues. Econometrics gives us a way to quantify our analysis and test our results. However in making policy recommendations economists must always make clear their own political and ideological biases.

## EFFICIENCY AND EQUITY

Economists often distinguish between efficiency and equity. Efficiency refers to producing output at minimum cost or getting the most satisfaction per dollar of income. More generally it means achieving our objectives in an efficient manner; in a manner that economizes on the use of inputs. Markets, if organized in a competitive manner with understood rules of the game, can be said to produce efficient outcomes. Equity, as it is used here, refers to fairness. Are the solutions that come out of a market economy fair? That depends primarily on their effect on the distribution of income. If property ownership is concentrated in the hands of a few people, then a market solution that is efficient might be considered unfair because it generates a highly skewed distribution of income. Matters of equity are usually dealt with through the political system. For example a progressive tax might be enacted to help reduce the skewed-ness of the income distribution. Or a negative income tax might be used to increase income of low-income people.

## ASSUMPTIONS AND REALITY

Economists often make assumptions that are simplifications of reality. Economic models, like models in other sciences, must be abstract. The economic world is very complex. Realistic models would be too complex to be understandable. Instead we try to pick out key variables that give us insight into economic behavior and make behavioral assumption that simplify actual behavior. For example we assume firms behave in a manner to maximize profits. Clearly not all firms have the knowledge of cost and revenues necessary for this behavior. However firm owners and managers learn over time what works to increase their profits. In the long run they must earn profits to survive. If they don't they face financial distress and possible bankruptcy. Likewise we assume that households maximize utility. This means that they want the most satisfaction per dollar of income spent. Not all households have the knowledge of preferences and prices and income that would allow this. Still if households don't behave in approximately this way, they to can face financial distress and bankruptcy. Households, like firms, do what is necessary to survive and grow.

We appraise economic models not on the realism of their assumptions but instead on two primary criteria: First, do they predict economic behavior. By this we do not mean predicting the future but instead predicting whether changes in certain variables lead to the changes predicted by the model. We usually test these predictions using econometrics. Second, do the models give us insight into how the economic world works? Do they help of to make sense out of a very complex world?

## WHY DO ECONOMISTS DISAGREE?

On policy issues economists often disagree. Why, since most economists use the same analytic techniques, do they often come to very different conclusion on important policy issues? First, economists, like every one else, hold different values about how the economic and political system ought to be organized. There are liberal economists and conservative economists. There are Republican economists and Democratic economists. A Republican President will choose a Republican (and conservative) economic advisor because he wants an advisor who shares his view of the world. A Democratic President will choose a Democratic (and liberal) economic advisor who shares his view of the world.

Second, economists may disagree about methodological issues. These issues are about the appropriate methodology to be used for analyzing certain issues. For example there are neo-Keynesian economists and new classical economists that have different methodical approaches as to how to analyze the workings of the macro-economy. Likewise on micro issues there is the approach of the "Chicago School" that has a strong anti-intervention bias when it comes to government regulatory issues. On the other side is the approach of most economists at Harvard and MIT that is more sympathetic to certain types of regulation. These approaches stem from differing views of how the economy operates. The Chicago School looks at the economy and sees mostly a purely competitive world. Harvard and MIT economists look at the economy and see what economists refer to as imperfect competition. These approaches lead to differing conclusion about the appropriate role for government in the economy.

Third, economists may have different beliefs about either factual or normative matters. Differing beliefs about factual matters often result because information is incomplete and facts are subject to differing interpretations. As we get better information, these beliefs may change. Also, we may have differing beliefs about normative matters. As we gain more knowledge about how the economic system actually works we may change our views about how the system ought to work. For example, the fall of the Soviet Union in the late 1980s, led to a relatively quick conversion of economists and political leaders in Russia and Eastern Europe from socialists views to free market democratic ideas about how to organize their economies.

## ECONOMIC THEORY AND ECONOMIC POLICY

Economic theory is our road map to economic reality. It helps us find our way through the bewildering landscape of economic reality. To discuss economic policy we first need the road map of economic theory. In the absence of theory we may come to very wrong conclusions on economic policy. For example we might conclude that higher wages will lead to higher income. However economic theory tells us that if aggregate income doesn't change higher wages will only redistribute income from receivers of property income to receivers of wage income. For the economy as a whole, the only way that income per worker can increase is for output per worker to increase. Knowing economic theory does not guarantee that we will always get the right policy solution. But it does reduce the probability that we will get a wrong solution. Economic policies do not depend just on the economics of the issue. We also need to know the institutional setting of the issue. And there may often be political considerations that override the economic considerations.

## ECONOMICS AS A SCIENCE

Economics is a social science, but it uses many of the analytic techniques of the physical and biological sciences. This is partly because economics deals with variables that can be measured either in dollars or in physical units. This means it lends itself readily to quantitative methods. The use of mathematical and graphical models is common in economics. Once one understands the math and knows how to read the graphs, they are a lot simpler than words. All scientific professions develop their own language for communicating with each other. These languages often involve math or graphs because they add precision and clarity to the ideas so that other researchers can understand them more easily. Also mathematical models lend themselves to estimation and testing using the methods of econometrics.

The scientific method involves developing theories and models about economic behavior and then testing these theories by estimating them using actual data to see if the estimated models are consistent with the theories. Also theories can be tested by history. Programs adopted during the great depression offered social experiments: We can now go back and look at the results and perhaps gain knowledge as to what might be done in similar circumstances in the future. The rule of the Soviet Union with its state socialism and the subsequent collapse of the system involved a social experiment that led many to reject the economic and political model on which the system was based.

## SUMMARY

In this chapter we have discussed the scope and method of economics. The emphasis has been on three things. Economic theory which is our road map to economic reality; economic and political institutions which give us the knowledge of how the system is organized; and economic policy which uses knowledge of theory and institutions to analyze policy issues

## REVIEW QUESTIONS

Multiple choices: Select the correct answer:

1. Macroeconomics is:
   a. The study of firms, households and markets.
   b. The study of the Federal Reserve System.
   c. The study of aggregate output, employment, prices and interest rates.
   d. The study of the financial system.
2. Microeconomics is:
   a. The study of the financial system.
   b. The study of the aggregate output, employment, prices and interest rates.
   c. The study of firms, households, and markets.
   d. The study of the Federal Reserve System.
3. Positive economics is concerned with:
   a. Proscribing how the economic system ought to work.
   b. Explaining how the economic system works.
   c. Explaining how the political process works.
   d. None of the above.

4. Normative economics is concerned with:
   a. Proscribing how the economic system ought to work.
   b. Explaining how the economic system works.
   c. Explaining how the political process works.
   d. None of the above.
5. Product (or output) markets coordinate economic decisions between
   a. Firms and their suppliers.
   b. Firms and their customers.
   c. Neither of the above.

### Essays

1. Explain how economic decisions are coordinated through the market system, through the political system and through the administrative system within large organizations.
2. Despite the fact that most economists use the same analytic tools, they often disagree on policy issues. Explain why this is the case.
3. The study of economic theory and economic institutions are crucial to our understanding of economic policy issues. Explain why.

## SUGGESTED READINGS

Friedman, Milton, "The Methodology of Positive Economics," in his *Essays in Positive Economics,* Chicago: Phoenix Books, The University of Chicago Press, 1966, 3–33.

Knight, Frank, "Economics", in his *On the History and Method of Economics,* Chicago, Phoenix Books, The University of Chicago Press, 1956: 3–33.

Kuhn, Thomas S., *The Structure of Scientific Revolutions,* 2nd ed. University of Chicago Press, 1970) (First Edition 1962).

Robbins, Lionel, *An Essay on the Nature and Significance of Economic Science,* 2nd ed. Revised and Extended, London: Macmillan, 1952, (First Edition, 1932).

Schumpeter, Joseph "The Development of Economics as a Science" in his *Economic Doctrine and Method* New York: A Galaxy Book, Oxford University Press, 1967, (First English Edition, 1954) (First published in German in 1912), 9–41.

Sowell, Thomas, *Basic Economics: A Citizens Guide to the Economy,* New York, Basic Books, 2000, 1–4.

## *Chapter Two*

# The Role of Markets: Production, Consumption, Distribution, Specialization and Exchange

### HOW MARKETS WORK

Markets work through the interaction of thousands of individual firms and millions of individual resource suppliers and millions of consumers. Firms decide what to produce and supply to the market. Resource suppliers decide where to employ their resources. Consumers decide what goods to buy (demand) from firms. Firms also must decide how many resources to use to expand capacity for generating additional future output. And households must decide how much current consumption to forego in order to save and invest for future consumption. As was pointed out in the previous chapter, product markets are markets for the output of firms. Demanders of the products may be final consumers or other firms, if the output is an intermediate good. For example auto firms demand components from firms that supply to the auto industry. Other demanders may be government when, for example, it buys defense goods from the defense industry. Or, of course, demanders may be foreign firms or foreign governments. Input markets are markets between firms and their suppliers. Suppliers may be suppliers of labor skills, of managerial skills, of raw materials, of capital goods (new plant and equipment for example) or suppliers of funds to finance the firms operations or its accumulation of capital goods.

Markets also work through many stages of production. We mentioned the wheat example in the last chapter. At each stage the producer produces an output that is an input in the next stage. Wheat is an output of the farmer; it is an input of the grain elevator. The wheat with storage services added is an output of the grain elevator; it is an input of the miller. The miller in turn sells flour to the baker, cereal producer, or macaroni producer for whom the flour is an input. And so on to the final stage where the final product is consumed.

Thus we have supply and demand operating at many stages and the final price to the consumer must, on average, cover all these costs at all the various stages with producers at each stage being able to make a return that covers their costs and allows a competitive return on invested funds. In some industries production is integrated from the original producer to the final consumer. This is true for at least part of the petroleum industry where production is integrated all of the way from the wellhead to the gas pump at the retail level.

The system is motivated by the desire for profits by firms and the desire for income by workers. Ultimately workers are motivated by the satisfaction they can get from the income in purchasing various consumer goods and services and saving for future consumption. And at each level producers, consumers, and resource suppliers are making decisions based on their own interest with no thought to the final outcome. With competitive markets the results end up being in general in the interest of consumers. However, the system only works with a set of institutions that allow the system to function. These institutions include property rights, rights of contract, long term capital markets, a monetary system that ensures relatively stable prices, environmental laws that prevent degradation of the environment and many more. These institutions have evolved over hundreds of years along with the evolution of the market system.

Also, what motivates the political and administrative system: Basically the same types of things that motivate firms and households? We can think of politicians as motivated by the desire to maximize their political support. This means getting votes, money to run their campaigns and political and organizational support from interest groups, individuals and their party. Corporations strive to maximize profits to the enterprise. Members of the bureaucracy are motivated to maximize their current and future income given the constraints they face in their particular position. Similar forces drive government agencies and non-profit organizations. Top administrators define the goals of the organization. Lower level administers are constrained to work in ways to achieve those goals.

Competition ensures that goods will be produced at least cost. When firms make excess profits there is an incentive for new firms to enter to capture these excess profits. This means that there must not be serious barriers to entry into industries. We will discuss these issues in more detail in later chapters. Also competition ensures innovation. Firms, to increase their profits attempt to lower costs through cost innovation and increase demand through demand innovation. Cost innovation means new methods of production or distribution or new lower cost inputs that lower unit cost of output. Demand innovation means ways to increase demand through advertising, brand names and product promotion. Firms may also innovate by introducing new products or new versions of existing products. Again, the gainers are consumers if innovation gets passed on to consumers in the form of lower cost products, new products or new varieties of old products.

## PRODUCTION POSSIBILITIES

What do we mean by production possibilities? At any given time we assume that the economy (say of the US) has a given supply of resources. These resources are usually classified as the services of labor (workers, managers and executives), the services of capital goods (such as land, plant and equipment and inventories), a given level of knowledge of production techniques and the way of organizing production and a given level of productivity of these various inputs. With these assumptions society will have a given level of output potential (or normal output) at any point in time. This potential may be somewhat exceeded if the economy is in a boom and producing beyond normal capacity. Or the economy may be producing at less than its potential if it is in a recession. At any point in time we assume that the economy faces diminishing returns if it tries to increase any one type of good relative to other goods. For example, if we decide to increase defense spending, it will mean that production of some other goods will have to be reduced. If we measure in dollars of constant purchasing power, if we have constant cost of producing each type of good, a 100 billion increase in defense spending will imply a 100 billion reduction of non-defense spending, with total GDP remaining constant (say at 10,000 billion dollars). However we cannot expect constant costs in the short run. Not all inputs and capital goods can easily be converted to defense production in the short run. This means that we can expect diminishing returns (or rising marginal cost) in the short run. A 100 billion dollar increase in defense spending might require a 120 billion dollar decrease in non-defense spending. Total GDP has fallen by 20 billion dollars. The point is that in the short run we face diminishing returns. If we wish more national defense we must be prepared to give up successively larger amounts of other goods.

Figure 2.1 shows a hypothetical production possibility curve for the aggregate economy with diminishing returns. We simplify things by assuming that the economy produces two types of goods: national defense (ND) and all other goods (OG). The sum of the two give the output for the economy measured in constant prices. If the economy produces all other goods (OG) real GDP would be 10.5 trillion dollars. If only national defense (ND) were produced real GDP would be only 2.0 trillion dollars. The reason is that many of our resources could not be easily adapted to defense production in the short run. The curve connecting these points represents all possible combinations

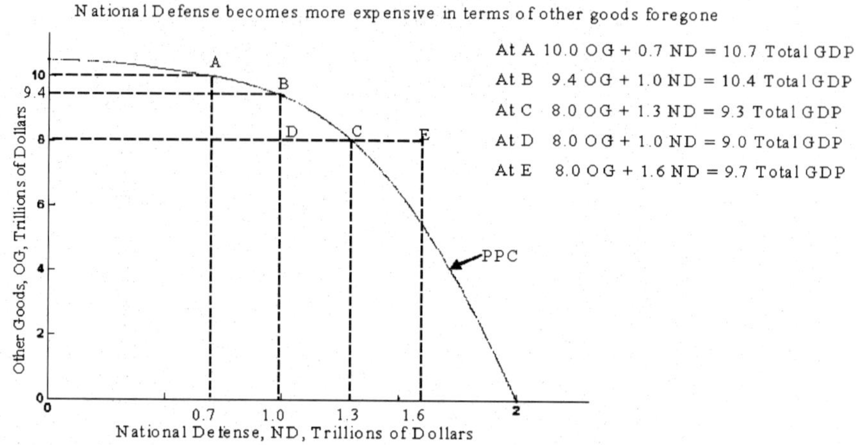


**Figure 2.1. Production Possibilities with Rising Marginal Cost**

of other goods and national defense that could be produced during a given time period, say one year. At point A, 10 trillion of other goods are produced and 0.7 trillion of national defense for a total GDP of 10.7 trillion dollars. At point B, national has increased by 0.3 trillion to 1.0 trillion dollars and other goods have fallen to 9.4 trillion dollars. Total GDP has fallen to 10.4 trillion. At point C national defense is increased another 0.3 trillion to 1.3 trillion. Other goods have fallen to 8.0 trillion for a total GDP of 9.3 trillion. The point is that each additional .3 trillion increase in national defense requires a larger additional sacrifice of other goods requiring decreasing GDP at an increasing rate. This is what we mean by diminishing returns or equivalently rising marginal cost of national defense in terms of other goods foregone.

If we are at D the economy is producing at less than normal output and would be in a recession. By moving back to normal output at C we could have more ND without having less OG. Or if we moved to B we could have more OG without having less ND. Or at some point between B and C we could have more of both. During an economic expansion we might be at E that is outside the production possibility curve. This means the economy is producing beyond normal output. Total GDP here is 9.6 trillion, greater than at either D or C. This would imply labor and capital being used at above their normal rates. This could not be sustained and would likely lead to inflationary pressures and moves by the Federal Reserve to slow the economy.

Over time the economies production potential increases. This increase results from growth of the work force, growth of the capital stock, growth of knowledge, growth of productivity of labor, of capital goods, and of the way production is organized. So, over time we can have both more defense spending and more spending for other goods. Then the relevant questions become (1) how fast does normal output grow over time? And (2) how do the shares of defense spending and other goods spending change over time? As we will see in a later chapter, growth of aggregate output must equal growth of the work force plus growth of output per worker. Growth of the work force depends on four primary things: first population growth about 20 years earlier, second the rate at which workers retire from the work force, third the rate of labor force participation, and fourth emigration rates of new workers from other countries. Population growth varies over time. Population growth in the US slowed during the Great Depression and World War II, first due to declining economic opportunity and then due to the disruptions caused by the war. After WWII there was an upsurge of population growth as people returned from the war and prosperity returned to the country. This period was from 1946 to 1965 and was called the baby boom generation. The post-baby boom generation was from 1966–1985 when population growth slowed again partly as a result of a big upsurge in labor force participation rates by women and a reduction in desired family size. The pre-baby boom generation is now mostly retired. The baby boom generation is now approaching retirement age. The post baby boom generation is now in its peak earning years. And the generation after that (sometimes called generation X) is now in its early earning years.

Combined with the baby boom generation was a big upsurge in labor force participation rates by woman. This occurred primarily between 1960 and 1990. This resulted from several forces. First, development of modern household appliances (washers, dryers, refrigerators electric stoves, microwaves, etc.), convenience foods and fast foods reduced the burden of housework; second, preferred family size fell; third, jobs for women became available in the increasing service economy and fourth, attendance of college by women increased so that today there are more women in college than men; fifth, higher divorce rates meant that many women had to enter or remain in the work force to support themselves and their families.

In addition the US has seen an upsurge in the rate of immigration over the last twenty or so years. The trend growth rate of the work force in the US is about one percent per year. With a work force of about 140 million workers that means about 1.40 million new workers per year. That is net of retirements so gross additions would be much higher.

Growth of output per worker is the other factor driving growth of output for the economy. Output per worker grows as workers become more productive and as workers are combined with more productive capital and more productive ways of organizing the production process. A person using a typewriter could achieve a certain level of output based on the person's skills and the technology of the typewriter. The typewriter has been replaced with the word processor. A person using a word processor has to gain a new set of skills. His or her productivity goes up both because of the new skills learned but also because of the new technology imbedded in the word processor. There are all sorts of things that can be done on a word processor that are impossible with a typewriter.

Trend growth in output per worker declined during the 1970s and 1980s but apparently increased during the 1990s. The slow growth of the last four years (2000–2003) has reduced growth of output per worker but the trend has probably not changed. When the economy recovers it will be moving back to the trend path. That trend path is currently about 2.5% per year. Trend growth in aggregate output thus is about 3.5% per year. (1.0% growth of the work force plus 2.5% growth of average output per worker.) As we will see later, aggregate output must equal aggregate income. Therefore growth in output must equal growth of income. So aggregate income is also growing at about a 3.5% trend rate. By subtracting the growth of the work force of 1% per year we get growth of income per worker of 2.5% per year that is equal to the growth of output per worker. This is a fundamental truth of economics based on the accounting identities we use to define income and output. For the aggregate economy, growth in income per worker must equal the growth in output per worker. The only way that average per worker incomes can increase is for average per worker output to rise. What is true for the aggregate economy is not necessarily true for any individual worker. A workers income can rise faster or slower than productivity for all kinds of reasons. It is only the averages that have to be equal.

Figure 2.2 shows the economies production possibility curve shifting over time. When this happen we can have more of both types of goods. At point A total GDP is 10.7 trillion the same as in Figure 2.1. At point B total GDP is 11.3 trillion and both national defense and other goods gave increased. The reasons why the production possibility curve shifts right over time were given above. Over time the relevant questions are how fast GDP grows over time and the share of GDP devoted to each type of good. From A to B, GDP increases from 10.7 to 11.3 trillion dollars. This is a 5.6 percent rate of growth. Suppose the time period involved was two years. This would be an average growth rate of about 2.8% per year. At A, 93% of output goes for other goods; 7% for national defense. At B 91 % goes for other goods and 9% for national defense. There has been an increase in the share devoted to national defense by 2% point of GDP. This is similar to the situation of the last few years. Because of the war on terror and the war in Iraq the share of GDP devoted to national defense has increased.

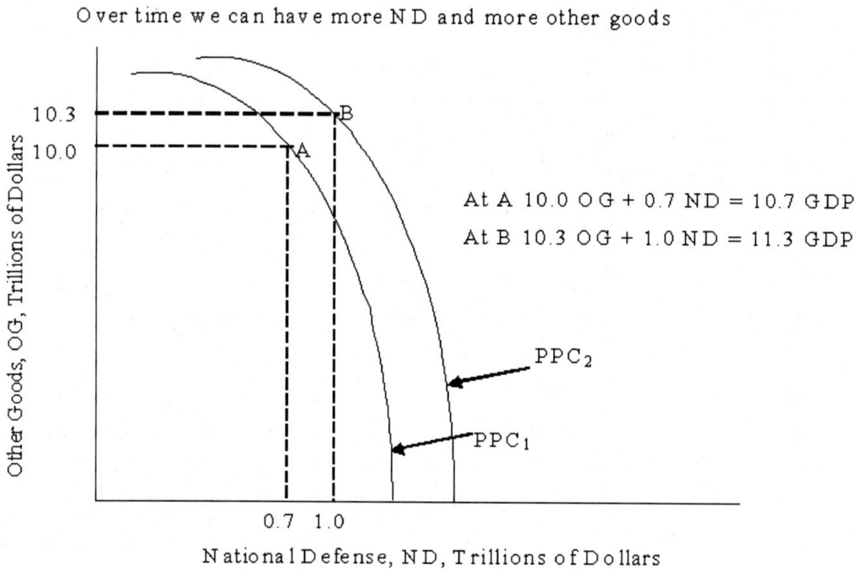


**Figure 2.2. Shifting Production Possibilities over Time**

## SPECIALIZATION IN PRODUCTION

One of the reasons that output per worker grows over time is specialization by workers, by firms, by industries and even by countries. People get an education to get a set of skills; they become accountants, financial analysts, computer engineers, airline pilots, etc. Their earnings in these fields depend on the skills they learn both in education and in on the job training. Specialization allows us to increase our potential income. But the same is true of firms. General Motors specializes in autos, Microsoft in computer software, Intel in computer chips, etc. By specializing they have a set of firm specific knowledge, skills and capital goods that are passed on to new generations of workers managers and executives. And even countries may specialize: Brazil in coffee, Saudi Arabia in petroleum, the US in computers and soybeans. Countries specialize for several reasons: First, natural endowments of soils, minerals, climate, topography, etc. may give countries advantages in special types of products. Brazil in coffee; the US in soybeans are examples. Second, the past history of development; at any point in time, a country has a given level of education, invested capital and institutional structure that give it advantages in certain types of production.

## EXCHANGE AND GAINS FROM TRADE

Specialization leads to exchange and exchange leads to gains from trade. When an individual goes to the grocery store and buys a hundred dollars worth of groceries the individual is voluntarily trading the $100 for the cart full of groceries. Presumably she is better off with the groceries to feed her family than with the $100. The grocery store on the other hand is better off with the $100. It can be used to pay workers, to buy more groceries and to pay dividends to shareholders. In economics we assume that people don't voluntarily trade unless they are made better off or, at the limit, no worse off. The grocery store specializes in the retail sale of groceries. The individual customer may specialize in being a computer engineer. But the reason for specializing is to have something to trade in order to buy the things she need to maintain a certain level of living. The same is true of countries. Countries export goods that they can produce relatively cheaply in order to earn income to be able to import goods that other countries can produce relatively cheaply. The same is true of countries as of individuals. They don't voluntarily trade if it makes them worse off. To trade they must be better off, or at the limit, no worse off. However, what is true for the country as a whole is not necessarily true for workers or owners of particular industries. The country may be better off to import apparel from China. Workers, managers and owners in the apparel industry in US are not. They may be out of a job and not have the skills needed to find alternative employment. And the owner may be stuck with a plant that has lost its market value.

## THE CIRCULAR FLOW OF GOODS AND SERVICES, EXPENDITURES, INPUT SERVICES AND INCOME AND SAVING AND BORROWING

Production of goods and services generate income in the form of payments to workers managers and owners. This income is in turn used to buy the goods and services produced. Some of the income is saved and reinvested in order to maintain productive capacity and to add new productive capacity. Financial markets allocate funds from savers to investors. These funds are used to finance current production or to finance inventories and new capital goods that are added to productive capacity. Households also borrow to finance current operation of their households; to add to the stock of household capital goods (housing, appliances, autos, etc.); to generate future earnings by investing in education; and sometimes to invest in financial assets to accumulate future consumption potential. Out of this circular flow government is financed primarily by taxes levied on both households and firms. If tax receipts are less than government expenditures the difference if financed by government borrowing.

Normally the circular flow of income and expenditures grows each year as the work force grows and as output per worker grows. However, if the system grows faster than trend growth, during an expansion, excess capacity will develop. This will lead to slowing investment, and slowing growth of income and a recession as output growth falls below the trend path. We will discuss this issue in more detail in later chapters.

Figure 2.3 shows a circular flow diagram for the economy. The top half of the diagram shows the flow of goods and services through output markets. The top arrow on the left shows goods supplied by firms. On the right side the upper arrow are goods demanded by households or what economists call household consumption. Flowing in the opposite direction is household expenditures for these goods and services. On the other side these expenditures become firm receipts. The bottom of the diagram shows flows of input services to firms from households. Households are suppliers of input services such as labor, capital goods, land and funds. Firms are demanders of these same services. These services flow though input markets. In the center of the diagram is the flow of financial assets. Household saving flows through the financial markets and becomes borrowings of firms, The flow of funds going

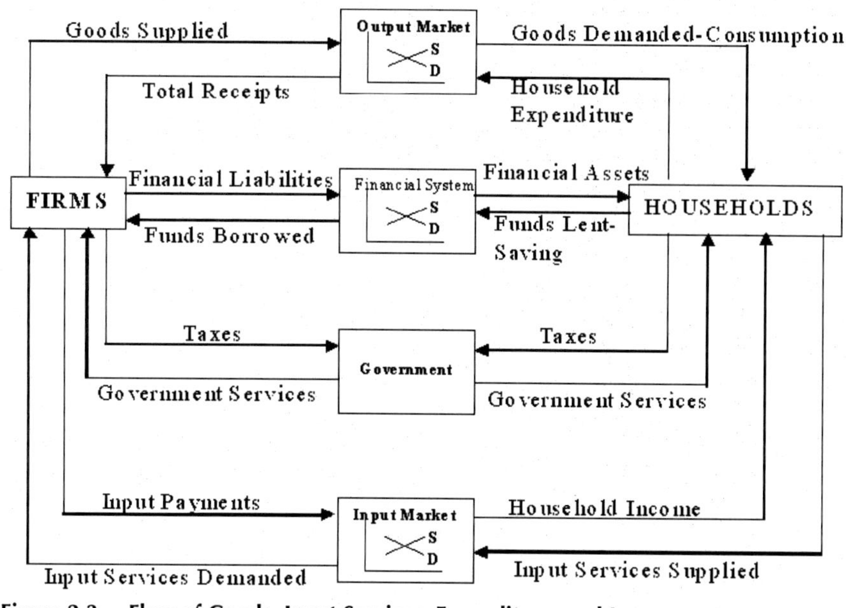


**Figure 2.3. Flow of Goods, Input Services, Expenditures and Income**

one way corresponds to a flow of assets going the other way. Financial assets purchased by households are financial liabilities issued by firms.

The other set of arrows in the bottom half of the diagram represent flows to and from government. The government (federal, state, and local.) supplies various collective goods and services to both households and firms. These include the government itself, executive, legislative and judicial branches as well as such government services as national defense, police protection, national parks, agricultural extension services and many more. Flowing in the opposite direction is taxes paid by households and firms. Because of the collective nature of the goods there is no direct relation for individuals or firms between the amount of taxes paid and the amount of government services received. All of these arrows could be filled in with dollar amounts from the national income accounts that we discuss later. However the numbers wouldn't add up because we have left out some important flows. We have left out business investment that is expenditure by firms to other firms for capital goods; we have left out exports and imports that are flows between the US and other countries, and we have left out government borrowing to finance part of its expenditures. All of this is to keep the model relatively simple. In chapter 16 we present a sector receipts and expenditure table that shows similar flows in dollar amounts. Here all of the flows do add up.

## THE ROLE OF INSTITUTIONS

What are institutions? Institutions are social systems that coordinate individual interests to group interests. They rely on human nature and arise either spontaneously or as a result of human planning and design. Markets rely on the natural self-interest of individuals and, if properly organized, channel this self-interest to the public good. The military channels the aggressive instincts of young people into group interest for defense or often aggression. Religious institutions rely on the moral instincts that we have as social animals to develop moral codes for society. Political systems channel the political interests of individuals and organized interest groups into the political institutions of society. Corporations channel the self-interest of workers, managers, executives, shareholders, creditors and customers into the interest of the corporate collective. A major benefit of social institutions is that they reduce transaction costs of coordinating economic and social activity.

With all of these social institutions there are two basic problems that must be dealt with. First, most social institutions develop interests of their own that are independent of the interest of their constituents. General Motors has interest of its own independent of the interest of its individual workers, managers, or shareholders. Labor unions have interest of their own independent of the interest of their worker members in part because they must form coalition with other interest groups in order to increase their bargaining power in Washington. The Department of Defense has interests of its own independent of the interest of Congress, the President, or the public. Top executives and Boards of Directors articulate these group interests. Internal control mechanisms like accounting and budgeting procedures, hiring, firing and promotion procedures, standard operating procedures and shared values of the organization ensure (in most cases) that the decisions of lower level workers and managers will be consistent with the overall objectives of the organization.

Second, social institutions must be held accountable to some broader notion of the public interest. With our political system we have the constitution and separation of powers to protect the governed from the government. In the market system competition is the primary way that individual producers, consumers and input suppliers are held accountable. But in addition to the competition of the market there is a whole set of institutional rules of the game that help, or sometimes hinder, markets to work. These include property rights, rights of contracts, legal enforcement of contracts, and a stable monetary system. Corporations are held accountable in several ways. First, there is the Securities and Exchange Commission that requires public accounting statements to be made available to investors. In addition there are various regulatory agencies such as the FDA (Food and Drug Administration), the EPA (Environmental Protection Agency) the FED (Federal Reserve System) and many more depending on the industry. The ultimate check is the market. A corporation must generate an income stream to survive. Failure to do so leads to insolvency and ultimately bankruptcy.

Economic progress depends on having social institution that encourages development. These include property rights, rights of contract, a legal and police system to enforce and protect these rights, a stable monetary and financial system, an open political system, access to education and jobs, a system to channel saving into investment in future productive capacity and a system of defense against external attack. Without these, development attempts are usually doomed to failure.

Economic systems evolve over time along with our political system and other social systems. Where we are today depends on our past history. Our current institutions have developed over the past several hundred years. This evolutionary path is sometimes called path dependency. Once on a particular path, it is often very costly to change even though the gains from change could be very great. To take a simple example, in the peasant agriculture of many developing countries output per worker is very low maybe only a few hundred dollars per year. The productivity of an agricultural worker in say

Iowa might be as much as $50,000 dollar per worker per year. Why don't developing countries convert to modern agricultural methods? There are many reasons. First, it would mean displacing thousands of workers who would have to find jobs in non-agricultural pursuits. Second, it would mean a major change in land ownership pattern. Third, it would require a major change in the educational system since modern agriculture requires educated workers. Fourth, it would require development of new systems of finance, new systems to supply inputs such as modern machinery, fertilizer, fuel, and seeds and new systems of transportation and distribution to get the products to market. Even though the new path would be much more efficient, getting there can be very difficult. This is why major change often comes after wars, revolutions or major economic crisis (such as the Great Depression). These events often break up existing institutional structures and allow new structures to develop.

## SUMMARY

Markets work to coordinate economic activity between firms and their customers and firms and their suppliers. Households, firms, markets and even countries specialize in activities where they have a comparative advantage either due to natural endowments, learned skills and technology or past history. Individuals, firms and countries trade because though trade they can be made better off. Although trade between countries may make the countries better off, it may make certain groups within the countries worse off. The same is true of domestic trade. If a computer software company closes its plant in Massachusetts and moves to North Carolina, some workers in Massachusetts will be worse off. Some workers in North Carolina will be better off. Assuming that production in North Carolina is cheaper than in Massachusetts, the country as a whole is better off.

## REVIEW QUESTIONS

Multiple choices: Select the correct answer:

1. Which of the following does not shift the economies production possibility curve right over time.
   a. Growth of the capital stock.
   b. Growth of the general level of prices.
   c. Growth of the labor force
   d. Growth of output per worker

2. Production possibility curves show diminishing returns because:
   a. In the short run it is easy to transfer resources from one line of production to another.
   b. In the short run it is difficult to transfer resources from one line of production to another.
   c. Neither of the above.
3. A production possibility curve tells us:
   a. How much a society can consume at a given point in time.
   b. The optimum amount of each good that should be produced at each point in time.
   c. The mixes of output that society can produce with given resources and technology.
   d. The optimum mix of consumption for society

### Essays

1. List and explain the major things that shift the production possibility curve right over time.
2. Why do we normally expect gains from voluntary exchange between individuals, between firms and their customers and suppliers and between individuals, firms or governments of different countries.

## SUGGESTED READINGS

Coase, Ronald, "The Institutional Structure of Production," in his *Essays on Economics and Economists,* Paperback ed. Chicago: The University of Chicago Press, 1995, 3–14.

North, Douglas, "Institutions," *Journal of Economic Perspectives,* 5, no. 1 (Winter 1991): 97–112.

Herendeen, James B. *The Economics of The Corporate Economy* , New York, Dunellen, 1975, 13–64.

Putterman, Lewis, *Dollars and Change: Economics in Context,* New Haven: Yale University Press, 2–52.

Sowell, Thomas, *Basic Economics: A Citizens Guide to the Economy,* New York: Basic Books, 2000.

# *Chapter Three*

# The Economic Role of Government

## THE ECONOMIC POLICY ROLES OF GOVERNMENT

What is the economic policy role of government in the economy? When we talk about government we will be referring primarily to the Federal Government. The four primary economic functions of the Federal Government are: public goods and services policy, macroeconomic policy, regulatory policy, and income redistribution policy.

### Public Goods and Services Policy

This is government policy regarding the provision of public goods and services. These are goods and services provided by the government. Examples would be national defense, public education, national parks, the Federal Court System, Agricultural Extension Services and many more. We can distinguish between pure public goods and quasi-public goods. A pure public good has non-separability of consumption and non-excludability. Non-separability means that one person's use of the good does not reduce the amount of the good available to others. My consumption of national defense does not reduce the amount of national defense available to others. Non-excludable means that once the good is available people cannot be excluded from using it. I cannot be excluded from the benefits of national defense. Quasi-public goods may be excludable but non-separable such as a highway or a bridge. In the absence of congestion one person's use does not prohibit use by others. But people could be excluded for example by charging a toll. Or a good could be separable but non-excludable. Fish in the ocean are separable but non-excludable. Government provides both pure and quasi-public goods as a result of the political process. It also provides goods that may have all the characteristics of a private good. Private goods are separable in consumption and excludable. If I buy a car it is no longer available to others. If I buy a loaf of bread it is mine to consume. Government provides fire protection and police protection because use of a market would prevent some people from having the service. With police protection you can also buy private protection. The same is true of education. It is provided at low cost by the government with the additional cost paid by taxpayers. But you can also buy private education if you don't want to use the public system. But you still have to pay your taxes to support the public system.

With public goods there is a free rider problem. This means that some people may benefit from the good without paying for it. Once national defense is available, I get the benefit whether I pay for it or not. Government prevents free riders by using taxes. Taxes must be paid irrespective of how much use you get from a public good. With a public good there is no direct relation between what you pay and what you get. With a private good you pay for it and you get the use of it. Government decides through the political process what public goods to provide and how much to provide.

## Macroeconomic Policy

Macroeconomic policy is policy by the government to influence the economic state of the aggregate economy. There are three types of macroeconomic policy. First is what we call stabilization policy. This is policy designed to stabilize aggregate real output over the business cycle. Stabilization policy can be either monetary policy or fiscal policy. Monetary policy is policy by the Federal Reserve System to influence interest rates, the money supply and credit availability. Fiscal policy is policy by the Congress and the President to influence government spending, taxes and the government budget deficit. Second is growth policy. This is government policy designed to increase trend growth of real GDP. Third is inflation policy. This is policy by the Federal Reserve to try to target a long run inflation rate. We will discuss these in more detail in later chapters.

## Regulatory Policy

This is government policy aimed at regulating price, quantity or quality or other conditions in specific markets. Examples would be regulation of the banking industry, of airline safety, of agricultural prices, of securities traded on securities exchanges and environmental regulation.

## Income Redistribution Policy

This is policy designed to redistribute income from taxpayers in general to specific groups. Social Security and Medicare redistribute income from the working to the non-working. Welfare programs and Medicaid redistribute income to low-income people. Social Security and Medicare make up the bulk of the income redistribution expenditures. All of the other policies listed above have income redistribution affects but their primary goal is not redistribution.

## MARKET FAILURE

Another way to look at the role of government is though the concept of market failure. Market failure refers to cases where markets may fail to give efficient or equitable results and where government action may be justified.

### Public Goods and Services

There is no guarantee that certain public goods and services will be provided by the private sector. National defense, property rights, the courts and legal system are examples. And most economists agree that such public goods are necessary for economic development.

### Monopoly and Oligopoly

As we will see in chapters 5 and 6, monopoly or oligopoly may involve cases where firms earn excess profits in the long run. Also, monopolies or oligopolies may produce at a higher prices and lower outputs than a competitive industry with the same costs. A natural monopoly is one where costs fall for the full range of industry output and it is only efficient to have one firm in the market. This is the case for some public utilities. Government ownership or government regulations are possible remedies. Also where we don't have natural monopolies, anti-trust policy is sometimes used to break up monopolies or oligopolies to attempt to create more competitive conditions. We will return to these issues in a later chapter.

### Externalities

Externalities refer to cases where external costs or external benefits are created by either production or consumption. External production costs would be the case of pollution. A firm might pollute a river by dumping chemical wastes in the river. The polluted river is a cost to society because it can no longer be used for fishing, or swimming, or boating.

A case of external cost in consumption might be smoking. The cost of lung cancer or emphysema may be borne by the Medicare System, not the smoker. In addition there are the cost of exposure to smoke by non-smokers. An external benefit from production might be the economies to other firms that are the result of suppliers or even competitors that locate in a particular area. Silicon Valley and the computer and software industry might be an example. An external benefit in consumption might be inoculation to prevent spread of disease like small pox. These issues are discussed in more detail in chapter 11.

### Asymmetric Information

This refers to the availability of information to various participants in production or consumption. Producers might have more information than consumers about the quality or safety, or reliability of certain goods or services. The FDA tests and inspects certain foods and drugs and has an approval process for new drugs. Financial institutions are required to disclose the terms on certain types of loans. The SEC requires publication of financial reports on publicly traded securities.

### Failure to Provide Normal Employment

Government stabilization policy is designed to stabilize the economy over the business cycle. The presumption is that in the absence of government stabilization, the business cycle might have swings in output, employment or prices that are costly to the economy and that government policy can reduce the fluctuations. However there is no guarantee that government stabilization policies will always be successful. Sometimes government policies destabilize the economy and actually make the fluctuations of the business cycle greater.

### Failure to Provide a Stable Value of Money

Monetary policy by the FED is designed to maintain relatively stable purchasing power of the dollar. This means attempting to target a long run inflation rate but may also mean attempting to stabilize the international value of the dollar. By stable value of money we mean stable purchasing power of money. This means low and stable inflation at home and approximate purchasing power parity between the dollar and other major currencies. These issues are discussed in chapter 20.

In all these cases of market failure, government intervention may be justified. However there is no guarantee that government policy will make things better. Poorly designed programs may end up making things worse not better.

## THE POLITICAL PROCESS

To understand what kinds of policies are possible and why some policies fail, we need to understand the political process. We gave a brief overview of the political process in Chapter 1. The key players in the political process are the electorate, organized interest groups, elected politicians, the government bureaucracy and the Office of the President. The electorate has the ultimate veto power in that it may either elect or not elect candidates for public office. Organized interest groups lobby Congressional Committees, the Bureaucracy and the Office of the President. They furnish to politicians funds to help finance elections. Large group interests promise votes, organizational support and information (or disinformation) to politicians. Congressional Committees have legislative jurisdiction over various policy areas such as agriculture, national defense or health care. Interest groups and the government bureaucracy lobby the committees. Interest groups also lobby the bureaucracy and the office of the President.

Proposed legislation first has to be passed by the Committees, next it goes to the full House or Senate. If both pass it, it goes back to a Conference Committee, made up of selected members of the House and Senate Committees where differences are ironed out; then back to the full House and Senate. If passed there, it goes to the President who may either sign it into law or veto it. If vetoed, it takes a two-thirds vote of both Houses to become law over the veto. The government bureaucracy has the knowledge of the policy areas and the expertise to help write new legislation. It has power with Congress because of the various constituencies it represents. The President and Vice President are the only elected politicians with a national electoral constituency. That means that the Office of the President usually initiates new legislation but is also often able to stop legislation that it disagrees with.

The essence of the political process is concentrated benefit and dispersed cost. The benefits of government programs are usually concentrated on certain groups that, if organized, can put pressure on the political system to act in their favor. The costs of the programs are spread over millions of individuals, businesses and taxpayers. Unless there is strong public opposition, interest groups can often get benefits at the expense of the public. This is sometimes called rent-seeking behavior. It means getting benefits through the political process that are unrelated to productive activity. It is income redistribution through the political process. A primary constraint on this type of behavior is competition from other interest groups. But interest groups often form coalitions with other interest groups to increase their bargaining power. Another constraint is the electorate. If the electorate strongly opposes the program, Congress is unlikely to pas it as they risk not getting reelected. And last there is the Constitution that stipulates in broad terms where the government can act.

## GOVERNMENT RECEIPTS AND EXPENDITURE

Table 3.1 shows Federal Government receipts and expenditures in billions of dollars and sources and uses as a percent of total receipts for 2006 (Figures are based on the third quarter at an annual rate.) Current receipts exceeded current expenditures by 165 billion dollars. This is the net deficit for that year. It is net because government capital expenditures are excluded. When capital expenditures are included the deficit is 244 billion dollars. This would be the difference between total receipts and current expenditures. Capital expenditures are spending for structures, equipment and software. On the receipts side note that the bulk of government revenue comes from two sources, personal taxes, 38%, and social security contributions, 33%, or a total of 71%.

**Table 3.1. Total Federal Receipts and Expenditures, Billions of Dollars and Percent of Total Expenditures by Sources and Uses, 2006**

| *Billions of $* | | *Billions of $* | |
|---|---|---|---|
| Current Receipts | 2565 | Total Current Expenditures | 2730 |
| Current Borrowing | 165 | | |
| Capital Account borrowing | 79 | Capital Expenditures | 79 |
| Total Government Receipts | 2809 | Total Government Expenditures | 2809 |
| Percent of Total Receipt | | Percent of Total Expenditures | |
| Current Receipts | | Current Expenditure | |
| Personal Taxes | 38 | National Defense, Current | 17 |
| Corporate Profits Taxes | 14 | Non-Defense, Current | 9 |
| Indirect Business Taxes; Misc | 6 | Transfers to Person | 43 |
| Social Security Withholding | 33 | Transfers to Rest of World | 1 |
| Gross Borrowing | 9 | Grants to State and Local Gov. | 13 |
| | | Interest Payments | 11 |
| | | Subsides | 2 |
| | | Capital Expenditures | |
| | | National Defense | 3 |
| | | Non-defense | 1 |
| Total | 100 | Total | 100 |

*Source: Economic Report of the President,* 2007

14% come from corporate profits taxes and 6% from indirect business taxes, and other miscellaneous receipts. Indirect business taxes at the federal level, come mainly from the gasoline tax, the tax on alcoholic beverages and the tax on tobacco products. On the expenditure side transfers to persons comes to 43%. This is mostly Social Security and Medicare but also includes welfare programs and Medicaid. National Defense is 20% (current plus capital). Non-defense expenditures (current plus capital) are 10% of the total. Federal grants to state and local governments are 13%. Net interest is interest on the Federal debt less any interest earnings of government and is 11% of the total. Transfers to the rest of the world are only 1%. National defense as a percent of the total has declined from its peak of about 29% of the total in the late 1980s but has increased again in the last few years.

## THE BUDGET DEFICIT

The Federal budget deficit rose during the eighties, peaking at about 5% of GDP in the late eighties. During the mid and late 1990s the budget deficit fell and there was a surplus in 1998, 1999 and 2000. However recession in 2000–2001 and the aftermath of the terrorist attack September 2001, turned the budget surplus quickly back to a deficit. The deficit rose in the eighties, first because of recession in 1981–1982, then due to increased defense spending and continued growth of spending on transfers in combination with the tax cuts of 1981 and 1986. In the 1990s, after the recession of 1991–92, the deficit fell steadily, mostly as a result of a growing economy that increased tax revenues. In addition there was a small tax increase in 1993 and slower growth of government spending during the 1990s. At the end of the 1990s policy makers and politicians were predicting 10 years of growing surpluses. Unfortunately the prediction turned out to be drastically wrong. The recession of 2000–2001 ended the surpluses as tax receipts dropped dramatically. After the terrorist attach of 9-11-01, government spending increased, both for defense and non-defense purposes. We may very well have another decade of deficits as we did in the eighties and early nineties. Once the government is in deficit it is very difficult to reduce the deficit. First cutting the growth of spending is never easy because every spending program has powerful constituencies that want to continue and expand the programs. Second, raising taxes is politically very difficult. All the pressures are to reduce taxes. And raising marginal rates might slow growth and contribute to falling tax revenues. To raise revenues and not slow growth, the average tax rate would have to be raised without raising marginal rates. This would mean closing many of the tax loopholes in order to broaden the tax base. But every important loophole in the tax structure also has powerful defenders. The other way to reduce the deficit is to increase trend growth. This brings in additional tax revenues. This is what happened in the 1990s. But much of the increased growth had little to do with government policy. The fourth way to reduce the deficit, at least in an accounting sense, is to change the accounting procedures. In the late 1990s the government went to a current account and capital account for the Federal budget. What this meant was that capital goods expenditures (structures, equipment and software) were no longer treated as current expenditures. The current account budget deficit became the difference between current tax revenues and current expenditures. This reduced the size of the deficit. With a surplus, the surplus became the difference between current expenditures and current revenue. The net surplus is current expenditures plus capital expenditures minus current tax receipts.

## SUMMARY

The Federal Government plays a major role in the economy. It is a major purchaser of goods and services. Government accounting treats salaries of government employee as a purchase of a service. Government also redistributes income from the working to the non-working and from the general taxpayer to low-income groups. The government also provides a multitude of public and quasi-public goods and services. Government expenditures and taxes have a major impact on the state of the economy and on its rate of growth over time. Monetary policy by the Federal Reserve System affects the money supply, short-term interest rates and credit availability. We will discuss these issues in more detail in chapters 18 and 19.

## REVIEW QUESTIONS

Multiple choices: Select the correct answer:

1. Stabilization policy is policy to:
   a. Stabilize nominal aggregate income over the business cycle.
   b. Stabilize real aggregate income over the business cycle.
   c. Stabilize the trend inflation rate.
2. Transfers as a share of national income have:
   a. Increased over time.
   b. Decreased over time.
   c. Neither of the above

3. Water pollution is an example of:
   a. An external benefit
   b. An external cost
   c. Neither of the above

### Essays

1. List and explain the four primary economic functions of government.
2. What do economists mean by the term market failure. Explain and give some examples of market failure.
3. What do we mean by concentrated benefits and dispersed costs when discussing the political process and the role of interest groups?

## SUGGESTED READINGS

Buchanan, James and Gordon Tullock, *The Calculus of Consent,* Ann Arbor: University of Michigan Press, 1962.

Friedman, Milton, "The Role of Government in a Free Society," in his *Capitalism and Freedom,* Chicago: Phoenix Books, University of Chicago Press, 1963, 22–36.

Herendeen, James B. *Economics of The Corporate Economy*, New York: Dunellen Publishing Company, 1975, 1–34, 225–45.

Lerner, Abba, "Functional Finance" in David Collander, Editor, *Selected Economic Writings of Abba P. Lerner,* New York: NYU Press, 1983.

Musgrave, Richard, *The Theory of Public Finance: A Study of the Public Economy,* New York: McGraw Hill, 1959.

Olson, Mancur *The Logic of Collective Action*, Cambridge: Harvard University Press, 1965.

# *Part II*

# MICROECONOMIC ISSUES

# *Chapter Four*

# Households and Markets

In this chapter we develop the concepts of supply and demand for individual goods and discuss how households (or other users) determine demand and firms determine supply. We have discussed supply and demand before but now we must develop the analytic concepts. To keep it simple we assume an industry where firms sell directly to households.

## HOUSEHOLD DEMAND

We will use as our industry the cola industry. First we assume an individual household that consumes cola. The units of cola are six packs. The first two columns at the bottom of Figure 4.1 give a set of prices for cola and the number of six packs consumed at each price by household A, our typical household. As we would expect as the price falls the number of six packs purchased rises. This assumes that the price of other goods, income and consumer preferences are given. At a price of $6.00 only one six pack is demanded. At $1.00 six are demanded. Column 3 shows the total number of consumer that we assume is constant at 100 million consumers. We assume that household A is our average or typical household. Therefore we can multiply the quantity demanded by household A by 100 million and get total market demand. This is given in column 4. Figure 4.1 is merely a plotting of the numbers of six packs in column 4 against the prices in column 1. When the price is $6.00 we have 100 million six packs demanded. At $5.00 we have 200 million six packs and so on until at $1.00 we have 600 million six packs demanded. This is our hypothetical demand for six packs of cola.

Why do we expect the demand curve to slope down? The primary reason is called the substitution effect. As we lower the price of cola holding constant

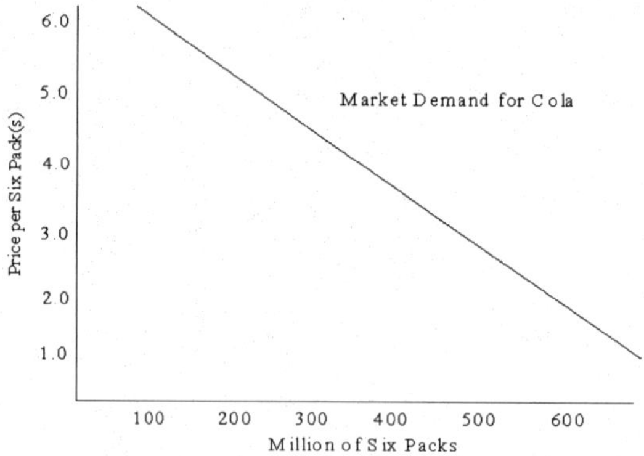


| Price/Six Pack | Number of Six Packs Consumer A | | No. of Consumers (millions) | | Number of Six Packs Market, Millions |
|---|---|---|---|---|---|
| $6.00 | 1 | * | 100 | = | 100 |
| $5.00 | 2 | * | 100 | = | 200 |
| $4.00 | 3 | * | 100 | = | 300 |
| $3.00 | 4 | * | 100 | = | 400 |
| $2.00 | 5 | * | 100 | = | 500 |
| $1.00 | 6 | * | 100 | = | 600 |

**Figure 4.1. Market Demand**

the price of other goods some of which are substitutes for cola, we expect consumers to switch to the now cheaper good. This means that as price falls quantity demanded will rise. The other reason is called the income effect. If we lower the price of cola holding constant the price of other goods and income, our same income can now buy more goods: either more cola or more other goods. If cola is a normal good its consumption will increase with an increase in income. For what economists call inferior goods, consumption will decrease with an increase in income. Income effects are minor as a determinant of the slope of the demand curve for goods that are a small share of the consumer's budget. However for goods or groups of similar goods that are a large share the budget, income effects can be quite important. Examples might be food, housing or automobile demand.

## HOUSEHOLD SUPPLY

The numbers in the first two columns at the bottom of figure 4.2 give the supply curve for firm X. Note that as the price rises the quantity supplied rises. We assume that there are 100 firms producing cola. Multiplying the number of firm by the amount supplied at each price gives total market supply. Again

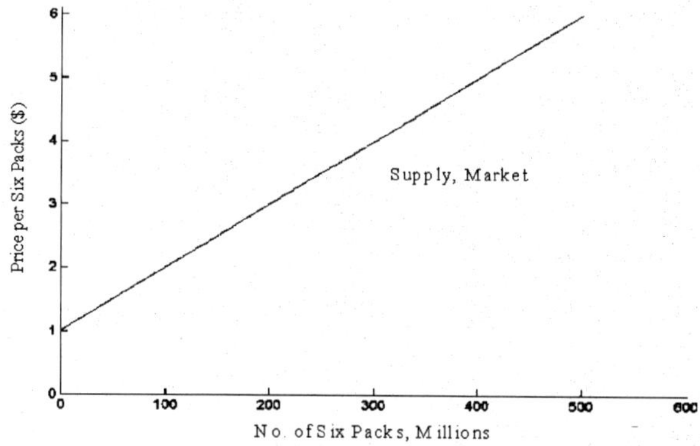


| Price/Six Pack | Number of Six Packs Firm X, Millions | | No. of Firms | | Number of Six Packs Market, Millions |
|---|---|---|---|---|---|
| $1.00 | 0 | * | 100 | = | 0 |
| $2.00 | 1 | * | 100 | = | 100 |
| $3.00 | 2 | * | 100 | = | 200 |
| $4.00 | 3 | * | 100 | = | 300 |
| $5.00 | 4 | * | 100 | = | 400 |

**Figure 4.2. Market Supply**

we are assuming that firm X is our average or typical firm. Note that for the firm, quantities are in millions of six packs. Multiplying by 100 give hundreds of millions of six packs. The supply curve is constructed by plotting the prices in column 1 against the quantities in column 4. Note that the supply curve is upward sloping. This is because if we hold constant other prices, the prices of inputs (such a labor) and the technology of production, an increase in price will make it profitable to increase output. Also the supply curve is upsloping because we expect firms to face rising marginal cost. This is because we assume that some inputs of the firm are given. Usually we assume that the firm has a given stock of capital goods but can vary its labor, raw materials and other inputs. The short run theory of the firm is based on the idea that as we increase the quantity of a variable input, given the quantity of the fixed input that the firm will eventually face diminishing returns, that is the additional output from each additional unit of variable input will decline. The inverse of this is that each additional unit of output will require successively larger quantities of input given the price of the input. This gives us rising marginal cost of output. In the long run all inputs are assumed variable and rising marginal cost depends of diminishing returns to scale or size. For now, we will stick to the short run analysis.

In Figure 4.3 we combine the demand curve from figure 4.1 with the supply curve in figure 4.2. Note that the supply curve intersects the demand

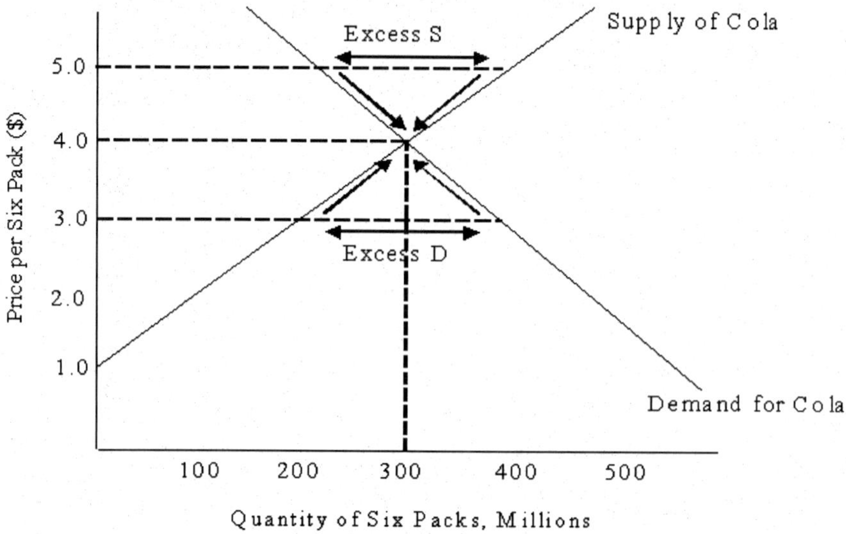


**Figure 4.3. Supply and Demand and Market Equilibrium**

curve at a price of $4.00 and quantity of 300 million six packs. Note from the table in figure 4.1 that our individual consumer A is buying 3 six packs at a price of $4.00. In figure 4.2 see that our typical firm if producing 3 million six packs at a price of $4.00. Back to figure 4.3 point A is where the price that consumers are willing to pay is just equal to the price that firms are willing to offer. This is what is called the market-clearing price. At this price the amount consumers are willing to buy is just equal to the amount that sellers are willing to offer. Realize that the market determines both the price and quantity. Both the firm and the household take the market price as given. The household decides how much to buy at that price. The firm decides how much to produce and offer for sale at that price. If the price is above the market-clearing price, say at $5.00 there will be excess supply. Firms will have an incentive to lower price to get rid of the excess. As the price falls households will buy more. If price is below the market-clearing price there will be excess demand and firms will have an incentive to raise the price. At a higher price consumers will buy less. Thus there will be incentives in the market for the price to adjust toward the market-clearing price.

## SHIFTERS OF SUPPLY AND DEMAND

Figure 4.4 shows an increase in demand with the supply curve unchanged. In this case both price and quantity will increase as a result of shifting up the de-

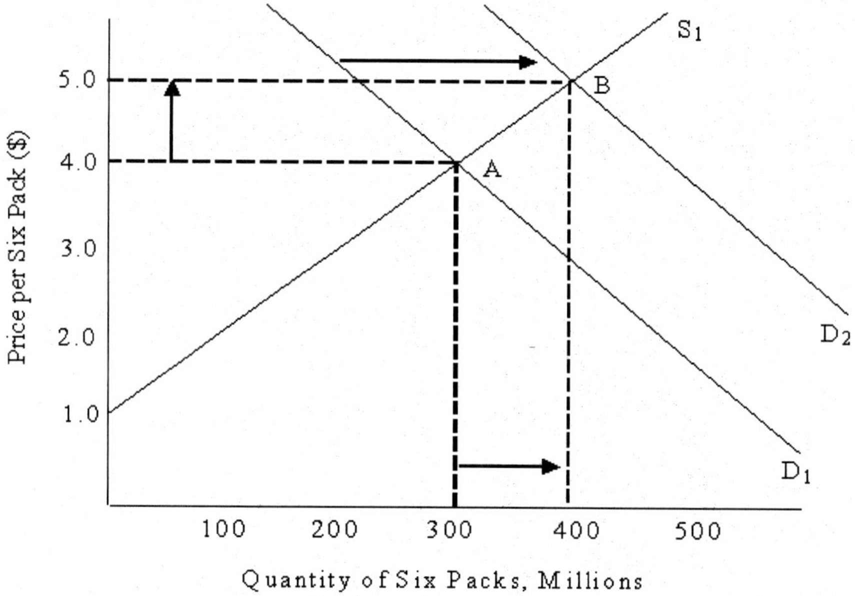


**Figure 4.4. An Increase in Demand**

mand curve from A to B along a given supply curve. What will shift the demand curve right? An increase in consumer income (for a normal good), an increase in the price of a substitute good (such as fruit juice), a change in preferences that leads consumers to demand more cola at any given price and income or an increase in the number of consumers.

Figure 4.5 shows a rightward shift in the supply curve for cola given the demand curve. The supply curve could be shifted right by a decrease in the price of inputs, such as labor or raw materials, a change in technology that reduces the cost of production of cola or an increase in the number of firms producing cola. An increase in input prices, a cost increasing change in technology or a decrease in the number of firms would shift the supply curve left. With a rightward shift in supply, with the demand curve given, the price of cola will decrease and quantity supplied will increase. We move from A to B on Figure 4.5. Price falls to $3.00 per six-pack and quantity supplied increases to 400 million six packs. If the supply curve were to shift left then the price would increase and quantity would decrease. Over time both supply and demand will shift and usually both will shift right this is because we normally have growth in demand as population and incomes grow; we have growth in supply as numbers of firms increase in response to rising demand and as costs decline due to technical change. What happens to price over time depends on which shifts faster, supply or demand. In most competitive industries where

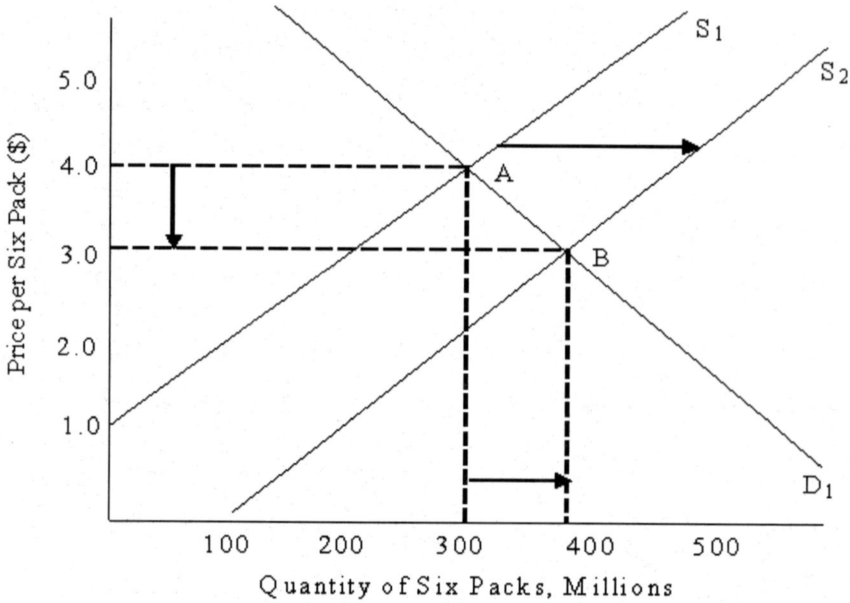


**Figure 4.5. An Increase in Supply**

there is rapid technical change, supply shifts faster than demand and the trend price is downward over time. Consumers benefit as the advantages of technological progress are passed on to consumers in the form of lower prices or higher quality products. Examples would be computer services and software over the last thirty years, or consumer electronics products over the same period.

For some other goods demand increases faster than supply over time. Land prices and thus real estate prices tend to rise over time, especially around growing urban areas. This is because land is limited in any given area and as demand grows prices will rise. Another example might be scarce metals or minerals such as crude oil or precious metals like gold or silver. In other cases prices of some services may rise over time because their supply is restricted by trade associations or by government subsidies to demand. This might be the case with lawyers, or investment bankers or health care services.

The crucial thing to remember is that supply and demand are independent because they are determined by the behavior of different groups of people. Demand is the result of decisions of consumers as to what goods to buy. Supply is the result of decisions of producers concerning what goods to produce. Each consumer takes the price of a product as given by the market and chooses how much to consume at that price to maximize her satisfaction.

Each producer also takes price as given and produces what it is profitable to produce at that price Collectively the price is determined by the interaction of supply and demand in the market. And if markets are competitive price will settle at a level that just covers the cost of production including a competitive rate of return on invested capital.

Households may be either individuals or family units. Households are viewed as demanders of goods and services and suppliers of productive inputs. The primary input they supply is labor services. But they may also supply owned capital goods (say a house for rent) and funds saved that are invested in financial intermediaries (such as a bank) or directly in the financial markets (by owning stocks or bonds). The goods and services consumed are food, clothing, gasoline, fuel oil, rent or mortgage payments on real estate, and many more.

Household demand curves show the relation between quantity demanded and the price of an individual good or service. Demand curves are normally downward sloping as we saw above. This assumes that consumers attempt to maximize utility subject to a budget or income constraint. What is utility? It is satisfaction. Or, put another way, we assume that consumers want to get the most satisfaction per dollar of income. Clearly, most consumers do not have the knowledge of individual goods, of prices and of their preferences to always make the correct decisions. But consumers will not trade money for goods unless they think they will be better off. Households like firms learn by doing. And, like firms, some are better at it than others. Individuals are driven by human nature to want to survive and reproduce. They are conditioned to prefer more income to less income and more goods and services to less goods and services. Households may save part of current income by accumulating financial assets. They may borrow against future income to consume more than current income in the current period.

Households may be thought of as having a dual decision problem. First, they must use the resources that they own to get as much income as possible. Second, they must use that income in such a way as to maximize utility in consumption and in saving. The first is the input supply problem; the second is the product demand problem. The household supplies labor or other resources that it owns to generate income because only with income can the household buy the goods and services it needs. In general, the higher the wage per unit of labor, the more labor will be supplied. On the demand side we usually assume that income is given, and the household uses that income to buy the goods and services that it needs to maximize utility or satisfaction from that given income. On the supply side the household chooses levels of employment of its resources to maximize income. In this traditional theory, the household is viewed as a consumer of goods and services, a net saver (or net borrower) of financial assets and a supplier of productive services. A net saver saves more in the current period than it borrows. A net borrower borrows more in the current period than it saves.

## CONSUMER AND PRODUCER SURPLUS

Return for a moment to figure 4.3. The equilibrium price is $3.00. The area above the price and under the demand curve is called consumer surplus. This is because at all units less than 300 million, consumers would have been willing to pay a higher price off the demand curve. Increases in supply will lower the price and increase consumer surplus. At the price of $4.00 and quantity of 300 million six packs the area below the price and above the supply curve is called producer surplus. This is because at all units less than 300 million, producers would have been willing to supply the goods at a lower price. Producers are receiving a price above cost on those units that represents a surplus to producers. If demand were to rise and price increase there would be an increase in producer surplus. If supply were to rise (shift right) there would be an increase in consumer surplus. At the equilibrium price marginal consumer surplus is zero. Also marginal producer surplus is zero. This means that given the supply and demand curves, consumer and producer surplus are maximized. This is a very useful result. It means that both producers and consumers gain from production and consumption and that their maximum gain is where supply equals demand. This assumes competitive markets and no externalities, issues that we will talk about later.

## THE NEW THEORY OF THE HOUSEHOLD

The new theory of the household that has developed over the past thirty years has added production to the theory of the household. (See Becker, Lancaster and Muth.) The household is viewed as a little firm that is a producer of consumption services. These include food services, entertainment services, shelter services, childcare services and more. These services are produced by combining household labor, household capital goods (house, furniture, car, etc.), and purchased inputs (consumer goods). Over time the household adds to its capital goods though investment, adds to its human capital through education and on the job training and adds to its financial assets through financial investment. At any given time the household has labor services that can be used at home for home production or rented in the market to earn an income. In the past the husband was the primary earner and the wife the primary home producer. That has all changed in the past 30 years or so. Now often both partners spend part of their time earning an income and part of their time in home production. This change has been the result of changes in the technology of the household, which released time for market work; from changes in the work force, which increased the demand for women workers; change in education, which opened up new career paths for women and changes in social attitudes about the role of women in society. In this new theory of the household, it is consumption services that give utility to consumers. Purchased consumer goods, durable goods (housing and other consumer durables) and household labor are inputs in this production process.

## FINANCING THE HOUSEHOLD

With this new theory, households, like firms, must be financed. They finance themselves partly from internal earnings and partly from borrowing. They borrow with a mortgage to finance their house, they borrow on car loans to finance their cars, they borrow on credit cards to finance vacations, gasoline for their cars and even to buy groceries. How much credit a household can obtain depends primarily on three things: The net assets it controls, its current and expected income; and the terms under which credit is available. Net assets are the value of assets minus value of debt or the net worth of the household. These provide collateral against which the household can borrow. Debt must be serviced out of income so the current and expected future income will help determine how much debt the household can service. This includes the expected growth of the income. With a growing income debt service can be relatively easy. However, if income stops growing or declines then debt service can become very difficult as it becomes a much larger share of income. It also includes the uncertainty of the income. It is much easier to service debt if income is relatively certain than if it is relatively uncertain. The terms of credit include the interest rate paid, the maturity of the loan, the down payment required and collateral requirements. As terms of credit become more generous, households can borrow more with any given income. But it also means that households might be more vulnerable to financial distress, in case income should unexpectedly fall.

In 2002, average real estate debt per worker was about $66,200. Average consumer credit was about $15,360 per worker. Of this consumer debt, 38% was revolving credit. ($5836 per worker) and 62% was non revolving (about $9523 per worker) .The revolving credit would be primarily credit card debt and would be unsecured. The non-revolving credit would be mostly auto or other consumer loans, much of which would be secured. Total debt per worker was about $81,560. Realize that these figure are averages for all workers and include workers with no debt. For workers with debt the figures would be higher. Also the mortgage debt figures include rental property as well as owned properties. With rental housing the household pay interest indirectly through rental payments.

Mortgage debt is usually issued for maturities of 25 or 30 years. The debt is amortized over the life of the loan. This means that each month the borrower's payment includes the current interest with the rest applied to principle. Each month the interest payment will decline as the principle declines and the amount applied to principle will increase. The loan will be paid in full by the end of the maturity. Most mortgage loans are fixed interest. This means the interest rate remains fixed for the maturity of the loan. Some are variable interest where the interest rate is periodically adjusted to current market rates. Mortgage loans are secured by the property that is being financed. Usually a down payment of about 10 percent of the value of the property is required. Most mortgages are not held to maturity. Instead they are often paid off and refinanced to remodel, to move to a new location, to move up to a larger or newer house or to refinance at a lower interest rate. The average life of a mortgage is about seven or eight years.

Auto loans are usually secured by conditional sales contract on the auto being financed. For a new car the loan may be amortized over five or six years. For a used car the maturity will be less. Credit card debt is an unsecured personal credit line. The cardholder has the option of paying off the full balance monthly with no interest charge. Normally an annual fee is charged. If the balance is not paid off monthly, the cardholder must pay a minimum payment that usually covers little more than the interest on loan. If the cardholder pays only the minimum payment the loan becomes an unsecured loan of almost infinite maturity. By choosing the monthly payment the cardholder is essentially choosing the maturity for the loan. Credit card debt is very convenient but also very expensive. Interest rates on an annual basis usually run 18 % or more. And penalties for late payment are very steep. High rates result from several things. First, the loans are unsecured. Second, the card issuer carries most of the risk of fraud. If a card is lost or stolen and charges are made on the card, the cardholder is usually only responsible for $50 or so assuming he reports the theft or loss promptly. Third, credit card companies issue cards to practically everyone with little or no attempt to check the credit worthiness of the borrower. This means that there is a lot of cross subsidization between cardholders. The customers with good credit subsidize the customers with bad credit. A customer with good credit would be much better off to pay the full balance monthly and if the person needed credit, to get a secured or unsecured credit line at a bank, credit union, or saving and loan association. The secured credit lines are cheaper. In many states secured credit lines are available as home equity loans. Unfortunately many people don't have access to credit lines through financial institutions.

The option of unsecured credit with near infinite maturity is more than many borrowers can handle. If they only pay the minimum payment, the balance continues to build until the borrower is in so deep that the debt cannot be re-paid. The issuer either writes off the loan or the borrower ends up in bankruptcy. This essentially invites people to get in too deep. A much better alternative would be to require borrowers to pay a minimum payment that would amortize the loan over a three or four year period. The borrower could continue to borrow, but his monthly payment would adjust to keep the amortization period. As the monthly payment increased the borrower would be deterred from further borrowing. Most credit card debt is for short-term purposes. Putting it on a high interest long maturity loan is asking for trouble. One way of reducing the likelihood of trouble would be to offer a lower interest rate to borrowers who are willing to accept the discipline of a shorter maturity. This would also reduce the amount of cross subsidization that now occurs.

## SUMMARY

Viewing the household as a little firm allows us to analyze many issues that are difficult to handle with the traditional theory of the household. Under the traditional theory anything that was not paid work was leisure. The new theory recognizes that much productive activity goes on in the household. It also recognizes that investment and financing decisions are crucial for the success of the household. The household like the firm faces market pressures that force it to follow approximately utility maximizing decisions if it is to survive and maintain its accustomed level of living.

## REVIEW QUESTIONS

Multiple choices: Select the correct answer:

1. Demand curves for individual goods are down sloping because:
   a. Households demand more of a good at higher prices.
   b. Households demand more of a good at lower prices.
   c. Firms produce more of a good at higher prices.
   d. Firms produce more of a good at lower prices.

2. An increase in the cost of cola cans (an input in production) to the cola industry shifts the:
   a. Demand curve for cola right.
   b. Shifts the supply curve for cola right.
   c. Shifts the demand curve for cola left.
   d. Shifts the supply curve for cola left.
3. An increase in the price of fruit juice (a substitute in consumption) shifts the:
   a. Demand curve for cola right.
   b. Supply curve for cola right.
   c. Demand curve for cola left.
   d. Supply curve for cola left.

### Essays

1. With rapid technical progress in production, supply shifts faster over time than demand and we expect trend price of the product to fall. Give some examples of industries or markets where this has been the case.
2. In markets where supply is limited such as land we expect trend price to be upward. Explain why.
3. In the new theory of the household, the household is treated as a little firm. What are some of the advantages of this approach over the traditional theory of the household?

## SUGGESTED READINGS

Becker, Gary, "On the New Theory of Consumer Behavior, *Swedish Journal of Economics*, (1973), 378–95.

Becker, Gary, *The Economic Approach to Human Behavior,* Chicago: University of Chicago Press, 1976: Chapter 17, 132–57.

Lancaster, Kelvin, "A New Approach to Consumer Theory," *Journal of Political Economy*, 72 no. 2 (April 1966).

Lancaster, Kelvin, *Consumer Demand,* (New York: Columbia University Press, 1971). Herendeen, James B. "The Role Credit In the Theory of the Household," *Journal of Consumer Affairs*, 8 no. 2 (Winter 1974), 157–181.

Muth, R., "Household Production and Consumer Demand Functions," *Econometrica*, 34.

Varian, Hal R., *Intermediate Microeconomics: A Modern Approach,* 4th ed, New York: W. W. Norton, 1996: Chapter 1.

*Chapter Five*

# Cost of Production and the Theory of the Firms

## COST OF PRODUCTION

Underlying market supply is firm supply that is determined by cost of production. Cost of production depends on two things. First is the firm's production function. This tells how the firm can combine inputs to produce output. Second, the cost of inputs hired by firms tells us how much it costs to produce that output. The theory of the firm usually assumes that in the short run firms have both fixed inputs and variable inputs. Fixed inputs are usually called the firms capital stock: its investment in plant, equipment, inventories and knowledge. Its variable inputs are its labor and raw materials and other inputs that vary with current output. In reality, the labor of top executives and managers is probably best considered a fixed input. The existence of fixed and variable inputs means that the firm faces diminishing returns in the short run. If the labor force is increased with a fixed stock of capital goods the firm faces diminishing returns to its variable inputs. If additional output per unit of additional input declines then the costs of each additional unit of output must rise.

In economics we look at the cost of both non-hired inputs and of hired inputs. Hired inputs include hired labor and raw materials and other purchased inputs. The firm pays the current market price for these inputs. Non-hired inputs are the cost of inputs furnished by the owners of the firm or by shareholders. It also includes the flow cost of capital goods. Capital goods are purchased at a point in time but give their services over a period of time. For example the firm may invest in a factory to produce output. That factory may be expected to give a flow of services over the next twenty or more years. This cost is then amortized over the expected life of the capital good. This cost is called depreciation. In addition to depreciation there is the cost of the funds invested in the capital goods and operating funds. This is interest cost.

It can be explicit interest on that portion of the funds that are borrowed. There is also implicit interest of funds furnished by shareholders or owners of the firm.

In addition for a proprietary firm or a partnership there may be implicit labor costs for proprietors or partners of the firm. This is the opportunity cost of what it would cost to hire the proprietor or partners to do their job. So the full cost of production includes both the cost of hired inputs and the opportunity cost of non-hired inputs. This is a crucial difference between economics and accounting. In accounting these non-hired costs are usually considered part of the net income of the enterprise. In economics the cost of these non-hired input is considered part of the cost of production. Economic profit is only the residual over and above the cost of all inputs, both hired and non-hired. In the short run economic profit may be positive, negative or zero. In the long run with competitive industries this economic profit will tend toward zero for the typical firm in the industry. This is because if there are economic profits in the industry, there will be an incentive for new firms to enter the industry to capture the excess profits. If there are negative profits in the industry there will be an incentive for firms to leave the industry.

For the competitive firm we expect the average cost of production to be a U shaped curve. As the firm expands output fixed cost per unit of output will fall as the fixed cost is allocated over more and more units of output. Variable cost per unit of output will eventually rise as we experience diminishing returns to the variable inputs. If labor and raw materials are increased and capital is fixed, we will get less and less additional output per unit of variable inputs. We expect average costs to fall as output rises until we reach the point where diminishing returns offsets declining average fixed or overhead cost; then average costs will start rising. In the long run all inputs are considered variable. However we still expect a U shaped long run average cost curve because of decreasing and increasing returns to scale or size. Marginal cost is the cost of additional units of output. It will be rising because of diminishing returns. If you get less additional output per unit of input then the cost of additional units output must be rising. This assumes that the unit cost of the inputs is given. The marginal cost curve will cross the average cost curve at its low point. This is because if marginal cost is above average cost it is pulling average cost up; if it is below average cost it is pulling average cost down.

## PROFIT MAXIMIZATION UNDER PURE COMPETITION

Figure 5.1 shows an average cost curves with average revenue curves. For a competitive firm. Price is taken as given and is equal to average revenue and

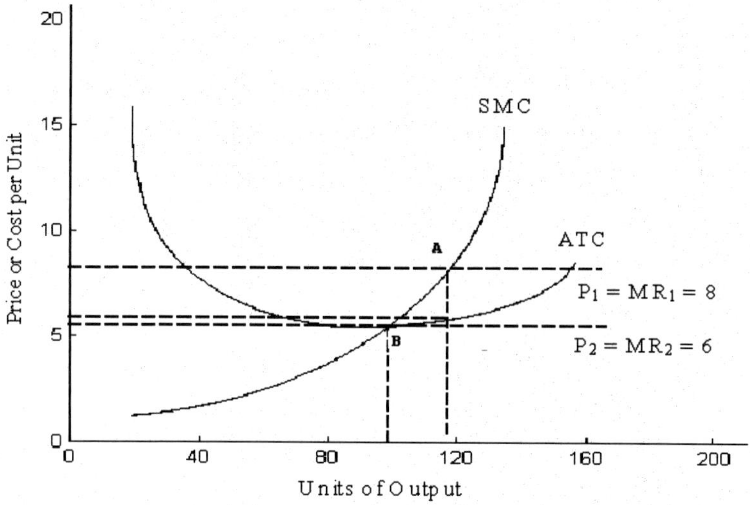


**Figure 5.1. Short Run Profit Maximization: Positive Profit and Zero Profit**

marginal revenue. Two price or marginal revenue curves are shown. One when the price is $8.00 and one when price is $6.00. Profit maximization requires that marginal revenue equal marginal cost when marginal cost is rising. If marginal revenue is above marginal cost, profit must be rising. When marginal revenue is below marginal cost, profit must be falling. Therefore, when marginal revenue equals marginal cost, profit will be at its maximum. With pure competition, price is given and equal to marginal revenue. As we will see, when price is not given at the firm level, this will no longer be the case. In Figure 5.1 at point A marginal revenue equals short run marginal cost. The profit maximizing output is found by dropping down to the horizontal axis where output is about 112 units. Average total cost at that output is $8.35. Average profit per unit is $1.65. Total profit is 1.65×112=$184.80. Total Revenue is 112×$8.00=$896.00. Total cost is $6.35×112=$711.20.

When there is positive profit for the typical firm, and thus for the industry, there will be an incentive for new firms to enter. This will shift the industry supply curve right and equilibrium will be achieved when profits for the typical firm are zero. Remember that costs include a competitive return on invested capital. This is shown in Figure 5.1 at point B where price is $6.00 and output is 100. Average total cost is also $6.00. Total revenue is $600.00 and total cost is $600.00. Total profit and average profit are zero. In the short run the price could fall below $6.00 and the firm could continue to operate as long as it covers variable cost. Fixed costs are sunk cost and must be paid irrespective of output. Firms with high fixed cost can continue to operate for a relatively long time even though economic profits are negative, especially if they don't have too much debt. They can live off the depreciation of their capital stock.

## THE FIRM AND THE MARKET: CONSTANT COST CASE; PURE COMPETITION

Next let us look at the interaction of the firm and the market. Figure 5.2A shows a hypothetical wheat farmer Joe Smith with initial equilibrium output at 30,000 bushels of wheat at $4.00 per bushel at point A This is a zero profit situation with average cost also $4.00 per bushel. In figure 5.2B shows the corresponding industry solution. The price $4.00 is determined by the intersection of industry supply and demand at point A. We assume that Joe Smith is our typical or average wheat farmer. Market supply is Joe Smiths supply multiplied by the number of wheat farmer. We assume there are 10,000 wheat farmers, so equilibrium industry output is 300 million bushels at point A. Now assume that there is an increase in demand for wheat. In the short run the number of wheat farmers is given and price increases to $5.00 per bushel at point B. Back in figure 5.2A we see that Joe Smith is now receiving $5.00 per bushel and producing 33,000 bushels of wheat. He is making an economic profit of $0.60 per bushel or a total economic profit of $19,000. This eco-

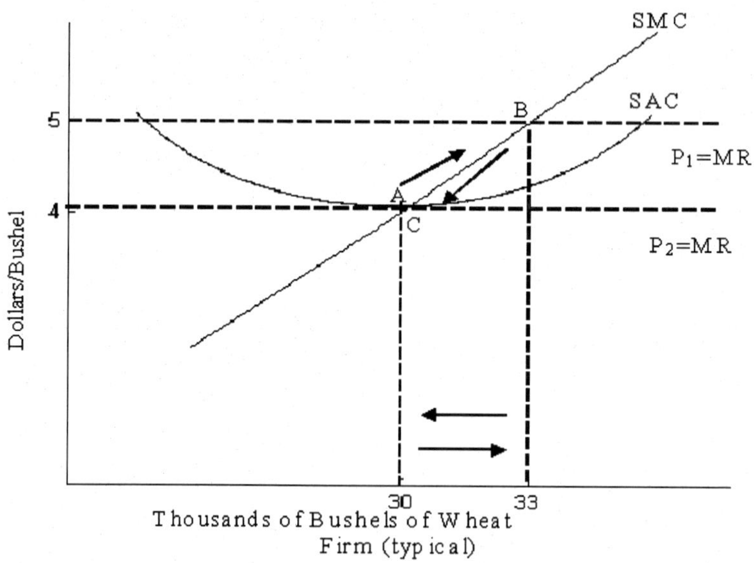


**Figure 5.2A. The Firm under Pure Competition; Constant Cost Case**

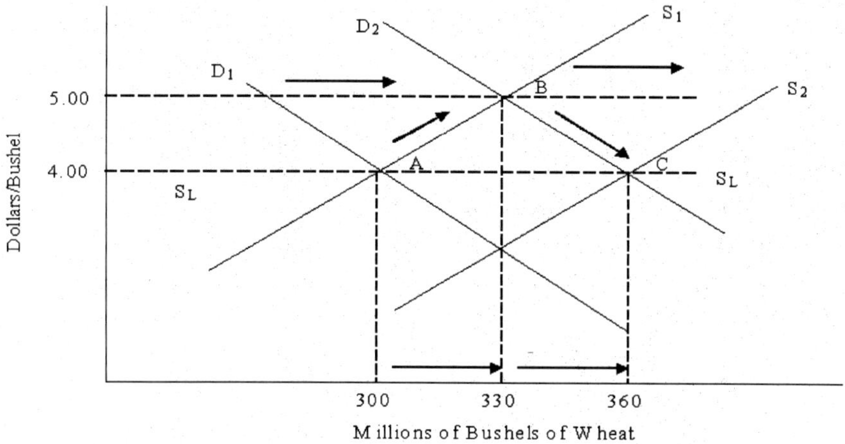


**Figure 5.2B. The Market under Pure Competition; Constant Cost Case**

nomic profit will induce new producers into the industry. The supply curve shifts in figure 5.2B and in equilibrium industry output will be at 360 million bushels of wheat at a price of $4.00 per bushel. Joe Smith in figure 5.2A will be back at 30,000 bushels of wheat again producing at A with zero profit. There are now 12,000 wheat farmers producing the new industry output. This over simplifies the process of adjustment by assuming that costs in the industry do not change and increased output in the long run is met by entrance of new firms.

Despite these simplifications it is an approximation of what happened in the wheat industry in the 1970s and 1980s. In the 1970s there was an increase in demand for wheat in the US. This was partly due to rising world demand and partly due to the falling value of the dollar that followed going to flexible exchange rates in the early 70s. With higher wheat prices wheat farmers enjoyed about seven years of prosperity. Wheat production increased as new producers entered and existing produces increased output. In the eighties the whole process was reversed. Falling world demand, and a rising dollar led to a fall in demand for wheat. Wheat prices fell and remained low for seven years. The wheat industry suffered from excess capacity and economic profits were negative for much of the industry; many farmers left the industry and gradually reduced capacity. Only with the falling dollar and rising demand in the late eighties did the industry recover back to approximate equilibrium.

Figure 5.2 A and B showed how a competitive industry adjusts to a change in demand, assuming costs remain the same. Figure 5.3A shows adjustment to a change in supply due to technological change. Again we use our wheat grower example. Joe Smith is in equilibrium output at point A in figure 5.3A

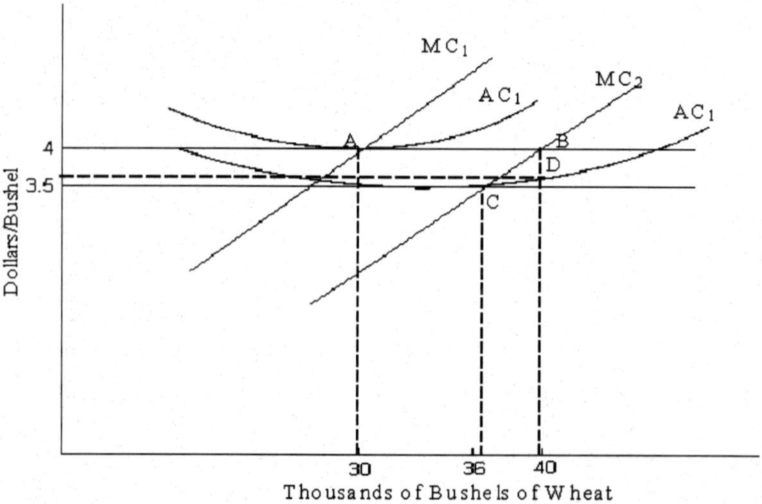


**Figure 5.3A. Innovators' Profits in a Competitive Industry; Firm Adjustments**

with price $4.00 per bushel and quantity of 30,000 bushels. The industry is in equilibrium in figure 5.3B at 300 million bushels of wheat and also a price of $4.00. Initially Joe Smith adopts an innovation, say a new variety of hybrid wheat that allows higher output for any given cost or lower costs for any given output. If he is the only adopter, the market price of wheat is not affected, as his output is a tiny share of industry output. He will make innovators profits of $0.40 per bushel on 40,000 bushels of wheat. Over time other

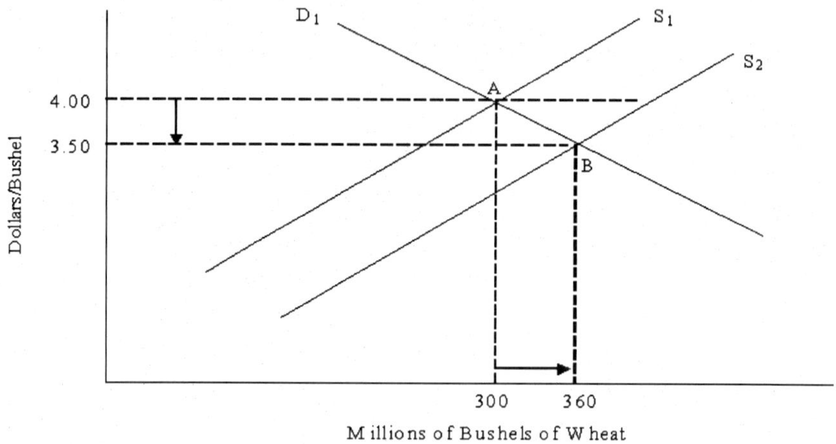


**Figure 5.3B. Innovators' Profits in a Competitive Industry; Industry Adjustments**

farmers will also adopt the innovation; supply will increase and when all farmers have adopted the new innovation, industry price will fall to $3.50 per bushel and industry output will be 360 million bushels. Joe Smith now produces 36,000 bushels and his costs will again equal price but now at $3.50 per bushel.

Again this has been going on in the wheat industry and many other competitive industries. Technical change is supplied to agriculture by the Land Grant Universities and State Experiment Stations as well as by the firms that supply farm inputs and buy farm output. Competition forces the gains to be passed on to the buyers of farm products and ultimately to consumers. The number of wheat farms has fallen dramatically over the past 50 years and farms have become much larger, more mechanized and more efficient. The same is true of the rest of agriculture in the U.S.

## PROFIT MAXIMIZATION UNDER IMPERFECT COMPETITION

Under imperfect competition in the output market firms face downward sloping demand curves. What this means is that the firm cannot sell unlimited quantities at a fixed price. It must either lower its price or increase advertising or product quality to sell additional output. This means that the firm is selling a differentiated product. Its product is different in some way from its competitor's products. Brand recognition is one of the most common ways of differentiating a product. Pepsi and Coke are very similar products but the two companies spend millions of dollars to maintain their brand image and keep their dedicated customers. The same is true in the auto industry. A Ford, a Chevy, or a Toyota may be very similar products but to their loyal customers they are definitely different. The same is true of the retail clothing market, the retail food market and many others.

Figure 5.4A gives a profit maximizing solution for a firm under imperfect competition in the product market. The line with the small d is the firm demand curve for this particular product, say, Brand X Cola. It assumes that the price of other brands in the product group is given. This means that the demand curve will be relatively elastic. A small change in price will bring about a relatively large change in output. The price along the demand curve represents average revenue. Because average revenue is falling, marginal revenue will be below it. Again if your average grade is falling, your marginal grade, the grade on your last exam, must be below the average and pulling the average down. Profit maximization requires that marginal revenue equal marginal cost. This is at point A in figure 5.4A. To find price we go up to the demand curve. Price is $5.20 per six-pack of cola. Quantity is found by going down

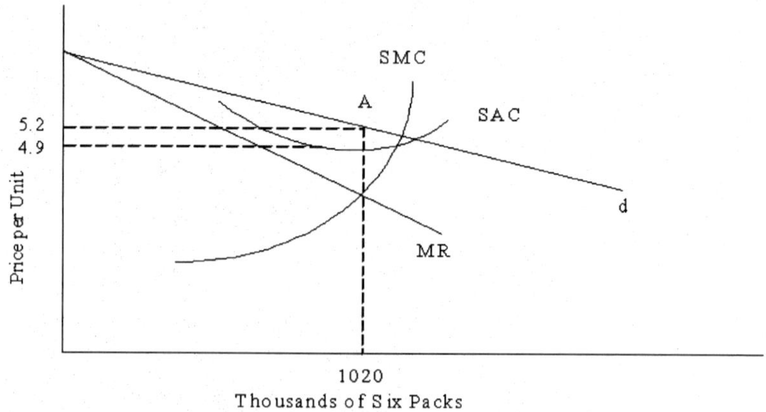


**Figure 5.4A. The Firm with Monopolistic Competition, Short Run, Positive Profit**

to the horizontal axis and is 1,020 thousand six packs of cola. Average cost is found on the average cost curve and is $4.90 per six-pack, a profit of $0.25 per six-pack and total profit of $255 thousand dollars ($0.25 x 1,020 thousand six pack).

Figure 5.4B shows the market solution. We assume that Brand X is the typical or average firm in the product group and that there are 100 firms in the cola industry. Industry output is 102 million six-packs. The industry demand curve is less elastic than the firm demand curve. This is because when we change industry price we assume that the price of all firms in the industry are changing together. This rules out substitution between brands. Substitution

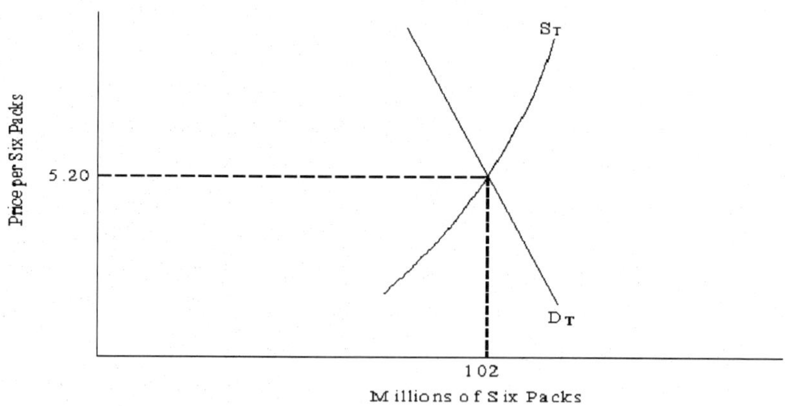


**Figure 5.4B. The Industry Solution Corresponding to the Firm Solution**

along the industry demand curve would be between cola and non-cola goods. Unlike pure competition the firm supply curve is not its marginal cost curve. Instead it would be above the marginal cost curve and trace out all the prices consistent with the profit maximizing outputs as demand and marginal revenue are shifted along the marginal cost curve. Likewise the industry supply curve will not be the sum of the marginal cost curves of the firms. It will trace out the profit maximizing output for all the firms when the industry price is changed. It will be more inelastic than the supply curve for the individual firm because supply substitution between firms is ruled out by assuming that prices for all firms change together.

Figure 5.5A shows the solution for the imperfectly competitive firm in the long run with zero profit. Note that the average cost curve is just tangent to the demand curve at point A. price is 4.50 per six-pack and firm output is 1000 thousand six packs. There are 100 firms in the industry and industry output is 100 million six-packs. However, under imperfect competition this tangency is not at minimum average cost. It cannot be as long as the demand curve is downward sloping. This means that firms are producing where price equals cost including normal profit but this is not at minimum average cost. This price above minimum average cost is usually considered the price of having product differentiation. Figure 5.5B shows the corresponding industry solution.

However it is possible to have a firm producing at minimum average cost even under imperfect competition. This is when advertising expense is treated as a variable cost and acts as a shifter of the demand curve. The long run average revenue with variable advertising will trace out the optimum prices at

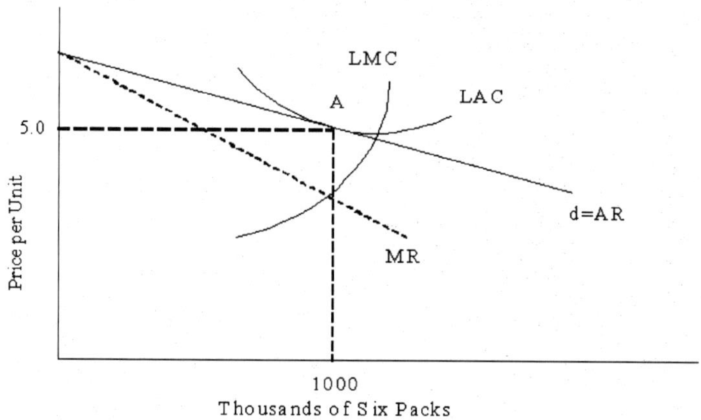


**Figure 5.5A. The Firm with Monopolistic Competition, Long Run, Zero Profit**

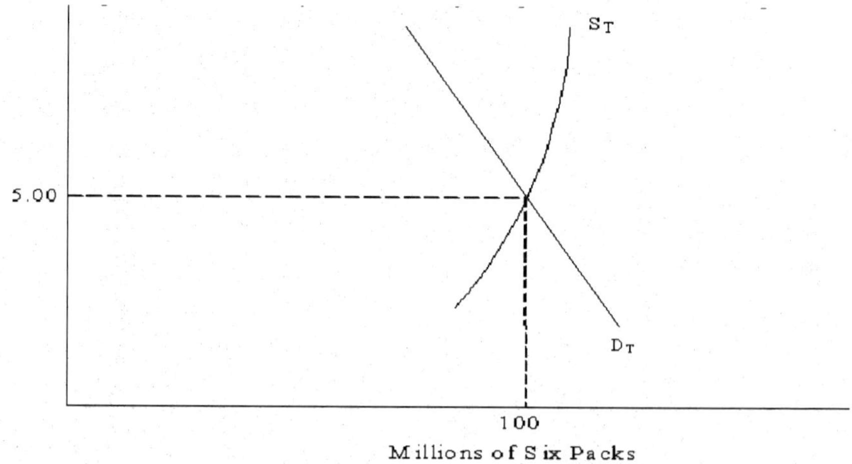


**Figure 5.5B. The Industry Solution Corresponding to the Firm Solution in Fig 5.5A**

each short-run solution with a fixed level of advertising and a given short run demand curve. Each point on the long run average revenue curve represents a point on successive demand curves as advertising is varied. Assuming diminishing returns to advertising we would expect a long-run average revenue curve that is rising, hits a peak and then declines. Likewise we will have a traditional long run average cost curve due to diminishing returns to scale or size in production and including variable advertising costs. This solution is shown in figure 5.6. The long run average revenue curve is just tangent to the long-run average cost curve at a price of $5.00 and output of 1100 thousand six-

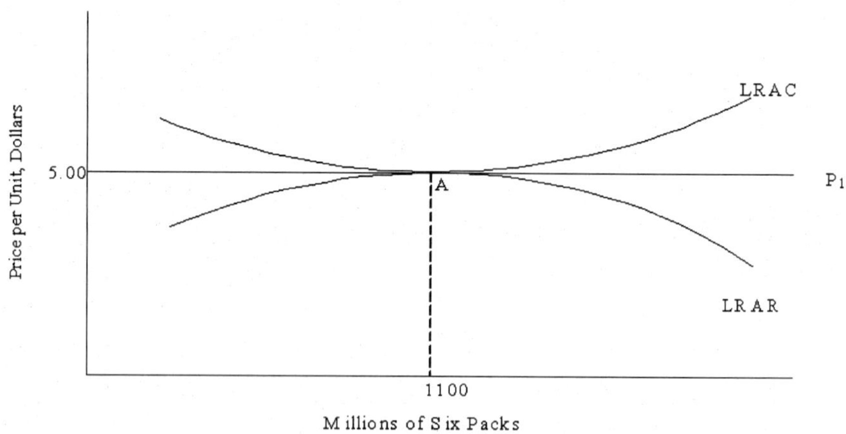


**Figure 5.6. The Long Run Solution; Monopolistic Competition; Variable Advertising**

packs at point A. If advertising effects firm demand but not industry demand then industry output will be 100 million six-packs, the same as in the case above. However, now we will have only 91 firms in the industry. With advertising each firm will be producing a larger output but there will be fewer firms in the industry. A similar solution can be shown where the firm is allowed to vary its product. The point is that under imperfect competition where entry into the industry is unrestricted and there are no fixed costs there are solutions that are similar to pure competition.

## MONOPOLY AND OLIGOPOLY

Under monopoly and oligopoly the same may not be the case. With monopoly there is only one firm and entry is restricted. This means that the firm may earn excess profits even in the long run. Figure 5.7 shows a comparison of a monopoly and pure competition solution. The monopolist will produce at C where MR=MC with price of $5.00 at point A and output of 100 thousand units. A competitive industry with the same average cost would produce at B with 120 thousand of output and a price of $4.00. The point is, if costs are the same the monopolist will produce at a higher price

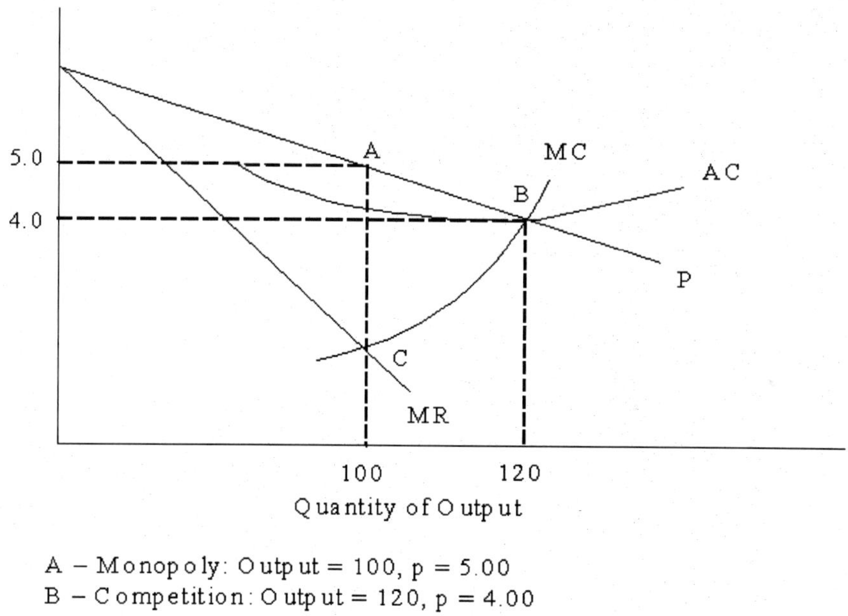


**Figure 5.7. Monopoly and Pure Competition Compared**

and lower output. In addition the monopolist will produce where price exceeds marginal cost and this implies a less efficient outcome. Efficiency requires that price equal marginal cost. This is because price represents marginal social value and marginal cost represents marginal social cost. This assumes no externalities; a subject that we will discuss is a chapter 11. Also, because it is a monopoly, entry into the industry is blocked. This means that the monopoly may earn excess profits, even in the long run.

With oligopoly we have restricted entry and mutual interdependence. (We discuss this in the next chapter.) The solution will depend on the degree of mutual interdependence and the number of firms. In Figure 5.8A we see the range of outcomes. $D_T$ represents the industry demand curve. Point A with output 1000 million and price $10.00 represents the monopoly or cartel solution. This is where total marginal revenue equals long run marginal cost. With a cartel if all firms have the same average cost each will produce at minimum average cost to maximize total profits to the group. If there are ten identical firms, each will produce 100 million units at cost of $5.00 and price of $10.00. Profit will be $5.00 per unit and $500 million for the group. Each firm will have a profit of 50 million dollars. This solution is shown in figure 5.8B. The problem is that each firm will have an incentive to produce more than 100 million units since, with rising marginal cost its optimum output will be

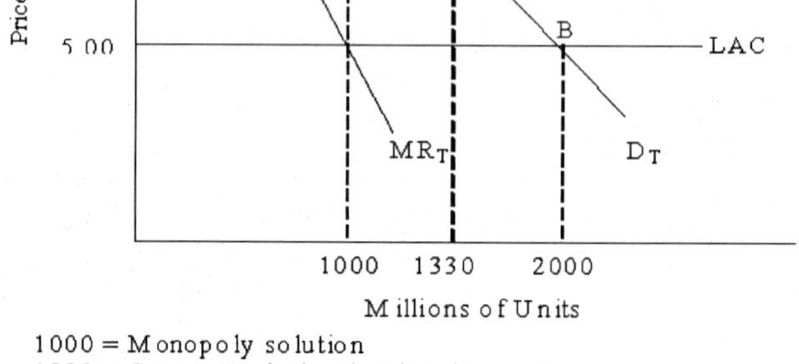


1000 = Monopoly solution
1330 = Cournot solution (2 Firms)
2000 = Competitive solution

**Figure 5.8A. Market Demand and Marginal Revenue Curves, Monopoly, Oligopoly and Pure Competition**

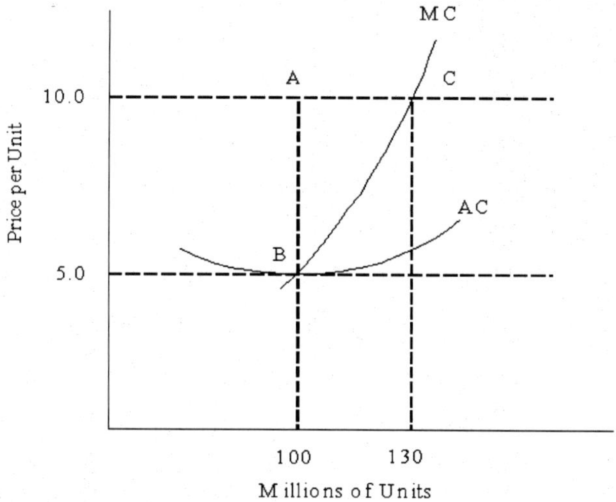


$10.00 = Monopoly Price
100 = Firm Output, 100 = Total Output, 10 Firm in Industry
2000 = Competitive Output
130 = Optimum Firm Output at Monopoly Price

**Figure 5.8B. Multi-Plant Monopoly, Joint Profit Maximizing Oligopoly: At the Firm Level**

greater than 100 million units. If all firms exceed the group optimum output, total output will rise and price will fall. This is shown in Figure 5.8B. Optimum firm output for the group maximization is at 100 million units with price of $10.0 at A and cost of $5.00 at B. However at a price of $10.00 the optimum output for each firm is 130 million units. This is where price equals MC at point C. If all firms produce this output then price will fall. At the limit it will fall to $5.00 the competitive price. This is the reason that most cartels ultimately fail unless backed by the power of government to impose discipline on the firms.

The monopoly or cartel solution is unlikely to result in most oligopoly situations unless there is a dominant firm or government able to impose the group interest on the individual firms. Instead the more common solution proposed by economists is called a Nash Equilibrium and derives from game theory. For a simple illustration take the two firm cases. Call them Firm A and Firm B. For each output selected by B there will be an optimum output for A that maximizes its profit given the residual demand. By varying Bs output we can trace out all of the optimum outputs for A. We can do the same for B. For each output for A there is an optimum output for B. This is shown in figure 5.9, using

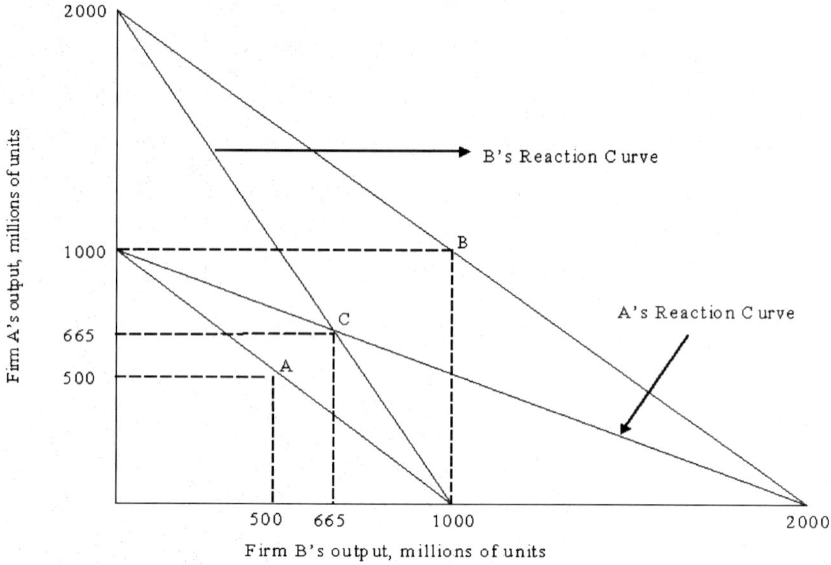


**Figure 5.9. Nash Equilibrium, Joint Profit Maximization and the Competitive Solution; the Two Firm Model**

the same demand, output, and cost as in figure 5.8A. Output for A can vary from O when B produces 1000 million units, its monopoly output, to 2000 units when B produces 0 units, its competitive output. The same is true for B. If A produces the competitive output of 2000 million B will produce 0. When A produces zero B will produce the monopoly solution of 1000 million. The lines connecting these points for A and B are called A's reaction curve and B's reaction curve. Where the two curves cross is the Nash Equilibrium. A is doing the best it can given B's output and B is doing the best it can given A's output. At A each firm produces 665 million units and total output is at 1330 units. This point is at C and corresponds to point C in figure 5.8A. If the two firms act as joint profit maximizing oligopolies they will produce at point A and each produce 500 million units for a total output of 1000 million. This corresponds to point A in Figure in figure 5.8A. If the two firms act as competitive firms they would operate at point B and each produce 1000 million units for total output of 2000 million units. This corresponds to point B in figure 5.8A. This would be the case if there was unrestricted entry and we had a perfectly competitive oligopoly that would in effect no longer be an oligopoly. The price for each solution if found off the demand curve in Figure 5.8A. The monopoly price is \$10.00; the Nash Equilibrium price is \$8.30 and the competitive price is \$5.00. These solutions are dependent on the simplifying assumptions we have made. First the two firms have constant and equal cost of $5.00 per unit. Second, they face a linear total demand curve. Third they each have the same share of total output. If we add more firms to the model the Nash price would be pushed down toward the competitive price. More complicated case can be solved mathematically but are difficult to illustrate graphically.

## SUMMARY

Over time firms compete by innovation. In a purely competitive market this involves cost innovation since the firm takes price as given by the market: new techniques of production, lower cost inputs and better ways of organizing the production process. With imperfect competition the firm can innovate either by reducing cost or by increasing demand: by advertising, by product promotion or by development of new products. In the short run innovating firms can earn excess profits by lowering costs or increasing revenues relative to other firms in the industry. In the long run, other firms copy the innovations and supply increases and excess profits are eliminated. This is why firms like patents and copyrights. They restrict the ability of other firms to copy their innovations and allow them to earn excess profits at least until the patent or copyright expires or until other firms find a competing product that does not infringe on the patent or copyright.

## REVIEW QUESTIONS

Multiple choices: Select the correct answer:

1. With an imperfect output market the firm faces:
   a. An up-sloping output demand curve
   b. A down-sloping output demand curve
   c. A horizontal output demand curve
   d. None of the above
2. A firm that is producing its optimum output will:
   a. Not be hiring its optimum quantity of input
   b. Be hiring its optimum quantity of input
   c. Neither of the above
3. A firm facing an imperfect output market
   a. Will produce where price is less than marginal cost
   b. Will produce where price is greater than marginal cost

c. Will produce where price is equal to marginal cost
d. None of the above

4. The trend price of land is upward because
   a. Land is plentiful and demand is falling
   b. Land is scarce and demand is falling
   c. Land is scarce and demand is rising
   d. None of the above
5. With perfect competition firms may innovate by:
   a. Cost innovation only.
   b. Demand innovation only.
   c. Demand innovation or cost innovation.
6. With imperfect competition in the product market:
   a. Price will exceed marginal cost.
   b. Price will be less than marginal cost.
   c. Price will be equal to marginal cost.
   d. None of the above.
7. With a cartel individual firms will have an incentive to:
   a. Produce more than the group optimum output.
   b. Produce less than the group optimum output.
   c. Produce the group optimum output.
8. Compared to a competitive firm, a monopolist will produce with:
   a. A higher price and output.
   b. A lower price and lower output.
   c. A higher price and lower output
9. The Nash solution for oligopoly says that:
   a. Each firm ignores the behavior of other firms in the market.
   b. Each firm does the best it can, given the behavior of the other firm (or firms).
   c. The firms act as joint profit maximizers.

## Essays

1. A competitive firm can earn innovators profits in the short run but not in the long run. Explain why.
2. Explain why we expect short run marginal cost to be up sloping.
3. Profit maximization requires that marginal cost equals marginal revenue. Explain why this is the case.
4. In the long run in a competitive industry firms will produce at minimum average cost and with zero excess profits. Explain why. Why is this good for consumers?

## SUGGESTED READINGS

Chamberlin, Edward Hastings, *The Theory of Monopolistic Competition,* Cambridge:Harvard University Press, 8th ed. 1962, Chapters 2, 5. (1st ed. 1933.)

Herendeen, James B. *The Economics of the Corporate Economy*, New York: Dunellen, 1975, 49–66.

Pindyck, Robert and Daniel Rubinfeld, *Microeconomics,* 2nd ed. New York, Macmillan Publishing Co. 1992, Chapters 7–10.

# *Chapter Six*

# Classification of Market Structure

Economists have a classification system for markets that helps us to see the varying degrees of competition under different market structures. Individual firms usually operate in several different markets on both the input side and the output side and these markets often have varying degrees of competition. However, the classifications are useful as they allow us to isolate the factors that determine competition in different types of markets. These different market structures can be looked at for both output markets and input markets.

## PURE COMPETITION: OUTPUT MARKET

Pure competition requires that firms be price takers in the output market. This means that all firms in the market take price as given by the market. Each individual firm is a small enough share of the market that its production decisions do not influence total output. The wheat farmer in South Dakota can sell all the wheat he can produce at the market price. If he doubles his output, the price will still be the same. A condition necessary for this to be true is for him to sell a standardized product. His wheat is no different from the wheat of thousand of other wheat farmers. Another condition is that there be a very large number of firms so that no individual firm can affect the price. And last, entry into the industry must be relatively easy. There are no substantial barriers to entry. We will discuss what those barriers are below.

Under pure competition in the output market, firms will maximize profits by producing where price is equal to the marginal cost of production. Since price is given it will equal marginal revenue. Marginal cost is the additional cost of producing another unit of output. Marginal revenue is the additional revenue from another unit of output. We assume that the firms face rising marginal cost because of diminishing returns to the fixed input. If marginal revenue exceeds marginal cost profits are rising. If marginal revenue is less than marginal cost profits are falling. Thus when marginal revenue equals marginal cost profits will be at a maximum. In the short run firms may have maximum economic profits that are positive, negative or zero. In the long run firms will produce at zero economic profit. Economic profit is profit above the normal profit required to keep the firms invested capital employed in the industry. If industry profits are positive (i.e., above normal) new firms will enter, supply will increase and excess profits will disappear. If industry profits are negative some firms will be forced to leave the industry, because firms must cover all costs, included normal profit in order to remain solvent. When some firms leave the industry, supply will fall and price will increase to cover costs. This implies that in the long run firms will produce at minimum average cost. A normal return on invested capital is considered part of cost.

## PURE COMPETITION: INPUT MARKET

Pure competition in the input market implies that the firm is a price taker in the hiring of inputs. If the input is labor it means that the firm can hire as many workers as it wishes at a fixed wage rate. For the wheat farmer, the better examples might be fertilizer, gasoline, chemical sprays and seed. For all of these the farmer would probably be a price taker.This implies that the farmer is hiring standardized inputs. Again this would be pretty much true for the ones listed. Another condition for pure competition is that there be a large number of firms hiring the input, so that no one firm can influence the price of the input. And, as with the output market, there must be easy entry into the industry.

In the input market, profit maximization requires that the price of the input (its marginal cost) be equal to the marginal revenue generated by the last unit of input hired. Also in the long run economic profit per unit of input will also be zero. It turns out that maximizing profit in the input market is equivalent to maximizing profit in the output market. You can't have one without the other.

## IMPERFECT (OR MONOPOLISTIC) COMPETITION: OUTPUT MARKET

Imperfect competition in the output market is also called monopolistic competition. The names come from the two people who first developed the ideas.

Joan Robinson, an English economist wrote a book called *Imperfect Competition* (1933) and Edward Chamberlain, an American economist wrote a book called *Monopolistic Competition* (1933). Although the two authors did not think their ideas were the same, economists have come to use the two terms to mean the same thing. With imperfect competition in the output market the firm is a price maker. This means it chooses a price off its demand curve that is the optimum price. (The price consistent with profit maximization.) This requires that the firm cannot sell unlimited quantities at a fixed price. Instead it must lower price to increase sales.

To have this condition firms must produce differentiated products. Each firm produces a product that is slightly different from the product of competing firms in the same industry. Examples might be the beer industry where there are a large number of competing brands. Or retail groceries where stores sell large numbers of closely competing brands of many different products. Products may be differentiated by small variations in quality, flavor, design, brand names, packaging, services provided and even by location.

With price declining with output, marginal revenue will be below average revenue (or price). To maximize profit the firm produces where marginal revenue equals marginal cost. This will be where price exceeds marginal cost. This means price is a markup over marginal cost. If the elasticity of demand is constant, the price will be a constant percentage (or ratio) markup above marginal cost. (Elasticity of demand measures the percent change in quantity divided by the percent change in price along the demand curve. It tells, in relative terms, how responsive quantity is to a change in price along a demand curve.) We know that in most retail trades markup pricing is the rule.

In he short run, average cost may be greater, equal or less than price: the firm may have positive, zero or negative economic profits. In the long run the firm will produce where price is equal to average cost and economic profits will be zero. This is because there are a relatively large number of firms in the industry and entry into the industry is relatively easy. When excess profits occur new firms will enter or existing firms will expand capacity and this will increase supply, force down price and eliminate excess profits. Even though a firm produces where price equals average cost, this is not at minimum average cost, as was the case with pure competition. This is because with a downward sloping demand curve the average cost curve cannot be tangent to the demand curve at its low point. However if we allow advertising in the model we can derive a long run average revenue, with advertising variable, and a long run average cost including varying advertising cost that can be tangent at minimum average cost.

## IMPERFECT (MONOPSONISTIC) COMPETITION: INPUT MARKET

In the input market imperfect competition is also called monopsonistic competition. In this case the firm cannot hire unlimited quantity of inputs at a fixed price. To expand employment of any given input the firm will have to pay a higher price to attract additional units, usually to bid them away from competing firms. For this to be the case we need differentiated inputs. You don't just hire workers you hire accountants, computer engineers, advertising specialists, assembly line workers and so on. To any given firm these skills will be limited in supply. The skills are often firm or industry specific. This further limits their supply. With an up sloping supply curve for the input, the marginal cost of the input will be above its average cost. The firm will produce where the marginal cost of the input is above the average cost of the input. The firm will equate the marginal cost of the input to the marginal revenue generated by the input to maximize profits. This requires that the price paid the input will be below the marginal cost of the input. There is an optimum markdown from marginal input cost. If elasticity of supply is constant, there will be a constant percentage markdown.

Again we assume relatively large numbers of firms and relatively easy entry into the industry. If this is the case, economic profits can be positive, negative or zero in the short run. In the long run, competition will eliminate excess profits and firms will earn only a normal return on their investment. The zero economic profit condition requires that the price of the input equal its average net revenue (average revenue minus the average cost of other inputs all per unit of the variable input). Again, this is equivalent to average cost equal average revenue in the output market. Optimum output always implies optimum input hired. Zero profit per unit of input implies zero profit per unit of output.

## OLIGOPOLY: OUTPUT MARKET

Oligopoly is also called competition among the few. It refers to a situation where an industry is dominated by a relatively small number of firms, each one of which has a relatively large share of industry output. When this is the case, each firm's major decisions such as pricing, output, advertising and new product development will depend on how other firms react to their behavior. This is called mutual interdependence. Under pure and imperfect competition above it was assumed that each firm acted independently. The market determined group decisions. With oligopoly things are not so simple. Oligopolies may have either standardized products or differentiated products. Entry into the industry is usually restricted. The things that can restrict entry are control of basic inputs, economies of scale, patents or copyrights on key technology or government regulation. With oligopoly the results depend on the assumption we make about inter-group behavior.

If we assume joint profit maximization, we get the monopoly result below. In this case we have what is called a cartel. With a cartel firms get together as a group and decide on the joint output that maximizes group profits. The problem is that cartel arrangements are difficult to enforce because at the cartel price each individual firm has an incentive to produce more than its allocated share of output. As more firms cheat, price falls unless the non-cheating firms further restrict output. OPEC was a relatively successful cartel in the seventies but it broke down in the early and mid eighties as non-OPEC countries increased their oil production and as many OPEC countries exceeded their production quotas. Saudi Arabia became the main country still restricting output and when it gave up in 1986 the crude oil price dropped dramatically.

The other primary oligopoly model is based on game theory. The result is known as a Nash-Equilibrium. (Named after John Nash, a Nobel Prize winning economist and mathematician.) This model assumes that each firm does the best it can, given the behavior of the other firms in the industry. When all firms do this we have a Nash-Equilibrium. This solution has a lower price and higher output than the monopolist or joint-profit maximizing solution but a higher price and lower output than would a competitive industry with the same costs. However if entry into an oligopolistic industry is not restricted then the solution approaches the imperfect competition solution with a differentiated product or the competitive solution with a standardized product. Small numbers, in itself, will not give an oligopoly solution: there must also be barriers to entry into the industry. If entry is affectively restricted then an oligopoly industry may earn excess profits even in the long run.

## OLIGOPSONY: INPUT MARKET

Oligopsony refers to competition among the few in the input market. This means a small number of firms hiring an input that may be differentiated or standardized. Each of the primary firms in the input market must have a significant share of industry employment. Examples might be the auto industry or the steel industry in their dealings with non-labor suppliers. Their labor suppliers are unionized so that in these markets there would be what is called bi-lateral monopoly or bi-lateral oligopoly. Again to have an effective oligopsony you need mutual interdependence and restricted entry. A profit maximizing solution in the input market implies a profit maximizing solution in the output market. Restricted entry implies that economic profits may be positive in the long run.

## MONOPOLY: OUTPUT MARKET

Monopoly means one firm in the market. It implies no close substitutes for the product. And this implies a differentiated product. Also entry into the industry must be blocked. AT&T was a regulated monopoly in the telephone business before the Federal Government broke it up in the early 1980s. A monopolist will maximize profits by equating marginal revenue to marginal cost. This will imply a price above marginal cost and usually above average cost. It will imply a higher price and a lower output than would be the case for a competitive firm with the same costs. However, unlike imperfect competition, profits may not be eliminated in the long run. This is because entry of other firms to capture excess profits is prevented by blocked entry. Blocked entry may result from control of basic raw materials, control of technology (usually by patents) control of key skills, economies of scale, or by government franchise. A monopoly position is difficult to maintain in the long run without some form of government protection.

## MONOPSONY: INPUT MARKET

In the input market the one firm solution is called monopsony. This means a single hirer of an input. Before its breakup, AT&T was the only hirer of telephone linemen. However, since they were unionized this would have been bilateral monopoly. For monopsony to occur there must be a differentiated input with no close substitutes. This implies an up-sloping input supply curve. The firm must pay a higher price to attract additional units of the input. With an up-sloping input supply (average cost) curve, the marginal cost of the input will exceed average cost. The firm equates the marginal cost per unit of input to the marginal revenue per unit of input. As with imperfect competition in the input market, this implies a price for the input that is below the marginal cost of the input. And even in the long run the price of the input (its average cost) may be less than its average net revenue. Even in the long run the firm may have positive economic profit. Again this results from the fact that entry into the market is restricted. Again a profit maximizing solution in the input market implies one in the output market.

## FIRMS WITH MULTIPLE MARKETS

Real world firms have multiple markets in both the output market and the input market. And these markets can exhibit varying degrees of competition. In the auto industry each major producer faces a variety of markets: small cars, mid size cars, luxury cars, SUVs, pick-up trucks and so on. The markup over cost in each of these markets will vary depending in part on the degree of competition. Mid-sized family sedans (such as the Honda Accord, Toyota Camry, or Ford Taurus) are a highly competitive market. The market for large SUVs is much less competitive and in general has a higher percentage markup than does the market for the mid-sized family sedans. Like wise on the input side. Firms hire all kind of labor from unskilled workers to highly skilled, including top executives. In general the more skilled the worker the higher the wage and benefit package he can command. Even a very large company may face relatively pure competition in the market for funds. The interest rate on loans may be constant for varying levels of funds hired. Thus a firm that is oligopolistic in the output market may be competitive in some of its input markets. Or a firm that faces an oligopsonistic input market may face some output markets that are highly competitive.

Also there are other market structures that we haven't discussed. We mentioned bi-lateral monopoly. This is when a monopolistic seller of output faces a monopsonistic buyer of that input. A labor union facing an auto firm might be an example. Here the solution may depend on the relative bargaining power of the two sides. Also we have price discrimination models to explain why the same product may sell at different prices in different markets. In order to have price discrimination you must be able to separate the markets and the different markets must have differing elasticity of demand. Elasticity gives the percent change in quantity for a given percent change in price. The less the elasticity of demand the smaller the percent response of quantity to a given percent change in price. An example might be a suit sold at a department store versus the same suit sold at a discount store. Because many people who shop at the department store do not shop at the discount store and vice versa the two markets are at least partially separate. The rule is that a higher price be charged in the less elastic market and a lower price be charged in the more elastic market. This is consistent with profit maximizing behavior. Demand at the department store is less elastic and there we usually observe the higher price. There are many other examples. Cars sold in the domestic market often command a higher price than when sold in the export market. Money loaned in wholesale markets usually carries lower interest rates than money loaned in retail markets. Retail customers for electricity usually pay higher rates than wholesale customers.

## THE FIRM AND THE MARKET

Under pure competition and monopolistic competition in either the input market or the output there is a clear distinction between firm and market. The output market is made up of hundreds or even thousands of firm suppliers and often thousands of consumer demanders. In this case impersonal market forces determine price. With pure competition both producers and consumers take price as given by the market. Under monopolistic competition there are still hundreds of firms and thousands of consumers and even though firms are price makers, price in the long run must reflect cost of production and price between firms will only vary because of product differentiation. With oligopoly things are not so simple. Price will depend on the degree of interdependence between firms and by the ability of other firms to enter the industry. Even with small numbers of firms, if entry into the industry is not seriously restricted, in the long run, price will settle near cost and we get a relatively competitive result.

In the US auto market there are five primary producers: General Motors, Ford, Chrysler (Daimler-Chrysler), Toyota and Honda. Despite this small number of firms the industry is relatively competitive. This is because the technology is relatively easily available. This was much less true in the 60s and 70s before the Japanese firms entered the US market. The US pharmaceutical industry also has a relatively small number of major firms. However, for them new drugs have about 20 years of patent protection, import and export of prescription drugs is not allowed and most drugs are paid for by third party payers (HMOs, insurance companies, and Medicaid). This means that the industry has a very protected market and drug prices are much higher in the US than in other countries. The drug industry has earned above normal profits for a long time. The crucial differences are ability to enter the industry and the ability to pass on high prices to third party payers.

With monopoly the firm is the industry and the concept of having price set by impersonal market forces loses its meaning. However, even a monopoly may lose its pricing power if it can no longer restrict entry. In a perfectly competitive monopoly, the ability of other firms to enter, removes its monopoly power. Basically, it is no longer a monopoly, even though it is the only firm in the market.

We have concentrated on price determination as most economic textbooks do. Actually there are many dimensions to the competitive process. Firms compete through advertising to increase demand; through product development to find new or better products; though new or better methods of distribution; through new and better ways to finance production and capital accumulation and even through new and better ways to organize the production process. And with all of these the same simple rule applies: equate marginal revenue of the new activity to marginal cost to maximize profits. Most firms have only a vague idea of what marginal revenue and marginal cost are but over time they learn what works. If markets are competitive firms are forced to develop these skills to survive. Many firms don't survive. They fall by the wayside, or are merged with, or taken over by, surviving firms. And even among surviving firms there are wide differences in profitability. It is only the average or typical firm that makes zero economic profit in the long run.

## REVIEW QUESTIONS

Multiple choices: Select the correct answer:

1. Which of the following is not a feature of pure competition:
   a. Differentiated product.
   b. Many firms.
   c. Price taker.
   d. Easy entry into the industry.
2. Which of the following is not a feature of monopolistic competition.
   a. Price maker.
   b. Price taker.
   c. Differentiated product
   d. Relatively easy entry into the market.
3. A firm that is competitive in its output market:
   a. Will also be competitive in its input market.
   b. Will not be competitive in its input market.
   c. May be either competitive or non-competitive in its input market.

### Essays

1. Discuss the key features of market structure for pure competition and monopolistic competition. Why is pure competition more efficient than monopolistic competition?

2. With Imperfect competition in the output market, the firm will face a downward sloping demand curve. Explain why.

## SUGGESTED READINGS

Chamberlin, Edward H., *The Theory of Monopolistic Competition*, Cambridge, Harvard University Press, 8th ed., 1962, First Published in 1933.

Herendeen, James B. *Economics of the Corporate Economy*, New York: Dunellen Publishing Company, 1975: 49–66

Robinson, Joan, *The Economics of Imperfect Competition*, London: Macmillan and Company, 1964, 1st ed., 1933).

Tucker, Irvin, *Economics For Today*, 3rd ed., Mason, Ohio: Thomson-Southwestern, 171–266.

## *Chapter Seven*

# Why Has Income Distribution Become Less Equal Over the Last 30 Years?

## MARGINAL PRODUCTIVITY THEORY

Marginal productivity theory is the primary theory of income distribution in economics. It explains the distribution of earned incomes, which as we shall see, is different than incomes received. Earned incomes are incomes earned by the primary inputs of production. Economists usually divide these primary inputs into labor and capital. Labor income is all income earned by labor and in the national income accounts includes wages, salaries, and bonuses. This includes income of workers but also wage income of managers and executives. Property income includes all income from the ownership of property or from ownership of claims against property income. In the national income accounts this includes interest income, rental income, net income of corporations and proprietors income. Or more generally what is called rental-income, interest income and profits (net income of firms). Marginal productivity theory says that the return to inputs of production depends on three things: productivity, scarcity, and the degree of competition. In other words if we are talking about labor, its return depends first on how productive the labor is. Productivity depends on education, on the job training, and, often, native ability. However, how much a worker earns also depends on how scarce his particular skill is. A professional football player gets a high income because he is very skilled at what he does but also because he has a skill that is relatively scarce. Most of us couldn't become professional football players no matter how hard we tried. Marginal productivity theory says that under pure competition each input will be paid the value of its marginal output.

This result follows from profit maximizing behavior. A firm hires inputs to the point where the marginal return is equal to the marginal cost. The marginal cost is the wage rate under competitive conditions. The marginal return is the marginal output times the price of the output or the value of the marginal output. We come to the very convenient result that workers are paid according to their contribution to output. However, even under competitive conditions, this return will also depend on the relative scarcity of the workers skill. A ditch digger may be very skilled at his job, but his skill is very plentiful so his return may be very low. Marginal productivity theory says that under pure competition, capital also gets the value of its marginal product. Again, this is for the same reason. The marginal cost of capital must equal its marginal return. The marginal cost of capital is its required rate of return that depends on interest rates and risk. The marginal return is the marginal output from the capital invested times the price of the output.

However under imperfect competition, things are not as simple. What a worker gets paid will also depend on the degree of competition in both the labor markets and output markets. And likewise what an owner of capital gets will also depend on the degree of competition in both the market for capital and the market for output. And with capital there is another complication. A worker is limited as to how much labor income he can generate by the skills he has. Capital is not limited in the same way. An owner of capital can own unlimited quantities and can pass this capital on to his heirs. Labor skills can be rented but in a non-slave economy cannot be bought and sold. And only a limited amount of labor skills can be passed on to the next generation.

These conclusions can be used to develop a share equation for aggregate income. The national income accounts define earned income as wages and salaries, rental income, interest income and profits. If we combine rent, interest and profits we have property income. Property income plus wage income give us national income. If we divide wage income and property income each by national income we have income shares. For the US economy these shares are about .65 for labor and .35 for capital or converted to percentages: 65 percent for labor and 35 percent for capital. Under competitive conditions these shares represent the relative productivity of the two primary inputs. Under imperfect competition the shares also depend on the average degree of competition in output markets and the average degree of competition in the two input markets. These relative shares for the US economy have been fairly stable over the past fifty or so years. However within the wage share and within the property share income distribution has become much less equal. We will return to the reasons for this below.

Over time incomes rise because of productivity increase. As we pointed out before, aggregate income per worker can only rise because aggregate output per worker rises. However, what about individuals who are in industries where there is no, or little increase in productivity. A barber that cuts hair has seen little or no increase in productivity over the last thirty years or so. But barber incomes tend to rise over time. The reasons are several. First, rising incomes in other areas increase the demand for haircuts assuming haircuts are a normal good. (For normal goods, demand increases with income at any given price.) Second, rising numbers of consumers of haircuts also increases demand. On the supply side, barbers will leave the industry is incomes for barbers does not increase along with, incomes in other areas with comparable skills. Also barbers will start offering additional service along with haircuts. They will do styling and sell hair spray and styling jells.

The point is that aggregate incomes rise because of average rising productivity. Competition between workers and industries spread those gains across other industries where productivity gains are smaller or non-existent. Average productivity growth for the economy is about 3.5% per year. However, industries with high productivity growth often have rates of 5–6% per year. Low productivity growth industries may be only 0–1% per year. Although wage gains may be higher in the high productivity growth industries, they will not be as much higher as productivity growth would suggest. And the low productivity growth industries will have wage gains exceeding their productivity gains. This is because competition spreads the gains across industries and workers to more or less equalize wages for workers of comparable skill and scarcity.

## NATIONAL INCOME AND DISPOSABLE INCOME

Also, there is a big difference between earned income, as discussed above, and disposable income. Disposable income is what households have left to either spend on goods and services (what we call consumption) or to save (to add to net financial assets). Disposable income is national income plus transfer payments minus personal taxes (including social security withholding) minus before tax business retained earnings. Consumption is both durable and non-durable consumption. Personal saving is the current period accumulation of financial assets by households less any new debt issued by households. Primarily the difference between earned income and received income is taxes and transfers that are determined by the political process. Both income taxes and social security withholding are tied to income so the more we earn the more we pay. Social Security and Medicare benefits go primarily to the elderly non-working population.

Table 7.1 shows recent figures (2006) for national income, disposable income and income shares.

**Table 7.1. National Income, Disposable Income and Labor and Property Shares, Gross Domestic Product and Incomes Per Capita, and Per Worker, 2006 (Third Quarter, Annual rate)**

w = average annual wage income per worker = $51,848
N = number of workers = .145 billion workers (or 144 million workers)
wxN = Total wage income = $7,518 billion
r = estimated return on capital invested = .15 or 15%
K = estimated invested capital = $27,907 billion
rxK = property income = $4,338 billion
NI = National income = $7,425 billion + $4338 billion = $11,763 billion
Wage share = $7,425 billion/11,763 billion = .63 or 63%
Property share = $4,338 billion/11,763 billion = .37 or 37%
National income share = 1.0 or 100%
Gross Domestic Product = $13,322 billion
Less: capital consumption allowance + net foreign transfers+ statistical discrepency = NI or $13,322 billion − $1,559 billion = $11,763 billion.
DI = Personal disposable income = NI − (personal taxes + corporate taxes + corporate retained earnings) + (transfers) = 9,598 billion
Per capita disposable income = $ 31,993 (about 300 million population)
Per worker disposable income = 66,193

*Source: Economic Report of the President*, 2007

As we can see, the labor share is about 63% the capital share about 37%. Average wage income per worker is $52,014. Realize that this includes salary income of managers and executives as well as workers. In property income is included proprietors income, some of which would no doubt be labor income. But that would not change the wage and property share greatly National income is earned income. Disposable income is national income minus (personal taxes plus corporate taxes plus corporate retained earnings) plus personal transfers. It is income that households have left to spend or save. Per capita disposable income is $31,993. Per worker disposable income is $66,193. About 48% of the population is in the work force. The rest would be children and young people not yet in the work force, elderly who are out of the work force and disabled and others not currently in the work force.

## WHY INCOME DISTRIBUTION HAS BECOME LESS EQUAL OVER THE LAST 30 YEARS

Although the wage and property shares have been fairly stable, the distribution of incomes within the wage share and the property share have not been stable. Over, the past thirty years income distribution in the US has become less equal. On average, people with a high school education or less have seen their real income fall over this thirty-year period. On average, people with more than a high school education have seen their real incomes rise. Table 7.2 shows changes in shares of income going to different quintiles of families by decades since 1970. Note that the shares going to the bottom three fifths have been declining over the period. The top fifth and the top 5% have seen their shares rise. Only the fourth fifth has been relatively stable.

Why has the distribution of income become less equal over this thirty-year period. There are several reasons: First, there has been rising demand for high skill labor. This is because our economy has become more technically oriented. The rising industries have been in computers, computer software the inter-net and telecommunications. Second, there has been a rise in service industries relative to manufacturing industries. This is partly because we consume relatively more services and relatively less manufactured goods. Legal services, health care services, educational services are all examples. Also more manufacturing jobs have been moving overseas.

On average service industries are lower paying than manufacturing industries (at least where the manufacturing industries are unionized). And over this 30–year period we have seen a relative decline in unionization in the US. 30 years ago about 35% of the work force was unionized. Now it is about 14%. And almost all of the growth in unionization has been in public employment: in education and in government employment such as postal workers, police-workers, and firemen. In general unionized workers have been paid more (for the same educational and skill level) than non-union workers. Third, there has been increased competition from overseas. The US economy has become much more open over this period. This tends to hold down wages in those industries where overseas competition and outsourcing are important. Fourth, there has been a major increase in labor-force participation rates by women.

Labor force participation rates measure the percent of the population over sixteen that is in the workforce. Since 1970 the ratio for women has increased

**Table 7.2. Shares of Before Tax Income by Quintiles and for the Top Five Percent of Families, by Ten Year Intervals, 1970-2000**

| *Year* | *Bottom Fifth* | *Second Fifth* | *Middle Fifth* | *Fourth Fifth* | *Top Fifth* | *Top 5%* |
|---|---|---|---|---|---|---|
| 2000 | 4.3% | 9.8% | 15.5% | 22.8% | 47.4 | 20.8% |
| 1990 | 4.6 | 10.8 | 16.6 | 23.8 | 44.3 | 17.4 |
| 1980 | 5.2 | 11.5 | 17.5 | 24.3 | 41.5 | 15.3 |
| 1970 | 5.5 | 12.2 | 17.6 | 23.8 | 40.9 | 15.6 |

*Source:* U.S. Bureau of Census, Taken from Mankiw, *Principles of Economics*, (2004): 431

from 43% to 60%. From 1950 it has about doubled, from a little over 30% to 60%. Male labor force participation rates have fallen from 80% in 1970 to 75% today. And in 1950 it was about 85% for males. The decline in male rates is partly due to the ageing of the population and partly due to increased educational levels. A higher percent of the population is retired now than 30 or 50 years ago. And more males over 16 are getting an education and entering the work force at a later age. The increase in women labor force participation rates have come about despite the aging of the population. Average women's salaries are still less than men. This is mainly because women did not begin entering the high paying professions until about 20 or 25 years ago. It takes time to reach the high paying jobs. But now about 55% of all college students are women. In another 10 or 15 years the salary differential will probably disappear. The change in labor force participation rates for women is the result of several causes. The US has moved in the last 50 years from a primarily agricultural and manufacturing economy to a high tech and service economy where the skills of women are just as valuable as those of men. The technology of the household has changed dramatically. Automatic washers and dryers, electric ranges, microwaves, TV dinners, take-out meal services, day care services and many more have dramatically reduced the time and cost of providing household services. And, average family size has fallen dramatically. All of these developments mean that much of the time that was once spent in caring for the family can now be used for market work.

Fifth, there has been a dramatic increase in single parent households partly as a result of the increase in divorce rates over the past 40 or 50 years and partly as a result of changed social attitudes about marriage and family. This means that any given income is being distributed over more families so that average family income has fallen. This is especially severe for low-income families where the female head of household does not have the education to be able to find good jobs or the income to afford child care services.

Sixth, there has been an increase in "winner take all" mentality in many fields. This means that in those fields there are relatively few highly paid winners and a relatively large number of relatively low paid non-winners. Examples would be professional sports, actors in television and movies, news broadcasting, popular music and many more. Partly this is the result of technology. Because of television, radio, music CDs, movie rentals, etc., everyone has access to the high quality performers. There is less demand for the less popular performers. In addition, people stay in these professions at relatively low rewards because there is always the chance that they might become winners.

Seventh, there has been an increase in rent seeking behavior. Rent seeking behavior is where people are able to get returns unrelated to productive behavior through political influence or through a position of power in an organization. Lawyers with class action suits are often able to redistribute millions to themselves and their clients. Top corporate executives often get incomes far in excess of their productivity. Special interest groups, through political influence, can often get returns for their constituents that are unrelated to productivity.

Eighth, the cutting of marginal tax rates in the eighties and again in the early 2000s may have contributed to the worsening of income distribution. This was probably especially true of the cut in capital gains and dividend taxes in 2004.

## INCOME DISTRIBUTION AND THE POLITICAL SYSTEM

The final distribution of income depends in part on the political and economic system we have inherited from the past. Access to voting, access to the political process, access to the legal system, access to property ownership, access to education, and access to jobs all help determine income distribution. The Southeastern US had remained primarily rural and poor from the end of the Civil War until the 1960s. Then the Civil Rights movement and changed political climate led to the Voting Rights Act of the late 1960s that allowed access to voting for most blacks. Over the next 40 years the Southeast saw a dramatic economic transformation. Other factors that contributed were technological. The development and adoption of the mechanical cotton picker in the 1950s and 1960s released thousands of poor workers from agricultural labor. Many migrated north, others to the cities of the south. At about the same time air conditioning was developed. This made tolerable work in offices and factories in the cities of the Southeast. This social and technological revolution had, over a 40-year period, a dramatic impact on income distribution in this region.

## POLICY OPTIONS

Over the last 30 years we have seen a multitude of programs aimed at helping low income people. Why is it that despite these programs, income distribution has become more skewed over this period? Does this mean the programs have failed? Not necessarily. Social Security and Medicare, and private retirement programs have dramatically improved the relative position of the elderly. Welfare programs and Medicaid have helped the poor. The problem is that these programs usually don't help the poor get jobs and escape the slums. Also programs that try to aid poor neighborhoods such as enterprise zones may only perpetuate poverty because they encourage the poor to remain in the slums. The best way to escape the poverty of the slums is to leave. The slum environment and the poor school systems tend to perpetuate low achievement and poverty. Better schools will help. But it's hard to improve the schools when parents, teachers, students, and school administrators are caught up in the slum environment. We will return to the problems of education in a later chapter.

Also, the big problem is the working poor. Because of poor education, because they often live in low-income areas, both urban and rural, they earn low wages. In addition their employers usually don't provide health care programs, and because they are working they are ineligible for Medicaid. We will discuss this problem in a later chapter. Again, one of the best ways to help the working poor is to get their children into good schools so they can escape the environment of poverty.

The problem is that most of these programs do not address the cause of the increase in income inequality discussed above. Increased demand for high skill jobs can be met by better and more technical education. Again, we discuss this later. Increase in service industries and decline in manufacturing will require improving wages in the services industries. This will probably come in time, as the service industries become part of the technological revolution. Unionization in these industries would help, but they are very difficult to unionize. Lower pay for woman will probably correct itself over time as more and more women become educated in high skill professions and move up into management and professional positions. The breakup of the family, is a serious problem, but requires more than economic solutions.

Another problem is the tax structure. It has become much less progressive over the last 25 years. The tax cuts of the 1980s and of the early 2000s benefited mainly the wealthy. Poor and middle-income people pay both income taxes and social security withholding. The wealthy pay social security withholding only on the first $90.000 of wage income (and none on property income). As a result many wealthy individuals end up paying lower average tax rates than low and middle-income people. Tax reform could help this problem but it is unlikely to happen. Without strong public support and strong leadership from the President, such reform is unlikely to get through the tax-writing committees of Congress.

One reform that could help would be to allow tax deductibility for social security withholding. This would have to be a deduction that did not require the itemized deduction form as a high proportion of taxpayers do not itemize deductions. Again this would be a difficult reform to get though the tax-writing committees. The lost revenue would have to be recouped elsewhere.

## SUMMARY

Economic theory concludes that earned incomes are determined by productivity of the inputs, by the relative scarcity of the inputs, and by the average degree of competition in output markets and in input markets for both capital and labor. Incomes received also depend on taxes and transfers that are determined by the political process. For the aggregate economy total income must equal total output; growth of income must equal growth of output and growth of income per worker must equal growth of output per worker. Income distribution has become less equal in the US over the past 30 years. There are many reasons for this: Some of them economic and some non-economic. Probably the most important economic reason is the continued growth in demand for high skill workers. Probably the most important non-economic reason is the breakup of the family and the rise in single parent households, especially among low-income workers.

## REVIEW QUESTIONS

Multiple Choice: Select the correct answer:

1. The property share is:
   a. Wage and salary income divided by property income.
   b. Wage and salary income divided by national income.
   c. Property income divided by national income.
   d. Property income divided by wage income.
2. The wage share is:
   a. Property income divided by wage income.
   b. Wage and salary income divided by national income.
   c. Property income divided by national income.
   d. Wage income divided by property income.
3. Over the past 30 years income distribution in the US has become:
   a. Less equal.
   b. More equal.
   c. Neither of the above.

### Essays

1. Under pure competition shares of aggregate income between labor and capital are determined by relative productivity of the inputs. Explain why this is the case. Under imperfect competition what else affects relative

shares. What determines the relation between national income and disposable income.

2. Discuss the major factors that have contributed to the worsening of income distribution in the US in the past 30 years.

## SUGGESTED READINGS

Blank, Rebecca, "Fighting Poverty,: Lessons From Recent US History," *The Journal of Economic Perspectives,* 16, no. 2, (Spring 2000): 3–19.

Blau, Francine, "Trends and Well Being of American Women, 1970–95," *Journal of Economic Literature,* 36, no. 1, (March, 1998): 112–65.

Freeman, Richard B., "Are Your Wages Set in Beijing," *Journal of Economic Perspectives*, 9, no 3, (Summer 1995): 15–32.

Murphy, Kevin M. and Finis Welch, "Occupational Change and the Demand for Skill, 1940–1990," *American Economic Review: Papers and Proceedings,* 83, no. 2, May 1993): 122–26.

Tucker, Irvin, *Economics for Today*, Third Edition, Mason, Ohio, Thompson Southwestern 2000, Ch. 12.

Wood, Adrian, "How Trade Hurt Unskilled Worker," *Journal of Economic Perspectives*, 9, no. 3 (Summer, 1995): 57–80.

## *Chapter Eight*

# Regulation and Deregulation

In this chapter we deal with the basic principles of government regulation of the US Economy. First we deal with theories of regulation, then we look at the history of regulation, then we look at the political pressures for both regulation and deregulation.

## THEORIES OF REGULATION

There are several main theories of regulation that have guided policy makers and economists over the past hundred years or so. First, is natural monopoly theory, sometimes called the classical theory of regulation. Natural monopoly theory said that some industries were natural monopolies in that it was only efficient to have one firm in a particular market. This occurred when average total cost declined for the full scale of market output. Under profit maximizing behavior there would be one firm producing at a price that was above marginal and average cost and an output that was too low relative to what would occur under competitive conditions. This was thought to be the situation with public utilities in the first half of the 20th century. The theory was developed during the early part of the 20th century as a way to justify and guide regulation of public utilities; especially, telephone, electric, natural gas and gas and oil pipelines. The theory basically said that there were three economic alternatives for natural monopolies. First, government regulation with private ownership, second, government ownership and third unregulated private monopoly. In the US regulated monopoly was considered the best alternative. In other countries, such as in Europe, government ownership was often preferred. In still others, unregulated monopoly was preferred. Regulation or government ownership was viewed as ways of protecting the public from the undesirable affects of monopoly. We will discuss this in more detail later in this chapter.

The second main theory of regulation is called "Capture Theory" or sometimes "The Chicago View." This view asked the question: why do we have regulation in many industries where natural monopoly is not a problem? Agriculture, airlines (before 1978), trucking (before 1979), banking the securities industry, insurance (at the state level) and many more. None of these were monopolies or even highly concentrated industries (with the possible exception of airlines). The Chicago School answer was that these industries were regulated because the industries involved gained economic benefits from regulation. These benefits included protected markets, regulated prices, control over basic inputs, patents and copyrights to deter entry, or restricted entry through government franchise and many more. How were industries able to get benefits that might not be in the public interest? These benefits came primarily through the political principle of concentrated benefits and dispersed costs. The benefits were concentrated on relatively small, well organized, groups; the costs were spread over millions of unorganized voters and non-voters. Thus the cost on any one voter or consumer would be very small.

The capture theory notion was that industries were able to "capture" the regulatory agencies that regulated them by using their political influence to get people sympathetic to the industry appointed to the agencies. It also referred to the fact that the industries had access to the political process and therefore had influence over the type of regulations that were enacted.

Capture theory was developed during the 50s, 60s and 70s primarily at the University of Chicago. It was very influential in the deregulation movement of the late 70s and during the 80s in the Reagan Administration.

The third main theory regards regulation to deal with externalities. Although the idea of externalities had been around since the early part of the 20th century, it did not become well known until the development of the environmental movement that started in the 1970s. Externalities may involve external costs or external benefits. For environmental issues, it was mainly external costs. The costs of air pollution, water pollution, soil pollution, noise pollution, destruction of forests and wildlife and more were viewed as costs to society that under current legal and institutional arrangements were not born by the firms, individuals or government agencies that were causing the pollution. In most cases it was decided that the market, by itself, would not solve these problems and that some form of government intervention would be required. We will discuss environmental issues in more detail in a later chapter.

A fourth theory of regulation involves asymmetric or imperfect information. In some cases producers have information that consumers do not. Regulations usually require that producers not provide misleading information. Examples are the Security and Exchange Commission, the Food and Drug Administration, Truth in Lending for financial institutions, and many more.

A fifth view of regulation is sometimes called the evolutionary approach. This approach says that to understand regulation in any particular market or industry we should understand how and why regulation first developed in the market or industry and how it has evolved over time. We will use this approach when we look at regulation in banking and in agriculture in later chapters.

There is a certain amount of overlap in these various theories of regulation. Each one arose in response to particular policy issues that appeared to require public action. In each case economists came up with theoretical explanation to justify the actions. The evolutionary view is useful because it allows us to see how the structure and competitive nature of the regulated industry changes over time and how this changes the pressures for regulation or deregulation.

## HISTORY OF REGULATION AND DEREGULATION

Modern regulation started with the Sherman Act in 1890. This act was in response to the excesses of capitalism during the period following the Civil War that was called the Gilded Age. The development of the railroads and the telegraph allowed the development of national markets and the growth of large national corporations many of which tried to monopolize particular markets. The excesses of the railroads, the oil industry, meatpacking and the steel industry were most notable. The Sherman Act prohibited combinations in restraint of trade and the monopolization of trade. It was passed in 1890 but did not get its first real enforcement until the early 1900s under the Administration of Theodore Roosevelt. The Clayton Act (1914) extended the Sherman Act by prohibiting price fixing, exclusive dealings, tying contracts, stock acquisition of competing firms and interlocking directorates. The Federal Trade Commission was established in 1914 to enforce consumer protection legislation, to prohibit deceptive advertising, and to prohibit collusion.

Public utility regulation came in the first part of the 20th Century. Most of this was done by state legislatures. In general Public Utility Commissions were set up to set prices for the utilities that allowed a fair rate of return on investment. The federal government also regulated public utilities when they did business across state lines.

Out of the Great Depression of the 1930s came regulation of agriculture, banking, labor markets and securities markets. All of these industries had been devastated by the Depression and Congress passed legislation to prevent past abuse but also to attempt to help the industries recover from the depression. All of these industries have continued to be regulated to the present but with many modifications.

In the late 70s and early 80s came the first major deregulation movement. Airlines were deregulated in 1978, interstate trucking shortly after and banking in 1980 and further in 1982. For airlines regulation of routes, of fares and restriction on entry were eliminated. The main result was a big drop in fares and a major increase in air travel. The government continued to regulate air safety. In banking it was the first major new legislation since the 1930s. We will discuss the banking industry in a later chapter. In addition in the 1980s there was a major relaxing of antitrust enforcement. In 1989 and 1992 came partial re-regulation of banking in response to the thrift crisis of 1982–89 and the banking crisis of 1989–92.

The 1970s saw the enactment of the first major environmental legislation. The Environmental Protection Agency was established in 1971 and was charged with enforcing pollution standards. Again we discuss this issue later in more detail. In 1996 came the first major deregulation of Agriculture since the farm programs were enacted in the 1930s. However, direct subsidies to agriculture have continued. We discuss agriculture in more detail in a later chapter.

Also, in the 1990s came further deregulation in the Financial Services Industry (Banking, Investment Banking, and Insurance). In 1994 came repeal of laws prohibiting interstate branching by banks. This, combined with high profits in banking in the 1990s, led to major mergers of banks across state lines so that many of the major banks became national in scope. Then in 1999 Congress passed the Financial Services Act that repealed Glass-Steagall, the Act that had separated commercial banking from investment banking in the early 1930s. This new law not only allowed banks to merge with investment banks but also allowed mergers of banks with insurance companies.

## MAJOR REGULATORY AGENCIES

The Food and Drug Administration (FDA) oversees safety of foods and drugs. This includes requiring extensive testing before new drugs can be introduced and also includes inspection of food processing plants and restaurants.

The Interstate Commerce Commission (ICC) oversees all surface transportation: trucking, rail, barges and oil and gas pipelines.

The Civil Aeronautics Board (CAB) regulates air travel.

The Federal Communications Commission (FCC) regulates telephone, telecommunications and broadcasting.

The Securities and Exchange Commission (SEC) regulates the Securities Industry.

The Occupational Health and Safety Administration (OSHA) regulates health and safety in the workplace.

The Environmental Protection Agency (EPA) enforces pollution standards.

The Federal Reserve System (the FED) is the nations Central Banker but also is one of the major regulators of the Banking System.

The Office of the Comptroller of Currency (OCC) is in the Treasury and charters all National Banks. In addition it shares regulatory power over National Banks with the Federal Reserve and with the Federal Deposit Insurance Corporation (FDIC).

The Federal Deposit Insurance Corporation (FDIC) runs the Deposit Insurance System for the Commercial Banks and for Savings Banks and Savings and Loan Associations and has regulatory authority to protect the soundness of the Deposit Insurance System.

## NATURAL MONOPOLY THEORY

A natural monopoly exists where there is declining average cost for the full scale of market demand. In this case it is most efficient to have a single firm produce industry output. Examples were electric utilities and telephone utilities. Under the technology of the first half of the 20th Century it would have been very inefficient to have several electric or telephone companies running their lines into any particular market. Under private ownership we could expect higher prices and lower output than would be the case for a competitive firm with the same costs. However you can't have a competitive monopoly unless entry into the market is relatively easy. This was not the case with a high fixed cost industry like the electric or telephone industries.

There were three possible solutions. One was private monopoly with its problems of high prices and low output. Many developing countries have privatized their public utilities only to find that private monopoly was little different from public monopoly. The second was public ownership. This was the preferred solution in Europe, Australia, Canada and many other countries. The problem was that public firms tended to be inefficient and staffed with political appointees and with pampered public unions. In the US we opted for private ownership and regulation. The regulation was by Public Utility Commissions that set prices that allowed a "fair rate of return" on investment. The system always had its problems. Determining the rate base on which to calculate the fair rate of return was always difficult. Also there was an incentive by the utilities to overcapitalize to increase the rate base on which they could earn the fair rate of return. In addition commissioners appointed were often sympathetic to the view of the industry or became sympathetic because the industry people had a lot more information than they did.

The natural monopoly theory is illustrated in figure 8.1. D=AR is the monopoly demand curve. The marginal revenue curve, MR, is below the demand curve with twice the slope. The average cost curve is labeled AC and is declining for all levels of output within the market demand curve. The marginal cost curve must lie below the average cost curve as long as average cost is declining. The profit maximizing solution is at point A with output $Q_1$ and price $P_1$. This implied a higher price and lower output and excess profits as compared to the other two solutions. The average cost pricing solution is at B with output $Q_2$ and price $P_2$. Here the firm is charging a price that just covers cost

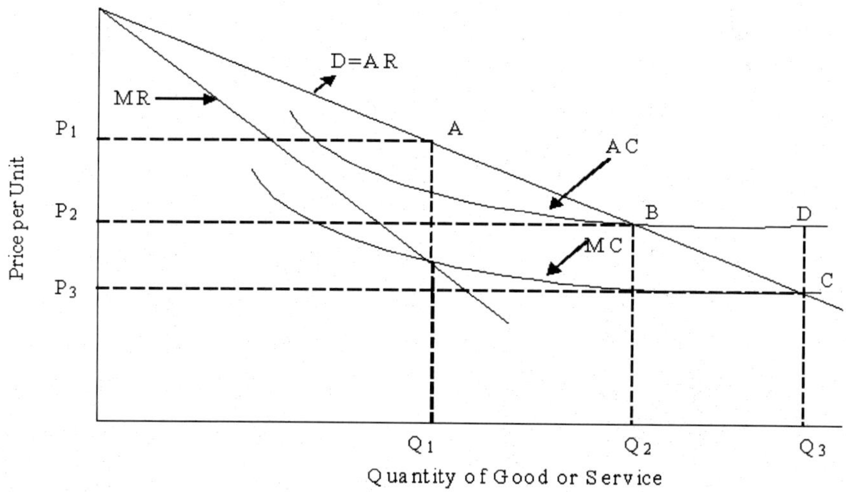


$P_1Q_1$ = Monopoly Solution
$P_2Q_2$ = Average cost pricing solution
$P_3Q_3$ = Marginal cost pricing solution
DC = Subsidy required per unit with marginal cost Pricing solution

**Figure 8.1. The Natural Monopoly Model**

where cost includes a fair rate of return on capital. The marginal cost solution is at C with output $Q_3$ and price $P_3$. This is the most efficient solution from the criteria of economic theory. However, at this output average cost is at D and the firm would have a per unit loss of CD. The firm could only stay in business is government provided a subsidy of BD per unit or if the firm was nationalized and run at a loss and subsidized by government. This was the impetus for nationalization of public utilities in many countries. In the US nationalization was never popular and we opted for regulation where average cost pricing and a "fair" rate of return was the goal. In recent years we have seen major moves toward deregulation in both electric and telephone industries. Much of this has been driven by technological change that has changed the natural monopoly status of the industry. In telephone making lines available to multiple servers changed the nature of the business. This came after the Federal Courts broke up the AT&T telephone monopoly in the early eighties. In more recent years the development of cell phones has made the industry even more competitive.

The electric utility industry has also seen major changes. Electric utilities have been required to allow other utilizes to ship electricity over their lines. This has meant the development of regional markets in wholesale electricity. This has tended to equalize costs across markets and made the old regulatory system obsolete. Deregulation has in some markets tried to separate generation, transmission, and retail distribution into the separate functions often performed by separate firms.

This was the model used in California where deregulation went badly awry in 2000. There were several flaws in the California system that led to its downfall. First, the utilities were required to sell off all of their generating capacity. Because of environmental regulations and other problems no new power plants had been built in California for several years. This meant that much of their electricity had to be imported from other states. Deregulation required by law that all of this imported electricity had to go through the spot market which was run by a small number of electricity trading firms (one of which was Enron). They were not allowed to buy electricity under long-term contracts. The retail price of electricity was regulated but the wholesale price was de-regulated. Electricity cannot be stored so the short run supply and demand at the wholesale level are very inelastic. When shortages developed in 2000, the wholesale price shot up rapidly and soon greatly exceeded the regulated retail price. The retail companies were quickly insolvent and the State of California, after causing the problem, had to step in to resolve the problem. The industry in California was partially taken over by the state. Several new power plants were contracted for, retail prices were allowed to rise, and utilities could again buy with long term contracts in the wholesale market. The taxpayers and electricity users paid a very high price for a badly designed system. Deregulation got a bad name and will probably come to a halt for several years. The moral of the story is that you can't deregulate wholesale prices when retail prices are regulated-especially when wholesale supply is very inelastic. And second, you can't rely on just the spot market when prices can be very volatile. Purchasing by long-term contract evens out the fluctuations in price and helps prevent disasters like the one in California.

## SUMMARY

In this chapter we have looked at theories of regulation. These theories have arisen over time as attempts to deal with specific policy issues. We also reviewed briefly the history of regulation over the last century and looked at the major regulatory agencies that have emerged from that history. Last we looked briefly at natural monopoly theory and regulation and deregulation of public utilities.

## REVIEW QUESTIONS

Multiple choices: Select the correct answer:

1. The capture theory of regulation says that:
   a. Regulation is designed to benefit the industry regulated.
   b. Regulation is designed to benefit the public.
   c. Neither of the above.
2. For a natural monopoly, setting price equal to MC will require:
   a. A subsidy to the firm.
   b. A tax on the firm.
   c. Neither.
3. A natural monopoly has:
   a. Falling long run average cost.
   b. Rising long run average cost.
   c. Constant long run average cost.

### Essays

1. Explain some of the reasons that deregulation of electric utilities went so wrong in California in 2000.
2. Explain how the concept of externalities contributed to environmental regulation in the early 1970s.

## SUGGESTED READINGS

Burton, Maureen, and Raymond Lombra, *The Financial System and The Economy: Principles of Money and Banking,* 2nd ed. Cincinnati, Ohio: Thompson Southwestern, Chapters 14–17.

Posner, Richard, "Taxation by Regulation," *The Bell Journal of Economics and Management Science*, 1, no. 1 (Spring 1971): 22–50.

Sowell, Thomas, *Basic Economics*, New York, Basis Books, 2000, Ch. 7.

Stigler, Joseph, "Theory of Economic Regulation," *The Bell Journal of Economics and Management Science*, 1, no. 1 (Spring 1971): 3–21.

*Chapter Nine*

# Why Are Farmers Doing so Poorly Despite All the Money Spent on Farm Programs?

## AGRICULTURE DURING THE GREAT DEPRESSION

During the great Depression between 1929 and 1939 agriculture was hit very hard. Much of agriculture was (and still is) highly dependent on the export market. This was especially true of crops like corn, wheat, soybeans, cotton and tobacco that were grown in the heavily agricultural areas of the Midwest, the Southeast, and Eastern Washington and Oregon. The Depression was worldwide and led to a shutdown of world trade. The Depression was brought about by the attempt of countries during the twenties to go back on the gold standard at pre-World War I prices of gold. This was only possible by deflating prices and wages back to pre-war levels. This led to severe recessions in England, in Europe and other countries. The US suffered a brief but severe recession in 1920–21 but then returned to prosperity. The same was not true in England and much of Europe.

The US economy entered recession in the summer of 1929. Then in October of 1929 came the stock market crash. The US dollar was overvalued relative to European Currencies because it remained at the pre-World War I price of gold. This depressed the demand for agricultural exports because an overvalued dollar increases the price of US goods relative to foreign goods. US prices have to fall to move toward equality between the dollar price of US goods and the dollar price of comparable foreign goods. The dollar price of foreign goods is the foreign price divided by the exchange rate. The problem was made worse when England and the Commonwealth Countries devalued in 1931. In 1930 Congress passed the Smoot-Hawley Tariff to try to protect domestic producers. This meant that foreigners could not sell to us to earn the dollars they needed to buy our goods. Other countries followed suit and barricaded their markets behind tariffs. Under President Hoover, the US refused to consider devaluing the dollar. If the US had devalued in 1931 when England did and if we had avoided passing the Smoot-Hawley Tariff, likely we would have had a much milder recession and the tragedy of the great depression might have been avoided.

President Roosevelt was elected in November of 1932 and took office in March of 1933. The collapse in prices led to failure of banks, especially in the rural areas of the south and mid-west. By 1932 the banking crises had moved to the urban areas. Many of the nation's banks were closed when Roosevelt took office in 1933. Roosevelt declared a Bank Holiday and closed the nations banks. Under emergency legislation, passed soon after Roosevelt took office, the Treasury Department examined the nation's banks and reopened those that were sound and closed the ones that were insolvent. There was no deposit insurance then, so many depositors lost their savings. Emergency agricultural legislation was also passed. There were two parts to Roosevelt's Farm Program. First was a passage of a program of price supports and production restraints that was to remain with us, with many modifications, until 1996. The second included enabling legislation to allow the devaluation of the dollar. Many of the farm interest groups and agricultural economist were convinced that devaluation would lead to a quick recovery of agricultural prices. In the summer of 1933 the Administration abandoned the gold standard and allowed the dollar to float. (Its price being determined in the market for foreign exchange.) Although agricultural prices recovered some, agriculture did not get a real recovery until World War II brought a recovery of export markets.

After six months or so of floating the dollar the Administration returned to the gold standard but at a much higher price of gold. Before devaluation, the gold price was $20.67 per ounce of gold. The new price was $35.00 per ounce of gold and amounted to a about a 40% devaluation of the dollar. We will discuss devaluation in a later chapter.

The farm programs helped reduce the hardships that faced agriculture during the depression but did not return agriculture to prosperity. The reason was that the world remained in recession. In the absence of programs to increase aggregate demand, all higher farm prices did was redistribute income from non-farmers to farmers. And the fall in income of non-farmers only contracted agricultural demand further.

One program for agriculture that was very successful was the farm loan program of the Farm Credit Administration. Government sponsored credit agencies were set up at the local level and administered by local Boards of Directors. The Federal Land Banks financed long-term mortgage debt and the Production Credit Associations financed short and intermediate term credit. During the 1930s they refinanced much of the farm debt that had been held primarily by banks and insurance companies. For mortgage debt they were able to do this by loaning on the basis of "normal" value for the property rather than the very depressed market values. They pioneered the use of amortized mortgages. They also pioneered the use of short term loans secured by crops to be repaid when the crops were harvested and sold. Also they pioneered the use of intermediate term loans secured by livestock and machinery. They raised their funds by borrowing in the money markets. Farmer customers were required to buy small amounts of capital in the system. The Federal Land Banks and Production Credit Associations are still important lenders to farmers. After World War II many banks in rural areas adopted many of the lending practices that had been pioneered by the Land Banks and Production Credit Associations.

## THE POST-WAR ERA

Agriculture enjoyed a brief period of prosperity during and after World War II up until the mid fifties. During the next 18 years or so agriculture was relatively depressed. A strong US dollar and overcapacity kept prices low. The Farm Programs were continued and were viewed as a way of saving the family farm. During the 70s, starting in late 1972, there was a brief period of prosperity in agriculture. This resulted from high world demand and from the fall in the international value of the dollar that occurred when the Nixon Administration abandoned the gold standard and allowed the value of the dollar to be determined in the international money markets. The first surge in farm prices came between 72 and 74 following the first fall in the dollar and partially coincided with the first energy crisis, which started in late 73. The FED tightened monetary policy in 75 and we had a brief recession. They eased again in 76 (an election year). By 1977 under the Carter Administration the dollar again started falling and farm prices again rose. In 1979 the Iranian Revolution set off the second oil crisis and inflation continued to rise.

The Carter Administration appointed Paul Volcker Chairman of the Federal Reserve in the spring of 79 and by the fall of 79 the Fed had pushed short-term interest rates to unprecedented levels. The Fed eased briefly in 1980 (another election year) but then pushed up interest rates sharply in 1981 and 1982. The dollar rose and inflation fell. Commodity prices dropped sharply and the boom in agriculture was over. From 1981–1987 agriculture experienced a major recession. This was caused by the sharp fall in world demand and the sharp rise in the dollar that further depressed farm prices in the US. Farm programs that had been deactivated in the 70s were quickly reactivated in the 80s. Recovery did not start until 1987 after the dollar started falling in

1986. Agriculture remained moderately prosperous from 1987 until 1996. This was partly due to high world demand and partly due to the relatively weak dollar. In 1996 congress passed the Farm Adjustment and Improvement Act (FAIR Act) also known as the Freedom to Farm Act. This act removed price supports and production controls from the major supported commodities. Excluded were sugar, peanuts, and rice. Direct payments were to continue at a declining rate for seven years but were to be unrelated to market price or output. This was the first major deregulation of agriculture since the programs were enacted in 1933.

Unfortunately, agriculture's problems were not over. Falling world demand starting with the Southeast Asian Crisis in 1997–98, a strong dollar during most of the period from 1997–2002, problems in selling US genetically altered food products to Europe, and rising output due to the removal of output restriction led to continued depressed prices for agricultural export commodities. Congress has continued to increase direct payments to agriculture and added new commodities to those getting subsidies in 2002.

## CHARACTERISTICS OF SUPPLY AND DEMAND IN AGRICULTURE

Agriculture has some unique features that have made it particularly vulnerable to economic conditions and have added to pressure for government support. First, both supply and demand at the farm level are very inelastic in the short run. This means that small changes in either supply or demand lead to proportionately much larger changes in price. And large changes in price lead to large changes in income because output responds very slowly to changes in price and because most costs do not decline when prices decline. Figure 9.1 shows supply and demand curves for supported commodity wheat. Note that supply and demand are both relatively inelastic. This means a small change in either supply or demand leads to a relatively large change in price. At point A supply and demand are equal and the equilibrium market price is $3.00 per bushel; the quantity is 100 million bushels. If farmers are paid a supported price of $4.00 per bushel supply exceeds demand and farmers have to restrict output to maintain the higher price. With inelastic demand this higher price would increase total revenue to farmers. It would pay each individual farmer to exceed his quota so government had to have some way to enforce output restriction. For most supported crops it did this by paying farmers to take land out of production in order to be eligible for the supported price. If output restriction is successful, output will be 90 million bushels. Note that at point A total revenue is $300 million dollar. ($3.00x100 million bushels.) At B total

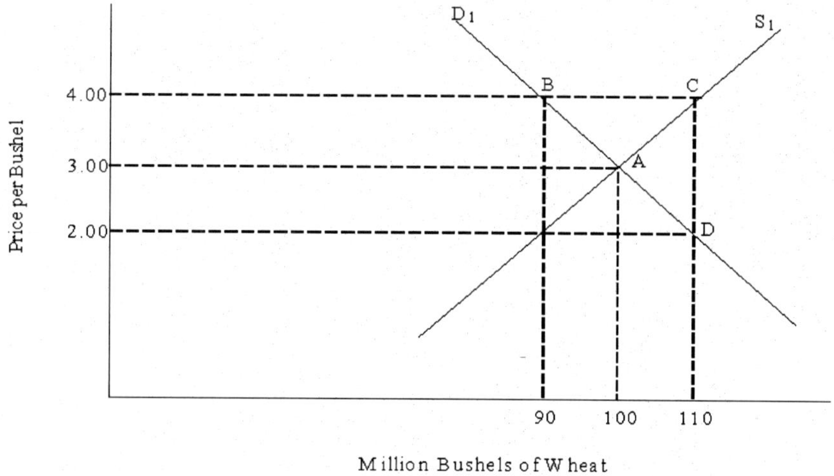


**Figure 9.1. Supply and Demand for an Agricultural Commodity with Price Supports and Direct Payments**

revenue will be 360 million dollars. ($4.00x90 million bushels.) In addition farmers would get rental payments on the land removed from production.

In 1996 the farm programs for the major commodities were changed. Farmers were no longer paid to restrict output and market prices were to prevail. Farmers were to be paid a direct subsidy based on past output. The subsidies were to be phased out over seven years. Unfortunately farm prices remained low and the subsidies were not phased out. Look at figure 9.1 again. If the subsidy were equal to the difference between the market price and the former supported price farmers would behave as if the price was $4.00 per bushel and produce 118 million bushels. Unfortunately, this quantity could only be sold at $2.00 per bushel and market price would fall to that level. Farmers, if they got the $1.00 subsidy would end up at $3.00 per bushel just where they would have been if the market had been allowed to prevail. And the taxpayer would be out $1.00 per bushel on 110 million bushel: hardly a winning proposition.

Second, in agriculture supply shifts faster than demand over time. This causes trend prices to be downward. The reason is that rapid technological progress continues to increase output and reduce costs. Technical progress is subsidized by the Agricultural Colleges and Experiment Stations and made available to farmers who can afford to adopt it. Early adopters gain temporary innovators profits. As more farmers adopt, supply increases and price falls. Late adopters, adopt just to survive. Those who don't adopt are gradually forced out of the industry. In the past 50 years the number of farmers has dropped substantially and farms have become much larger. In 1965 there were about 3.4 million farms and about 1.0 million commercial farms (sales over $10,000 in 1965 prices). In 1997 there were about 1.9 million farms and about 350 thousand commercial farms (sales over $100,000 in 1997 prices). Sales over $100,000 would imply a net income of about $20,000. A large number of the non-commercial farms would be part-time and would have some family members receiving non-farm sources of income. Commercial farms in 1997 produced 87% of farm sales and comprised only 18% of all farms.

Figure 9.2 shows how technical progress shifts supply right faster than demand, Demand grows primarily with population growth. Supply grows more rapidly due to relatively rapid technical progress in agriculture. As a result price falls over time. In figure 9.2 the line through points A, B and C represents the trend price, here we are ignoring price supports or subsidies. Third, agriculture is heavily reliant on the export market. This is particularly true of the main crops that have received government support. The US is still the world's largest exporter of food grains and feed grains. The main crops would be wheat, corn and soybeans. Production of these crops is concentrated in the Midwest and Great Plains as well as Eastern Washington and Oregon. The other big export crops are cotton and tobacco, both grown in the Southeast and cotton also grown in Texas and California. For these crops changes in export demand can have a big affect on prices and incomes. Export demand can

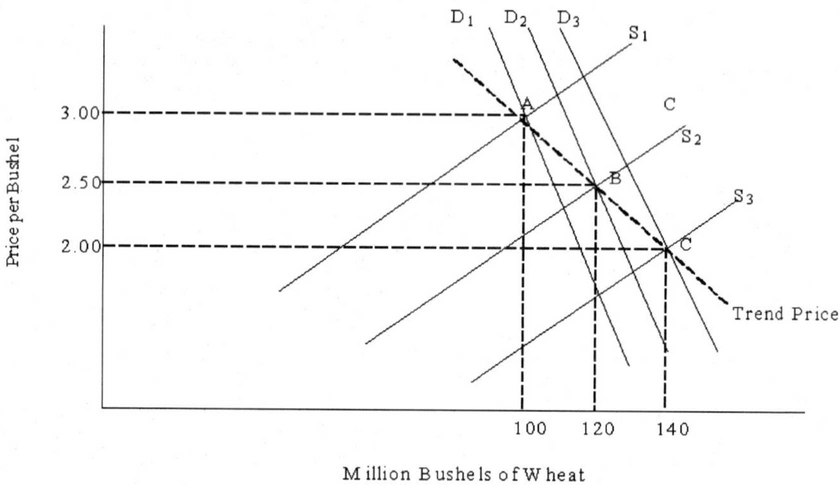


**Figure 9.2. Supply and Demand in Agriculture with Technical Change and Downward Trend Price**

change either as a result of changed demand in the rest of the world or as a result of major changes in the international value of the dollar or some combination of the two. The other commodity to get major government support is milk production. Milk producers have benefited from programs to buy up surplus dried milk, butter and cheese, from milk marketing orders and from direct subsidies.

## JUSTIFICATIONS FOR FARM PROGRAMS

Over the years we have had various justifications offered by agricultural economists and policy makers for continuation of farm programs. One justification was to stabilize farm incomes. Given the inelastic supply and demand, farm incomes are highly vulnerable to economic conditions in both the US and the rest of the world. However farm programs have always done more than stabilize farm income. They have increased incomes over what they would be in the absence of the programs. Second, it was argued that since farm incomes were below non-farm incomes, that the programs were designed to equalize that difference. However, for the last twenty or thirty years farm incomes have been equal to or greater than non-farm incomes so that argument has lost its force. Over the last thirty years or so it has been argued that farm programs were justified to offset the affects of rapid technical progress. Rapid technical progress has meant that farmers are caught in a continual cost price squeeze. Because of the competitive nature of the industry, the gains of technical progress are quickly passed on to consumers in the form of lower prices. Farm subsidies allow some of the gains to be kept by the farmers. Unfortunately because subsidies are tied to production (or past production) the biggest subsidies go to the largest and most successful producers. A last argument for farm programs is to help poor farmers. As we have just pointed out, the programs have never been designed to help poor farmers. Poverty programs and social security are much more likely to benefit poor farmers.

The other thing that needs to be pointed out is that farm programs affect only a portion of agriculture. Fruit and vegetable producers, beef producers, chicken and egg producers, pork producers, and fish and seafood producers get little or no support. Government payments go to only about 36% of all farms. The average payment per farm receiving is about $7,400. For commercial farms the figure would be much higher. Tobacco, sugar and peanuts get indirect support through quota programs and import restrictions. Ultimately, who get support depends primarily on the political power structure.

## SUMMARY AND CONCLUSIONS

Government has spent billion to support farm incomes. Despite all the support farmers still are not doing well. There is little evidence that the supported farmers are doing any better than those who do not receive support. The reason is that the supported crops are primarily crops that are also major export commodities. All of the developed countries pay generous supports to their farmers. This results in excess capacity for the major food-grains, feed-grains, tobacco, and cotton and sugar crops. In the absence of output restrictions the subsidies merely add to the excess capacity. The US did away with its production controls with the FAIR Act of 1996 mainly because it realized that all it was accomplishing was holding up prices for Europe and Japan, since they made little attempt to restrict output. Once we stopped restricting output their programs became even more expensive. The restrictions by Europe against US genetically altered US crops can be seen in part as retaliation against cheap imports from the US after we did away with output restrictions. As long as the present programs continue in the US, Europe, Japan, Canada and Australia, we will continue to have excess capacity and depressed farm prices and governments of the countries will continue to feel compelled to pay farm subsidies. And it also means that developing countries that would like to export agricultural commodities to the west are also stymied by depressed prices. Only rarely do we have periods of temporary prosperity like the 1970s when we had high world demand combined with (for the US) a falling dollar.

## REVIEW QUESTIONS

Multiple choices: Select the correct answer:

1. In agriculture rapid technical progress causes:
   a. Downward trend prices.
   b. Upward trend prices.
   c. Neither of the above.
2. Rapid technical progress in agriculture has:
   a. Given consumers higher food prices.
   b. Caused food prices to consumers to fall.
   c. Neither of the above.
3. Over the last 50 years agricultural income as a share of aggregate income has been:
   a. Falling
   b. Rising.
   c. Remained about the same.

## Essays

1. Discuss the characteristics of supply and demand in agriculture that have contributed to the farm income problem.
2. How do farm subsidies in the developed countries contribute to depressed farm incomes in the developing countries?

## SUGGESTED READINGS

Gardner, Bruce L. *American Agriculture in the Twentieth Century, How it Flourished and What it Cost,* (Cambridge, MA, Harvard University Press, 2002).

Hallberg, Milton, *Policy for Commercial Agriculture: Choices and Consequences*, Ames, Iowa: Iowa State University Press, 1992.

Herendeen, James B. and Milton Hallberg, "What Drives Agricultural Cycles," *Challenge: The Magazine of Economic Affairs,* 40, no. 1, (January-February, 1997): 72–86.

Herendeen, James B. and William Grisley, "A Dynamic 'q' Model of Investment, Financing and Asset Pricing: An Empirical Test for the Agricultural Sector," *Southern Economic Journal,* 55, no. 2 (October 1988), 360–73.

Pasour, E. C., Jr. *Agriculture and the State,* Oakland, Calif., Independent Institute, 1990.

## *Chapter Ten*

# What's Wrong With Our School Systems?

### STRUCTURE OF THE INDUSTRY

Our educational system faces great problems. What has gone wrong and what might be done? First, we present a brief explanation of the structure of the educational system. At the elementary and secondary level we have both public and private schools. Many private schools have a religious affiliation, but others do not. The taxpayers, mostly at the state and local level, support public schools. People who send their children to private schools still have to pay taxes to support the public system. In addition in recent years we have seen the development of Charter Schools and Magnet Schools. These are schools that get public support but are outside the traditional public school administrative structure. Also in some states vouchers have been adopted allowing parents to send children to private schools with public support.

At the level of higher education there are Two-Year Community Colleges, Two-Year Technical Schools, Four-Year Colleges and Four-Year Universities. Again we have both public institutions and private institutions. Some of the private institutions have religious affiliation but most do not. Examples of major private Universities are Harvard, Stanford, MIT and Yale. Examples of major public Universities are Texas A&M, Penn State University, The University of California-Berkeley and the University of California-Los Angeles. Some of the public universities are what are called Land Grant Universities. These were established by States but funded by Grants of Land from the Federal government. Originally they were mandated to teach Agriculture and the Mechanic Arts. Land Grant Universities were established under the Morrill Act passed during the Civil War. Mechanic Arts was what we now call Engineering. So these Universities were originally mainly Agriculture and Engineering Schools. Examples would be Texas A&M, Penn State, Iowa State, and Wisconsin. They have all developed into general-purpose Universities. Other public universities started out as Educational Schools. Their original mission was primarily the training of teachers for elementary and secondary schools. Others started out as State Universities that taught Law, Medicine, and the Liberal Arts but without Land Grant Status. They too have evolved into general-purpose universities. Included would be University of Iowa, Indiana University and the University of Washington. There are even a few Federal Universities: West Point, The Naval Academy, The Air Force Academy and The Naval Post Graduate School.

## PROBLEMS IN THE PUBLIC SCHOOLS

First, at the elementary and secondary level there has been a deterioration of quality in the public schools, especially in the central cities. In the middle class and upper income suburbs, the public schools have remained quite good. There are several reasons for this deterioration of quality. First in the central cities, especially in the East, there is a lack of tax base to support good public schools. The suburbs are separate political jurisdictions and therefore have their own tax base to support good schools. The central cities are left with low-income housing, public buildings and downtown office buildings. Low-income housing generates little tax revenue; public buildings often generate none so the tax base falls on the office buildings. This in turn drives more of them to the suburbs. In the west city limits often extend out to include the suburbs.

Second, in the 1970s there was developed a philosophy in the educational colleges that de-emphasized subject matter and instead emphasized "how to teach" courses. The idea was that if education majors had enough education courses they could absorb the subject matter from packaged subject matter, textbooks and other curriculum materials. Unfortunately, subjects like math and science cannot be learned that way; instead education students must take subject matter courses to learn the material. This philosophy has changed in recent years but there are still a lot of teachers out there that were trained in the 70s and 80s.

Third, during this same period social passing became popular. This meant that students were passed to the next grade without having to pass the subject matter and ended up dropping out or even graduating without having basic knowledge of writing, reading, and arithmetic, to say nothing of history, social science, geography or science.

Fourth, teacher certification required extensive training in education. When teacher shortages developed, qualified people, often with Master's Degrees in history, or math or science could not get jobs in the public schools without first taking a year or two of education courses. Only recently have States begun to relax certification requirements.

Fifth, in the central cities the environment of poverty and crime make improving the educational system very difficult. Peer group pressure discourages educational advancement. Poverty means a low tax base to support schools and means that schools cannot attract high quality teachers or administrators. Teachers unions and administrators fight any reform that might drain resources from the public schools.

## POSSIBLE REFORMS

Many reforms for the public school system have been proposed and several are being tried. Most controversial has been vouchers. Vouchers would make funds available directly to the family of students and could be used to send students to the school of their choice, public or private. The idea is that schools would have to compete for the funds of students and this would force schools to improve quality to attract students. The primary opposition has come from four groups: first public school administrators who fear that vouchers would divert funds away from the public schools; second, teachers unions who represent primarily public school teachers and who also fear the diversion of funds from public schools; third, people who fear that vouchers would be a subsidy to religious schools and this would violate separation of church and state; last there are people who fear that vouchers would become a subsidy primarily for the middle class and rich to sent their children to private schools. The GI Bill, which followed World War II, was essentially a voucher system and students were allowed to use funds for higher education and no distinction was made between public and private (religious or not). The primary supporters of vouchers believe that competition is the best way to force an improvement of public schools and to give students and their parents more choice. The problem is that not all public schools are bad. It is mainly the schools in the central cities and in poor rural areas.

A second remedy has been to support Charter Schools and Magnet Schools. Charter Schools and Magnet Schools get public funding but are outside the traditional educational bureaucracy. Charter schools and magnet schools have met with mixed success and are now common in many states. Magnet schools are usually aimed at particular student clientele. Often they have a math or science or technology orientation. Charter and magnet schools have been a way for supporters of school reform to get around the strong and well-organized opposition to vouchers.

A third remedy, supported by the public school administrators, teachers unions and many others is to spend more money on the public schools. The problem is that there is little relationship between per-pupil spending and the quality of the schools.

Progress is being made on certification and many states have eased the strict certification requirements that have made it very difficult for people not trained in the educational colleges to get into the public school system. The teachers trained in the 60s and 70s will be retiring and will be replaced by students trained more recently.

The big problem is the students in the slums of the central cities and in poor rural areas. Here the problem is environment as much as any thing else. Poverty leads to joblessness and crime and to an anti-education attitude on the part of parents and students. Pressures from other students discourage intellectual pursuits and the teachers and administrators face rebellious and uninterested students. As a result the schools have difficulty attracting good teachers and good administrators. Students from a slum background whose parents go in the military and sent their children to military or non-slum schools do much better academically than those who remain in the slums. This is because the parental and peer group pressures are much different once you leave the low-income areas. The best way to escape the slum environment is to move out. Unfortunately, it is often very difficult to do so. But, in looking for cures to the problems of schools we should recognize that not all public schools are in trouble. There are lots of very good public schools, mostly in the middle and upper income suburbs where pressure from parents and other students ensure a good education.

## PROBLEMS IN HIGHER EDUCATION

Two-Year Community Colleges and Technical Schools: The problem here is that many of the community colleges spend much of their time training students to get into four-year colleges. Partly it is because high schools do not adequately train students for entrance into a four-year college; partly it is because of parent and peer group pressure to have a four-year degree. The problem is that many students of two-year colleges do not end up going on to a four-year school. And if their courses have been mainly requirements to go to a four-year school they end up with a degree that is relatively useless. If high schools do an adequate job of training students to enter college, they should go directly to a four-year school. Two-year schools should become mainly technical schools that train students for specific jobs: nursing, computer programming, word processing, photography, dental hygienists and many more. The purpose of an education should be to get a job. Not everyone is qualified for, or interested in, a four-year degree.

Four-Year Colleges and Universities: The biggest problem with four-year schools is the sharp escalation of cost. Part of the problem is the third party payer problem that we will talk about later with respect to health care. Most students pay only a small fraction of the cost of their education: Parents, the state government, the federal government and various private donors pay for the rest. This means that it is relatively easy for the schools to pass on higher costs to these third parties. In all of the Educational System, students (or their parents) pay much less than the cost of the private or public education. Private or public donors make up the additional cost. For all Universities the price charged is about 31.5% of the cost. For public Universities, price is only 12.5% of costs; for private Universities price is 45.5% of cost. (See Winston.) With State Governments, taxpayers ultimately pay for the cost. The Federal Government finances primarily research which subsidizes graduate training. Again, the cost falls ultimately on the taxpayer. Vouchers have been proposed for higher education as well as elementary and secondary schools. The idea is to make the universities compete for the money of students. This would, hopefully, increase efficiency and reduce the amount of money that goes into administration and other overhead costs that tend to escalate at both public and private universities. Other than the GI Bill, there has been little use of vouchers in higher education. Another idea is that students could pay higher tuition in those fields that offer the higher incomes: business, science, computer science and engineering for example. State support of education has been declining relatively for years and Universities have been forced to rely more on tuition and private donors to maintain their programs.

The Diversity Issue: For the last thirty years or so minority students have been given preferential treatment for admission to many of the countries best Universities. This was designed to overcome past injustice of discrimination. In recent years this policy has come under attach because many non-minority students are being denied equal access to these universities. It is much easier to get accepted to many of the prestige universities if you are Black or Hispanic than if you are Caucasian or an immigrant from say Europe or Asia. This program does little for low-income Blacks and Hispanics. It mainly benefits middle and upper income Blacks and Hispanics who would have got into college anyway but at slightly less prestigious institutions. These are no longer disadvantaged students and perhaps should no longer get preferential treatment.

## SHOULD THE PUBLIC SUPPORT EDUCATION?

What is the justification of public support of education? Democratic governments seldom work where there is not an educated middle class. The United States has always been a land of immigrants and we pioneered mass public education in the 19th Century. The idea was that there were gains to society over and above the gains to the students and their families. These gains included the political gain of having a relatively educated population that was crucial to the stability of the democratic system. Second, with a large immigrant population, free and compulsory public education ensured that the children of immigrants learned English as well as learning the basic education skills necessary to find jobs and move up in society. After the Civil War the US became an industrial and agricultural society. The country needed trained engineers, agricultural specialists, as well as teachers, doctors, lawyers and preachers. The Public Universities provided them. It is doubtful that the US could have become the democratic economic power that it is today without public support of education. Economists call these positive externalities. Positive externalities exist when the gains to society exceed the gains to the individuals. In the late twentieth century we went through a technological revolution involving personal computers and the inter-net. Silicon Valley is the center of this revolution. Spurring the revolution were Stanford (a private University), but also University of California-Berkeley, University of California-Santa Cruz and San Jose State (all public). In addition other universities around the country (public and private) also played a major role.

## REVIEW QUESTIONS

Multiple Choice: Select the correct answer:

1. The main justification for public support of education is that:
   a. Social benefits exceed private benefits
   b. Private benefits exceed social benefits
   c. Neither of the above

### Essays

1. Describe briefly how voucher programs for elementary and secondary schools would work. Why are voucher programs apposed by teachers unions and public school administrators?

2. Why are public schools, especially in the central cities, in trouble? What are some of the ways that have been proposed to improve their performance?

## SUGGESTED READINGS

Blau, Francine, "A Symposium On Primary and Secondary Education," *Journal of Economic Perspectives,* 10, no. 4 (Fall, 1996): 3–8.

Card, David and Alan B. Kruger, "School Resources and Student Outcomes: An Overview of the Literature and New Evidence from North and South Carolina," *Journal of Economic Perspectives,* 10, no. 4 (Fall 1996): 9–30.

Clotfelter, Charles T., "The Familiar but Curious Economics of Higher Education: Introduction to a Symposium," *Journal of Economic Perspectives,* 13, no. 1 (Winter 1999): 3–12.

Hanushek, Eric A. "Measuring Investment in Education," *Journal of Economic Perspectives,* 10, no. 4 (Fall 1996): 9–30.

Hoxby, Caroline Minter, "Are Efficiency and Equity in School Finance Substitutes or-Compliments," *Journal of Economic Perspectives,* 10, no. 4 (Fall 1996): 51–72.

Kane, Thomas J. and Cecelia Elena Rouse, "The Community College: Educating Students at the Margin Between College and Work," *Journal of Economic Perspectives*, 13, no. 1 (Winter 1999): 63–84.

Winston, Gordon C. "Subsidies, Hierarchies and Peers: The Awkward Economics of Higher Education," *Journal of Economic Perspectives,* 13, no. 1 (Winter 1999): 13–36.

# *Chapter Eleven*

# Environmental Economics: Does Saving the Environment Require Slower Growth?

## WHAT IS THE ENVIRONMENT?

The environment is the air we breath, the lakes, streams, and oceans, the land we farm, the forests, the wild life that live in the lakes, streams, forests and oceans and the land and forests and on a world scale, the atmosphere that protects us from the harsh rays of the sun and makes life on earth possible. The environmental movement probably started at the turn of the last century under such leaders as President Theodore Roosevelt and the creation of our system of National Parks and National Monuments. The modern environmental movement stated in the 1970s with the realization that many of our lakes and streams and even the air we breathe were becoming seriously polluted.

## THE EXTERNAL COST OF POLLUTION

The primary economic justification for protecting the environment was the externalities argument. Pollution was an external cost that was a cost to society but not to the firms, organizations or individuals that caused the pollution. A paper mill on a river treats the river as a free good and dumps its sewage in the river. If it doesn't other competing firms will and their costs will be lower. In other words the firm does what is in its self-interest. The problem is that what is in the firms interest is not in the interest of society, or at least some members of society. If the river, becomes polluted fishermen can no longer fish the river, swimmers can no longer swim in the river, owners of summer homes along the river see their property values diluted. What are the economic solutions to the problem? First, law could ban pollution. The problem is that enforcing the law might be difficult. It is costly to police firms and unless the law applied to all firms doing the pollution there would be a strong incentive to ignore the law. A second solution might be to give property rights to the river to the government or a public authority. The public authority could then charge the polluting firms for the use of the river as a way to get rid of their pollutants. If the charge is high enough the firms will find it in their interest to find other ways to get rid of the pollutants. Alternatively, the government could put a tax on the firm that would cover the cost of the pollution. Again if the tax is high enough the firms will find other ways to get rid of their pollutants. What about consumers? They are now faced with a higher price for the product. But this higher price merely reflects the full cost of producing the product. Before these costs were born by the fishermen, the swimmers, the boaters and the property owners that also used the river.

Air pollution is a similar example but with more complex problems of control. If the air becomes polluted people suffer from respiratory diseases. The problem is that these diseases may develop over long periods of time and it may be difficult to prove the cause of the illness. One method of controlling air pollution is for government to sell rights to pollute. The government decides how much pollution is acceptable and allots these rights to firms. Firms that don't pollute or pollute below their allotted levels can then sell their rights to other firms who are exceeding their allotments. But having to pay for the right to pollute gives polluting firms an incentive to find ways to reduce their pollution. The EPA has used this method for several years.

### Environmental Damage from Destruction of Forests

Clear cutting of forests for the production of lumber and paper leaves hillsides denuded and subject to erosion, destroys the habitat for wildlife, and leaves the scenery scared in a way that may take decades to recover and sometimes may never recover. Selective cutting of mature trees would be a much better way to harvest the trees. The problem is that this is more expensive for the lumber industry and may even be opposed by some environmentalists who would prefer no cutting at all. We need lumber, so no cutting is probably not an option. Somehow we must make it in the interest if lumber companies to selectively cut so as to preserve the forests for future generations.

## GLOBAL WARMING

Another problem with air pollution is that it may be global in nature. Many scientist believe that we are experiencing global warming and that it is being caused by chemicals being added to the atmosphere mostly by exhaust from automobiles and trucks and by the burning of coal by electric power plants. The burning of coal, wood and cow dung in developing countries also causes pollution. Great Britain a hundred years ago was covered with soot from coal and wood burning homes and factories. With the advent of fuel oil, gasoline and natural gas and electricity as alternative sources of energy and with the decline of manufacturing in Great Britain, much of the soot has disappeared or been cleaned up.

## DOES SAVING THE ENVIRONMENT REQUIRE SLOWER GROWTH?

This brings us to a crucial point. Does economic development cause environmental problems? Is slower economic growth necessary to solve our environmental problems? Many environmentalists believe that the industrial and developed west, that is, the US, Western Europe, Canada and perhaps Australia, are the major causes of global warming and that only slower economic growth in the west will stop global warming. In an absolute sense it is true that the west is the biggest polluter. Since the West produces most of the worlds GDP, it also produces most of the world's pollution. In a relative sense it is not true. The fast growing countries of the west have by far the best environmental record, at least in the last 30 years. The reason is that they can afford to try to clean up the environment and political pressure has forced them to do so. Poor countries have very poor records of taking care of the environment. Eastern Europe and the former Soviet Union had terrible environmental records. The same is true of most developing countries. Slow growth and poverty mean that they cannot afford the measures necessary to protect the environment.

If the west grows slower that will make the problems of the poor countries even worse. The reason is that their growth depends on selling goods to the West. And if the West grows slower their environmental problems will also become worse as money to clean up the environment dries up. This does not mean that we shouldn't try to clean up the environment or that we should ignore global warming. It means instead that slower growth is not the way to deal with the problem. The Bush Administration was probably right to reject the Kyoto Accords in 2001. It would have imposed much slower growth on the West (especially the US) and therefore on the developing world too. Where it was wrong was to not offer an alternative. Its position being that global warming is not a problem. Although the scientific evidence is probably not yet conclusive we cannot afford to wait too long. Life on earth as we know it may be at stake.

We can expect development of more fuel-efficient cars. Already available are small cars using a combination of self generated electricity and gasoline. These can get gas mileage of 40 to 50 miles per gallon or so. Within a few years this technology will be available on larger cars, SUVs and trucks and busses. In the longer run hydrogen fuel may be available. This could reduce auto pollution to zero. Technology exists to reduce pollution from coal burning power plants and in time coal will be replaced by natural gas as a much cleaner fuel. Also nuclear power plants are making a comeback as new technology makes them safer. They also are much cleaner than coal or fuel oil. Also developing countries can be expected to follow the path of England. With economic development will come the use of more fuel-efficient and environmentally cleaner sources of energy.

## SUMMARY

Over the last 30 years great progress has been made in cleaning up the environment in the developed countries. 30 years ago Lake Erie and Lake Ontario, two of the Great Lakes bordering the US and Canada, were severely polluted. The lakes were dying and fish life was becoming extinct. Today both lakes are relatively clean and again support abundant fish life as well as boating and fishing. The point is that our environmental problems are solvable. What it takes is the political will to act. On international issues like global warming, this means international cooperation. The best way to help developing countries is to help them grow. With growth in per-capita incomes they will be able to afford to tackle their environmental problems.

## REVIEW QUESTIONS

Multiple Choice: Select the Correct answer:

1. Water pollution is an example of:
   a. An external benefit
   b. An external cost
   c. Neither of the above.
2. With external costs of production:
   a. Private cost is less than social cost
   b. Private cost is greater than social cost
   c. Private cost is equal to social cost.

3. With external benefits in consumption
   a. Private benefits exceed social benefits
   b. Private benefits are less than social benefits
   c. Private benefits equal social benefits
4. Private interest groups can get benefits from the political process because:
   a. Benefits are concentrated and costs are dispersed
   b. Benefits and costs are concentrated
   c. Benefits and costs are dispersed
   d. Costs are concentrated and benefits are dispersed

## SUGGESTED READINGS

Coase, Ronald, "Economists and Public Policy", in his *Essays on Economics and Economists,* (Chicago, University of Chicago Press, 1994): 47–63.

Diamond, Jared, *Guns Germs and Steel: The Fates of Human Societies,* (W. W. Norton and Company; Paperback Edition 1999; Hardback Edition, 1997).

Diamond, Jared, *Collapse: How Societies Choose to Fail or Succeed,* (Viking: The Penguin Group, 2005).

Tietenberg, Tom, *Environmental and Natural Resource Economics,* 5th ed., Reading, Mass: Addison Wesley, 2000.

*Chapter Twelve*

# Economics of the Health Care System: Can The System be Reformed?

## INTRODUCTION

Health care expenditures in the US have been rising for at least 30 years and are now about 15% of GDP. On both a per-capita basis and as a percent of GDP, health care expenditures in the US are higher than any of the other developed countries. But do these rising health care expenditures represent rising quality of care or do they represent a health care system lacking the discipline of competition where incentives to control cost are often lacking? Slowing the growth of health care expenditures has become an important policy issue at the national level. Extending prescription coverage to the elderly with Medicare was an important issue in the last Presidential Election and has now become part of the Medicare System. This Chapter will attempt to give a broad overview of the economics of the health care system and a brief discussion of the policy issues involved. It will look primarily at the national system.

## STRUCTURE OF THE INDUSTRY

The health care industry will be defined broadly to include all the major participants. First, there are the hospitals, both public and private. These provide both in-patient and outpatient services. Doctors usually refer users of these services to the hospital. Emergency services are also provided which do not require a referring doctor. In addition there are Hospital Management Associations (HMAs), which are companies that own several hospitals as well as related facilities (such as nursing homes). Second, there are Health Maintenance Organizations (HMOs) and Preferred Provider Organizations (PPOs). HMOs are organizations that provide health care services to large groups of users usually through place of employment. They contract with a network of doctors, hospitals and other providers to furnish services to clients to whom they provide insurance coverage. PPOs are similar but they also allow the use of service providers that are out of the network but at lower rates of coverage. Third, there are doctors including: private practitioners, group practice, and network providers. Fourth, there are insurance companies that provide insurance coverage. These include individual policies, group plans, and plans through HMOs and PPOs. Fifth, there are Medicare and Medicaid, which are public programs. Medicare is a federal program that provides health insurance to people over 65 who also are part of the Social Security System. In addition, Medicaid is funded by the Federal government but administered by the States. It provides health insurance to qualifying low-income people. Sixth, there are the pharmaceutical companies that provide prescription and non-prescription drugs that are sold though retail outlets. Seventh, there is the Food and Drug Administration (FDA), which tests and approves new drugs. Eighth, there are the Medical Schools that train doctors and conduct medical research. Medical Schools are usually affiliated with a hospital where medical students do their residency training. Last, there is the National Institute of Health (NIH), that is a federally funded research institute which funds research conducted through Medical Schools, Universities and Research Institutes.

## WHY IS HEALTH CARE SO EXPENSIVE?

Third party payers pay most of the costs of health care services. These third party payers are insurance companies, the government (through Medicare and Medicaid), HMOs and PPOs. Once deductibles have been met the programs picks up a high share of the cost. This means that the marginal cost to the user is substantially below the cost of providing the service. As a result, more services are used than would be the case if users paid the full cost when the services were provided. Providers of services pass the costs on to the insurance companies, the government and the HMOs and PPOs. They in turn pass it on to the members of the plan and the taxpayers. Employers who furnish plans and cover all or part of the cost can deduct the costs for tax purpose. Individuals cannot deduct medical costs except over a very high tax deductible.

Another reason that costs are high is that health insurance is not like other insurance. It covers routine health care as well as catastrophic health care. As an analogy, auto insurance covers only unforeseen events such as an accident. It does not cover routine maintenance or the cost of driving the car. Life insurance covers only in the event of a death. Health insurance is, in fact, a combination of insurance and a time payment plan for paying medical bills. But it is a time payment plan with a lot of cross subsidization of costs. In effect the people who have low routine health care cost subsidize the people with high routine health care cost. Cross subsidization is to be expected with catastrophic health insurance. With private insurance plans, people in higher risk classes pay higher premiums. All of this separates the cost from the service provided and makes it easier to pass on costs.

Technological change in health care has also been cost increasing. New medical procedures are usually very expensive. This is in part because of the insurance system. Doctors and hospitals adopt these procedures in part because they know that the costs can be passed on. There are no cut-rate hospitals and doctors offering to do it for less. How many people would have $100,000 dollar heart surgery if there were no insurance? But even with insurance, if the system was more competitive, the cost might only be $80,000. In competitive industries technological change is usually cost reducing. Witness the computer and software industry in the past 20 years.

Another reason that health care is expensive is that expenditures tend to be concentrated in the retirement years. The elderly tend to have much higher health care costs both because they have more serious illnesses but also new technology allows many of these illnesses to be treated and life extended. Once a person is retired Medicare becomes the major provider and private insurance (for those who have it) is secondary.

Another reason that costs are high is the cost of prescription drugs. Drug companies have 20 years of patent protection on new drugs and even after patent expiration are often able to delay introduction of new lower cost drugs. The US market is a protected market. The same drugs are often available in other counties at much lower prices. Many people near the borders with Mexico or Canada go across the border to buy prescription drugs. Import or re-import of drugs from other countries at lower prices is not allowed. The FDA has a long, complicated and expensive process of testing before new prescription drugs can be introduced. And at the retail level, prescription drugs can only be sold in stores that have a prescription drug department and who hire licensed pharmacists. Generic drugs can usually only be introduced after patents have expired. Last, for doctors and hospitals, malpractice insurance is very expensive because successful lawsuits often lead to high punitive damages over and above any economic damages. In many areas the cost of malpractice insurance is forcing doctors out of business.

## WHAT HAPPENS TO LOW INCOME PEOPLE?

Low-income people without insurance have been priced out of the system. The working poor are not eligible for Medicaid and often do not have health insurance with their employment. The high prices make even routine health care unavailable. Instead, they do without routine health care until they are seriously ill and then go to the emergency room of a public hospital. At private hospitals insurance is usually required. Public hospitals are usually required to serve the poor. Because they cannot ration customers by price, they use long lines. People in dire need are taken in, the rest wait in line often for many hours. Those whose needs are not dire often give up and go home. Ultimately the costs are born by insured clients and taxpayers. The problem is that this is a very expensive way to provide health care to the poor. In border cities such as El Paso, TX, the problem is made more difficult. Thomason, the public hospital in El Paso, must serve many people from Juarez, Mexico, as well as El Paso.

The poor have also been priced out of the market for prescription drugs. People with Medicaid do get limited prescription coverage. People with Medicare did not until the new Medicare act was passed in 2003. This act goes into affect in January 2004. The elderly who lived on social security did not have coverage unless they also had private insurance. Prescription for the elderly can easily run several hundred dollars a month. This was a major issue in the last Presidential election. Congress has now passed a prescription drug program called Medicare D. It went into affect at the beginning of 2006. Primarily private insurance companies that get a subsidy from the Federal Government administer the program. With the new law prescriptions for people with Medicare will be available with the payment of a deductible of $250, payment of a monthly fee for the plan you select and a co-pay of 25% of the cost of prescriptions. There are special provisions for qualified low-income people. They may have no deductible and no monthly fee and only a small co-pay. For people who do not qualify as low income the program is not inexpensive but is better than no coverage as was the case before.

## CAN THE SYSTEM BE REFORMED?

Getting reform of the health care system will be very difficult because there are so many vested interest in the system: the hospitals, the insurance companies, the pharmaceutical companies, the HMOs and PPOs, the American Medical Association (AMA), The American Association of Retired People (AARP), the Unions, and many more. Serious reform would require a consensus among the major interest groups or strong pressure from the public or both. More likely to happen are small piecemeal reforms.

## MEDICAL SAVINGS ACCOUNTS

One proposal that has been around a long time is medical saving accounts with catastrophic insurance. Under this plan a person's insurance payment would be divided into two parts. One part would be for catastrophic insurance to cover major unforeseen illnesses (heart disease, cancer, diabetes, etc.). The other portion would be to cover routine medical expenses. The routine portion would go into a medical savings account out of which medical bills would be paid directly by the client. If the client did not use the entire routine portion, the client would get to keep the money and earn interest on it. If the person exceeded the routine portion, it could be applied to the catastrophic insurance after a deductible had been met. Or the person could be allowed to carry over a surplus to future years.

The primary advantage of this type of plan is that the clients pay their own routine bills and thus have an incentive to economize on cost. Providers of services would have to compete for the business of the clients. Unfortunately, it would only work if it were widely adopted. Providers will not offer lower prices to individuals or small groups when most other clients are still paying higher prices. So far these types of programs have only been available to small numbers of users not in existing plans. To be workable, the HMOs and PPOs would have to offer the programs. Also large corporation who offer their own plans would need to offer medical savings accounts. HMOs and PPOs now dominate the health care business. HMOs and PPOs could still deal with preferred providers but would have to allow patients to pay for their own services. The biggest problem is that different clients would require different levels of services. Clients could be offered different levels of service and pay higher premiums for higher levels of service. This seems to be the biggest difficulty with medical saving accounts. If clients pay their own routine medical bills it will be difficult to have the amount of cross subsidization that current plans allow. The new Medicare act of 2003 allowed much broader use of medical savings accounts and these plans have been gaining popularity, especially with large corporation that are under great pressure to slow the rapid growth of health care expenditures, especially for their retired employees.

## PRE-FUNDING OF MEDICARE

In order to avoid the big transfer from working to non-working, it has been suggested that Medicare be converted to a pre-funded program rather than a pay as you go program. (See Feldstein.) Workers would be required to buy a medical retirement account as soon as they started paying into social security. The contributions would buy an annuity that could be used at retirement to purchase a health care plan. These accounts have been referred to as medical retirement accounts. These accounts would be mandatory and would replace the current Medicare program. Under the present program, private insurance covers workers during their working years but Medicare takes over for the retirement years with private insurance becoming secondary. But for most people these are the really expensive years as far as health care is concerned. But Medicare is paid for primarily out of social security contributions and general tax revenue. Thus it is a major redistribution from working to non-working. If it was pre-funded it would be paid for over the earning life of the recipients and the funds would be invested and earn interest. This would make the system much less expensive in the long run. But in the short run it would be more expensive because existing retirees and future retirees would still have to be funded during a lengthy transition period. These are the same problems that exist with plans to convert social security from a pay as you go to a pension (pre-funded) system.

## LONG TERM CARE INSURANCE

In the last few years, private long-term care insurance has become available and some employers are now offering it to their employees. (Including The University of Texas System.) This type of insurance does not cover medical expenses since, for the elderly, they are covered by Medicare. Instead it covers nursing home care and in home care. These are expenses that are not usually covered by Medicare. Medicaid will cover nursing home care for low-income people. But to qualify most people have to give away their assets several years before the care is needed.

## PEOPLE NOT COVERED

Most large business and government and non-profit organizations offer health care plans. Many small businesses do not. This means that there are a large number of people who are out of the system and either have no health insurance or have to buy their own. The result is more expensive polices and no tax exemption. So far the small business lobbies have been successful in stopping legislation that would require them to provide health care plans. The other problem is part time workers and temporary workers. In most cases they are also not provided with medical coverage. Thus we have millions of relatively low-income workers who either have no insurance or who pay much more for their own policies. Many firms rely on temporary workers specifically because they will not have to provide benefit packages. These exemptions probably should be eliminated but overcoming the power of the lobbies will not be easy. At a minimum the tax laws should be changed to allow tax deductibility for individuals who pay for their own insurance. And this should be a deduction from gross income before calculation of itemized exemptions so that it would be available to people who do not fill out the long form for income tax.

Congress would need to pass a law allowing medical savings accounts for all employers and allow and encourage medical saving accounts for all HMOs. If HMOs were allowed to offer medical saving accounts they could put the burden of how much expensive health care to use on the individual and his health care providers rather than the HMO. The biggest complaint about HMOs is that they often limit or prohibit services that doctors and users desire in an attempt to hold down costs. Attempts by Congress to pass a bill of rights for health care consumers deal directly with this issue. Unfortunately, mandating certain levels of care and making HMOs subject to lawsuits if the care is not provided will be a big windfall for trial lawyers and make health care even more expensive. Much more sensible would be to introduce a comprehensive system of medical savings accounts and catastrophic insurance to allow more of these decisions to be made by user and providers rather than HMOs. This would also allow more competition in the provision of health care services, as providers would have an incentive to compete for the consumer's health care dollars.

Hospital management companies developed in part as a way for hospitals to have more bargaining power with HMOs, PPOs, and insurance companies. Unfortunately, under the current system they have little incentive to reduce the costs of service. Instead they are more interested in maintaining their share of the pie. There are no Wal-Mart's in the hospital business. There would be if hospitals had to compete for business. Unfortunately, public hospitals have been caught in a squeeze between the HMOs, PPOs, private hospitals and Medicare. Medicare determines how much will be paid for services that are paid by them. And public hospitals are required by law to treat indigent clients free. The costs of these patients have to be born by higher charges to paying customers or by the taxpayers who fund public hospitals. As a result many public hospitals have been losing money and many have decided to go private to escape some of these burdens. In many cases large hospital chains have bought out public hospitals.

## PRESCRIPTION DRUGS

With respect to prescription drugs, what can be done? First, Congress could reduce the patent protection for new prescription drugs. The drug companies argue that they need this protection in order to make the high-risk investments necessary to develop new drugs. However, we have had rapid technical progress in other industries without the protected markets of the drug industry. Second, the FDA could shorten the time it takes to get new drugs approved. Third, Congress could open up the international market to allow import and re-import of drugs from abroad at prices below the protected prices in the domestic market. The US has long been a supporter of free trade. Why not have free trade extended to the drug companies? Unfortunately, none of this is likely to happen soon. The pharmaceutical company lobby is one of the most powerful in Washington. Congress and the President have passed legislation allowing prescription drugs to be covered by Medicare and by private plans with a government subsidy.

## LOW INCOME PEOPLE

In many states people who draw social security disability income (SSDI) are ineligible for Medicaid because the states set income limits that are below the SSDI income. This means that they are eligible for Medicare (as dependents of Social Security recipients or as Social Security recipients themselves) but are ineligible for Medicaid. In many cases these are mentally ill patients who take medications that are very expensive. The laws could be changed so that state eligibility for Medicaid would be at an income level that doesn't exclude SSDI recipients. Congress has now given prescription drug coverage to Medicare recipients with special provisions for low-income clients. This should help solve the problem.

What about low income people who are not eligible for Medicaid? Most of the working poor are ineligible for Medicaid and if they work for small businesses, often do not have insurance with their employer. Private insurance is expensive and as pointed out above is not tax deductible. Health insurance laws could be reformed to require small businesses to furnish health insurance for their employees. Eventually some sort of subsidized insurance will have to be provided. Once you make health care very expensive, its difficult to leave large segments of the population without coverage. They are effectively priced out of the system. The poor who do not have either Medicaid or private insurance are forced to use the emergency rooms of public hospitals or, where available, public health clinics. Subsidized public health clinics are probably much cheaper than emergency rooms. Unfortunately the waiting time to get accepted into a public clinic is often very long. Alternatively, cities could provide subsidized health insurance for the poor so they could have the same access to health care as the insured population. This would probably be much cheaper for taxpayers than the current emergency room system.

Thomason Hospital, in El Paso, has recently started an HMO called El Paso First Health Plans. It was started to provide for Medicaid patients but now is planning to start offering low cost insurance to people without Medicaid or Medicare. It hopes to keep premiums low by limiting benefits and believes that the program will be much cheaper than providing emergency room care for the uninsured. The hope is that this program will appeal to small businesses that do not now offer coverage. The City of El Paso is supporting the plan and plans to look at health insurance provision when granting contracts to businesses that contract with the City. The County and School Districts may follow suit. If this plan is successful it will likely be copied by other cities in Texas and around the Country.

## MODELS OF HEALTH CARE PROVISION

The Social Security system works reasonably well. One reason it does is that the money is paid directly to the recipients, and they get to spend it as they wish. The health care system has lots of problems and many of these problems stem from the fact that most of the medical bills are paid by third party payers, not by the recipients of the services. These payers are insurance companies, HMOs, PPOs, and the government. They have an interest in holding down costs. But on the other side are doctors and hospitals whose interest is in providing as much service as possible irrespective of cost. There are basically two models of health care. The one espoused by the doctors and hospitals is basically a public goods approach. All medically desirable services should be furnished. Cost should not be a primary consideration. On the other side, espoused by the HMOs and Insurance Companies, is the economic model. Health care is an economic service and should by provided as efficiently as possible. The problem is that attempts to hold down costs have made them the "bad guys" by people who accept the public good model. Both approaches have their problems. Even public goods cannot be exempt from economic consideration. In principle they should be provided at a level where the marginal social benefit equals the marginal social cost. There is, hopefully, a limit to how much taxpayers will be willing to pay. For the HMOs and Insurance Companies there must be a way to hold down costs without denying crucial services.

## MALPRACTICE INSURANCE

There have been attempts to reform the legal system for many years. These attempts have failed in part because the Trial Lawyers have one of the strongest lobbies in Washington. Most reforms would limit the amount of punitive damages. Punitive damages are damages over and above economic damages that are intended to punish the individual or organization for damaging behavior. Evidence indicates that most medical errors that lead to malpractice suits are not the result of incompetence by doctors or other medical professionals. (See Gawande.) Instead, they result from errors in procedures that often can be avoided by doctors and hospitals adopting standardized procedures and fail-safe checks to avoid error. Malpractice suits force doctors to follow procedures designed to avoid lawsuits which are often more expensive and may not be best for the patient. There appears to be no evidence that malpractice suits actually reduce malpractice.

## SUMMARY

The health care system is expensive because there is little incentive for third party payers to hold down costs. This is partly because doctors, hospitals and patients who face them want all medically desirable service provided. And this in turn results from the fact that the patient faces very low marginal cost for additional services and providers like to provide as much service as possible, as long as third party payers will pay. One way of reducing costs is to return the incentive for controlling costs to the patient and the care provider rather than third party payers. Medical savings accounts and medical retirement accounts would help achieve this goal. Increased competition in the pharmaceutical industry could help reduce the costs of prescription drugs. Also removing the restrictions on export and import of prescription drugs could also help, Limitation on punitive damages in malpractice suits could also hold down costs. As long as health care is very expensive there will be continued pressure to extend the system to those not covered.

## REVIEW QUESTIONS

Multiple Choice: Select the correct answer:

1. Because of third party payers health care is:
   a. More expensive
   b. Less expensive
   c. Neither of the above
2. With health insurance the marginal cost of services to consumers is:
   a. Reduced and consumption of services is decreased
   b. Increased and consumption of services is increased
   c. Reduced and consumption of services is increased
   d. Increased and consumption of services is decreased

### Essays

1. Explain how third party payers increase the cost of health care and also increase the use of health care services.
2. Explain how health saving accounts and catastrophic health insurance might reduce the cost of health care.
3. What are the major reasons that prescription drugs are so expensive? What are some possible remedies that might reduce the cost of prescription drugs.

## SUGGESTED READINGS

Antos, Joseph R and Linda Bilheimer, "Medicare Reform: Obstacles and Options", *American Economic Review: Papers and Proceedings,* 89, no. 2 (May 1999): 217–21.

Cutler, David M, "Walking The Tightrope of Medicare Reform," *Journal of Economic Perspectives*, 14, no. 2 (Spring 2000): 21–44.

Cutler, David, M., Mark McClellan and Joseph Newhouse, "What has Increased Medicare Spending Bought," *American Economic Review, Papers and Proceedings*, 88, no. 2 (May 1998): 132–36.

Freedland, Robert, "Medicare: Short-Term Answers and Long-Term Questions,“ *Challenge: The Magazine of Economic Affairs*, 40, no. 1 (January–February, 1997): 30–45.

Feldstein, Martin, "Pre-funding Medicare", *American Economic Review: Papers and Proceedings,* 89, no. 2 (May 1999): 222–28.

Gawande, Atul, "When Doctors Make Mistakes," in *The Best American Science Writing: 2000*, Guest ed., James Glick, New York, The Ecco Press, An Imprint Of Harper Collins, 2000, 1–22, 2000. (Originally published in *The New Yorker*, 2000.)

Goodman, John C. and Gerald L. Musgrave, "Patient Power: The Free Market Alternative to Clinton's Health Plan," *Cato Institute*, Washington, DC, 1994.

Hudson, Robert, "Long-Term Care: The New Risks of Old Age," *Challenge: The Magazine Of Economic Affairs*, 40, no. 3 (May-June, 1997): 103–15.

McClellan, Mark, "Medicare Reform: Fundamental Problems, Incremental Steps," *Journal of Economic Perspectives*, 14, no. 2 (Spring 2000): 21–44.

Saving, Thomas, "Making The Transition to Prepaid Medicare," *Journal of Economic Perspectives*, 14, no. 2 (Spring 2000): 85–98.

Scanlon, William J. "Possible Reforms for Financing Long Term Care", *Journal of Economic Perspectives*, 6, no. 3 (Summer 1992): 43–58.

# *Chapter Thirteen*

# International Trade and Exchange

## DOMESTIC TRADE AND FOREIGN TRADE

There are some crucial differences between domestic trade and foreign trade. When we go to a grocery store or a department store we buy goods that come from all over the US and, more and more, from all over the world. We take for granted domestic trade and think nothing of buying lettuce from California or beef from Iowa. The reason is that the US Constitution gave to the Federal Government the power to regulate interstate commerce and the power to regulate the currency. As a result there are almost no barriers to trade between states and we all use the same currency, the dollar. There are no exchange rate problems between states. With foreign trade the same is not the case. We have trade barriers in the form of tariffs, export subsidies and import quotas. Also, most countries have their own domestic currency and so we have exchange rate problems. The European Union did not get a common set of trade policies until about 20 years ago. And it was not until 2002 that it got a common currency. Many economists attribute the relatively rapid growth of the US economy during the latter half of the 19th century and during much of the 20th Century, in part to the fact that we had a huge domestic market with no barriers to trade and a single currency.

## WHY IS THE FOREIGN SECTOR IMPORTANT?

The foreign sector is important to the US economy for several reasons. First, net exports are a component of aggregate demand. An increase in net exports increases demand and a decrease in net exports decreases demand. Net exports are only about four or five percent of GDP and have been negative for the last 20 years. That means that they have been a drag on demand. However, along with our trade deficit has come a large import of funds from abroad. This has helped keep interest rates low and has led to substantial investment in real productive capacity in the US by foreign firms. This of course could change if the dollar weakens against other major currencies.

## GAINS FROM TRADE

Economic theory tells us that trade occurs because there are gains from trade. If the US can produce computers relatively cheaply and Brazil can produce coffee relatively cheaply then it pays for us to export computers to Brazil and for Brazil to export coffee to the US. Or if we can produce soybeans relatively cheaply and Korea can produce apparel relatively cheaply, then we should export soybeans to Korea and they should export apparel to us. These relations tell us that there are gains from trade, normally for both countries. Each country will have a higher income and higher level of consumption with trade than would have been possible without trade.

## GAINS FROM TRADE: AN EXAMPLE

Figure 13.1 shows hypothetical supply and demand curves for soybeans. The first diagram at the top shows supply and demand for soybeans in the US. $6.00 per bushel is the equilibrium price in the US with no trade. 60 million bushels is output and consumption in the US with no trade. The second diagram in the upper right shows supply and demand in the rest of the world (ROW), excluding the US. The equilibrium price in ROW is $10.00 per bushel without trade. The quantity produced and consumed is 75 million bushels. By adding demand in the US to demand in the ROW at each price we get world demand in the lower diagram. Likewise if we add US supply at each price to supply in the ROW at each price we get world supply in the lower diagram. The intersection of world supply and world demand gives the world price with trade of $8.00 per bushel. The US price of $6.00 without trade reflects the fact that the US is a low cost producer. The ROW price at $10.00 without trade reflects the fact that the ROW is a high cost producer.

If the US and the ROW trade, they face the world price. At the world price the US will produce 100 million bushels where the world price intersects US supply. Domestic supply is 43.8 million bushels. The US will export 56.2 million bushels, the difference between US demand and US supply. For the US,

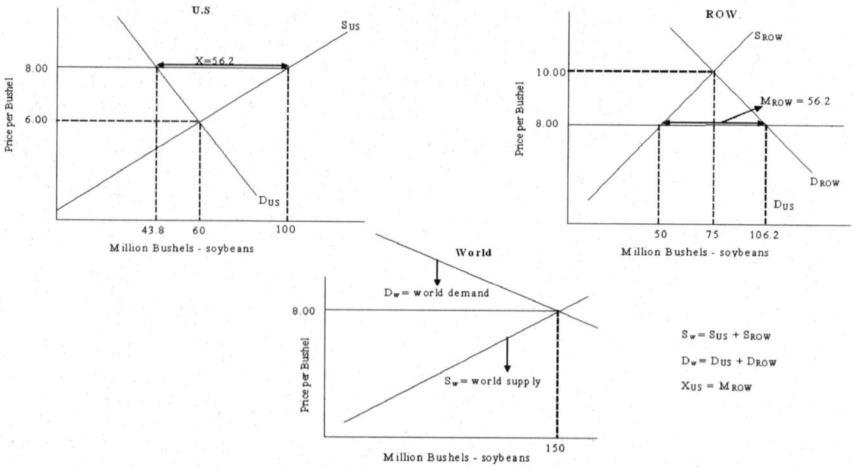


**Figure 13.1. Supply and Demand in a Two-Country Model**

demand beyond domestic demand is the world price as long as the US takes the world price as given. The ROW will produce 106.2 million bushels at the world price. Domestic supply at that price is 50 million bushels. The difference is made up of imports of 56.2 million bushels. The world price becomes the ROW supply curve beyond domestic supply as long as the world price is taken as given. At the world price US demand of 43.8 million bushels plus ROW demand of 106.2 million bushels is equal to world demand of 150 million bushels. The same is true for supply. US supply of 100 million bushels plus ROW supply of 50 million is equal to world supply of 150 million bushels. Also US exports of 56.2 million equals ROW imports of 56.2 million. These identities are shown in symbol form in the lower right hand corner of Figure 13.1.

Figure 13.2 shows a similar set of diagrams where the US is an importer. In this case our example is cotton shirts. The diagrams are again the US supply and demand for cotton shirts, the ROW supply and demand for cotton shirts and world supply and demand for cotton shirts. Again world supply is US supply plus ROW supply. World demand is US demand plus ROW demand. The US price without trade is $40 per shirt; quantity without trade is 20 million shirts. In the ROW the price without trade is $20 per shirt and the quantity is 25 million shirts. With trade, it is world supply and demand that determine price. The world price of $30.00 per shirt is determined where world supply and demand is equal. World quantity at that price is 50 million shirts. At the world price of $30.00 with trade the US will produce 15 million shirts. At that price demand is 30 million shirts. The US will import the difference between supply and demand of 15 million shirts. The ROW will pro-

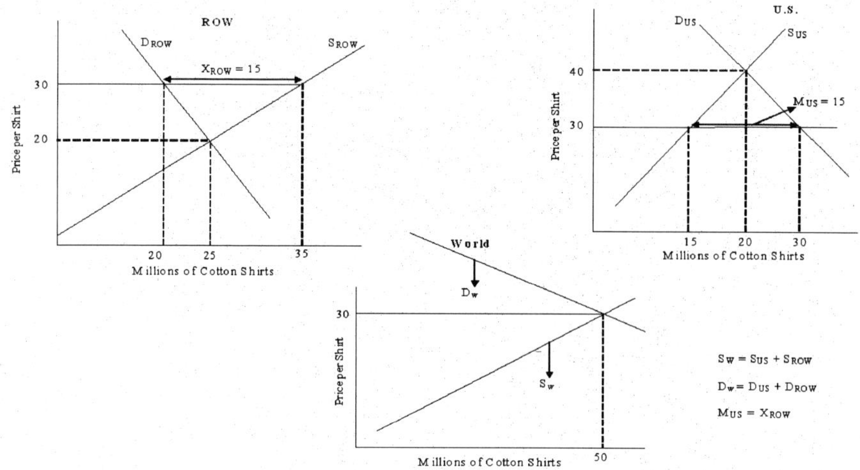


**Figure 13.2 Supply and Demand in a Two-Country Model; US as Importer, ROW as Exporter**

duce 35 million shirts at the world price. At that price domestic demand is only 20 million shirts. The ROW will export the difference of 15 million shirts. US supply of 15 million plus ROW supply of 35 million equals world supply of 50 million shirts. US demand of 30 million plus ROW demand of 20 million equals world demand of 50 million. World supply equals world demand equals 50 million shirts. US imports of 15 million equals ROW exports of 15 million. These identities are shown in symbolic form in the lower right hand corner of figure 13.2.

Figure 13.3 shows budget lines and production possibility curves for the US and the ROW for soybeans and cotton shirts. Recall our discussion of production possibility curves in Chapter 2. In Chapter 2 we were dealing with aggregate output measured in constant dollars. Here we deal with output measured in physical units. But the basic idea is the same. Each country at a point in time has a production possibility curve for producing soybeans and cotton shirts given the underlying resources available and given the productivity of those resources in producing each good. Each country faces diminishing returns as it increases the production of shirts and decreases production of soybeans or vice-versa. This means that as we increase units of shirt production we will have to give up successively larger units of soybean production. This is because many resources used to produce soybeans cannot be easily transferred to shirt production. Point A and A* shows US production of soybeans and shirts from figures 13.1 and 13.2 with trade. The US produces 100 million bushels of soybeans and 15 million shirts. The production possibility curve is drawn going

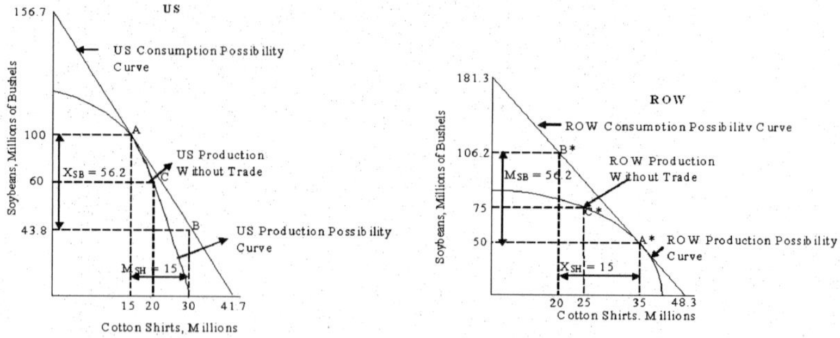


**Figure 13.3. Production and Consumption Possibilities and Gains from Trade in a Two Country Model**

through that point. The diagram for the rest of the world shows the production possibility curve for the ROW. Again production of soybeans and shirts are taken from figures 13.1 and 13.2 with trade. The ROW produces 35 million shirts and 50 million bushels of soybeans. This is at point A* in the diagram for ROW. The ROW production possibility curve will go through this point.

We can now calculate gross income generated by the production of soybeans and shirts both for the US and for the rest of the world. For the US it will be 100 million bushels of soybeans times $8.00 per bushel plus 15 million shirts times $30.00 per shirt or a total of $1250 million dollars. For the rest of the world the gross income is 35 million shirts times $30.00 per shirt plus 50 million bushels of soybeans at $8.00 per bushel. The total is 1450 million dollars. If the US were to use all of its income from the two goods to buy only soybeans it could purchase 156.3 million bushels of soybeans (1250 million dollars divided by $8.00, the price of soybeans.) This gives total soybeans if all income was spent on soybeans. That point is given on the vertical axis on the US diagram. Similarly if we divide the same income by $30.00 the price of shirts we get 41.7 million shirts if all income all income were spent on shirts. This point is shown on the horizontal axis. A straight line between these two points will be just tangent to the US production possibility curve at point A, the point of optimum production. If the US exports 56 million bushels of soybeans and imports 15 million shirts we end up at point B that is also on the budget line or consumption possibility curve. Total value of consumption of soybeans of 43.8 million bushels times $8.00 per bushel plus consumption of 30 million shirts at $30.00 per shirt gives $1250 million dollars Total value of production equals total value of consumption. But at point B, the US is outside its production possibility curve. By exporting and importing it is able to consume more than it produces.

The same is true for the ROW. If all income were spent on soybeans they could buy 181.25 million bushels. (Income of 1450 million divided by $8.00

per bushels.) If they were to spend it all on shirts they could buy 48.3 million shirts. (1450 million divided by $30.00 per shirt.) These points define the end points of the budget line. The budget line will be a straight line between these two points. The budget line defines all combinations of shirts and soybeans that could be purchased with the total income generated from production of the two goods. It will be tangent to the production possibility curve at A*. At this point $30.00 per shirts times 35 million shirts plus $8.00 per bushel times 50 million bushels equals $1450 million, the value of production. Point B* gives consumption of the two goods taken from the demand curves at the world price for each goods. These numbers represent the value of production with trade from figures 13.1 and 13.2. The value of consumption is 20 million shirts times $30.00 per shirt plus 106.2 bushels of soybeans times $8.00 per bushels equals $1450 dollars. The consumption of each good also falls on the budget line. This is because we assume that all income generated from production of the two goods is spent on consumption of the two goods. Implicitly we are holding constant production and consumption of all other goods. The point of all of this is that both countries are able to have higher levels of consumption through trade.

Also each countries income without trade is lower. Income without trade can be calculated from figures 13.1 and 13.2 at the intersection of domestic supply and demand. For the US it is $6.00 times 60 million bushels of soybeans plus $40.00 times 20 million shirts equals $1160 million. It was $1250 million with trade. For the ROW it is $10.00 times 75 million bushels of soybeans plus $20.00 times 25 million shirts equals $1250 million dollars. Recall that with trade income for the ROW was $1450 million dollars. Thus in our example both countries end up with both higher levels of income and higher levels of consumption with trade. Also in figure 13.3 production without trade is shown on both countries production possibility curves at points C and C*. Note that both of these points are inside the optimum consumption possibility curves and represent lower income than is attainable with trade. Realize that this assumes that the US has a comparative advantage in producing soybeans and the ROW has a comparative advantage in producing cotton shirts. Or put another way the US is a low cost producer of soybeans and the ROW is a low cost producer of shirts.

## PROBLEMS WITH TRADE

However, with trade between countries there are several problems. First, what is good for the country as a whole is not necessarily good for individual industries. When the apparel industry moves to Mexico, or Korea or China, it leaves domestic producers and workers unable to compete and often out of a job. These workers and firms will often organize and lobby Washington for protection against what they view as unfair competition. And often their lobbying is successful. Unfortunately, attempts to protect industries usually fail. The apparel industry moved from New England, to the Southeastern US, to the border States of Texas, and California, and finally to Mexico, Honduras, Korea, India and China. The steel industry has gone through a similar experience. Despite numerous attempts to support the industry, it has continued to decline and only recently sought temporary tariff relief from the Bush Administration.

Second, although goods, services and capital funds move relatively freely across borders labor is much less mobile both because many countries, including the US, have barriers to immigration and because workers and their families are reluctant to leave their native lands. However despite these barriers millions of people have immigrated to the US in the past two hundred years: First from Europe, then Mexico and Central America and now from Asia and the Middle East. Likewise in the last 50 years Western Europe has seen major migrations from the Middle East and Northern Africa.

The third major problem is what is called out-sourcing. American companies out-source parts of their production process to other countries that have lower labor costs. This has been especially true in manufacturing where jobs have been outsourced to Mexico and China as well as many other countries. This moves American jobs to other countries where labor costs are much cheaper. This gives cheaper goods for US consumers but means the loss of relatively high paying jobs in the manufacturing industries.

What is often ignored is in sourcing. Foreign companies investing in productive capacity in the US have created millions of jobs. This occurred throughout the eighties and nineties. Foreign companies, using funds earned from our trade deficits have built plants in this country. The Japanese started coming in the eighties and now assemble here most of the autos they sell in the US. The British also came in the eighties and nineties. British Petroleum has gas stations and convenience stores all over the Northeastern US. The Germans, Swiss and French came in the nineties. The Germans are concentrated in North Carolina, South Carolina, and Alabama, and include such well-known brands as Mercedes, BMW, and Siemans. The French, Swiss and Japanese produce pharmaceuticals in New Jersey. These companies came to the US for four primary reasons: First they wanted easy access to the huge US domestic market; second, they wanted the get the cheaper labor costs that the US provided (compared to Western Europe or Japan); third, they wanted to escape the highly regulated markets of Europe; and fourth, they were attracted by lower taxes in the United States. If the dollar were to weaken, these foreign investors may be less willing to invest in the US. A falling dollar reduces the return on foreign investment in the US.

Although we have lost jobs in many areas; we have gained jobs in many other areas. If out-sourcing meant a net loss of jobs we would see rising trend unemployment. Instead unemployment has remained low during most of the last decade. It was up briefly with the recession of 2001–2002. But on average unemployment in the US was about half what it was in Western Europe for the past decade.

## WHY DO WE HAVE BARRIERS TO TRADE?

If the economic argument is right that there are gains from trade, why do we find so many barriers to trade? Even in the US, which is a relatively free trade country, there are many barriers to trade. Protectionist policies result from several factors. First, we protect industries to try to save jobs and profits in the industries. Even if trade is good for the country as a whole it is not good for the affected industry. In the political process, concentrated interests can often override the general interest. Second, in developing countries, infant industries often need protection so that they can become competitive. The problem is that they don't want to give up protection once they have it. Third, some industries are protected because they produce strategic materials that may be necessary for national defense. Fourth, export and import of some food, fibers and animal products may be restricted to prevent spread of harmful plant and animal diseases and parasites. Fifth, labor is less free to migrate and thus equalize wages for comparable skills across countries. Still, the major differences in wages across countries appear to be due primarily to differences in productivity (output per worker).

## SUMMARY

Given that some countries have comparative advantage in the production of certain goods and other countries have comparative advantage in other goods we have shown that countries can gain from trade. The reason that there are barriers to trade is primarily because what s good for the country as a whole is not usually good for domestic industries. Export industries may benefit from trade. Trade may hurt import industries as production moves overseas and domestic prices fall. Out-sourcing may hurt domestic industries as production moves overseas to take advantage of lower labor costs. In-sourcing may help the domestic economy as foreign firms move to the US to take advantage of the huge domestic market that the US provides and to gain the advantage of cheaper skilled labor, less restrictive regulations and lower taxes.

## REVIEW QUESTIONS

Multiple Choice: Select the correct answer:

1. Comparative advantage says that:
   a. We should export those goods that are relatively costly for us to produce and import those goods that others can produce relatively cheaply.
   b. Restricting trade will help the US economy and make us better off.
   c. We should export those goods that we can produce relatively cheaply and import those goods that others can produce relatively cheaply.
2. Domestic trade differs from foreign trade primarily because:
   a. There are no barriers to trade and no exchange rate problems.
   b. There are barriers to trade and exchange rate problems.
   c. There are barriers to trade but no exchange rate problems.
   d. There are no barriers to trade but there are exchange rate problems.

### Essays

1. What are the major differences between domestic trade and foreign trade? Explain.
2. Discuss some of the major reasons that we have barriers to trade.

## SUGGESTED READINGS

Salvatore, Dominick, *International Economics*, 4th ed., New York, Macmillan, (1993): Chapter 3.

Ayers, Ronald M. and Robert A. Collinge, *Economics: Explore and Apply,* Enhanced Edition, Upper Saddle River, NJ, Pearson Prentice Hall, (2005): Chapter 28.

Sawyer, Charles and Richard Sprinkle, *International Economics*, 2nd ed. Upper Saddle River, N.J: Pearson Prentice Hall, 2005.

*Chapter Fourteen*

# The Recent Corporate Scandals: To Whom Are Corporate Executives Accountable?

## INTRODUCTION

To whom are corporate executives accountable? Most economists, financial analyst, and accountants would say that they are accountable first to the shareholders as owners of the corporation. However this view is based on a misconception of the nature of the shareholder claim. In reality the corporate collective owns all real assets of the corporation. In the nineteenth century the courts ruled that the corporation was a legal person that could own property, issue debts, engage in contracts, buy and sell assets, etc. The shareholder only owns a claim against the corporation. This claim is for dividends (paid at the discretion of executives), for capital gains (or losses) and for a residual claim against assets in case of insolvency. In addition the shareholder holds a voting right which most do not exercise. It is valuable mainly in that it can be sold, with the stock, to those who may wish to use it in an attempt to take control of the corporation. Owning fifty one percent on the shares allows an outside group to name the Board of Directors and to hire and fire the top executives of the corporation.

And who owns the shares? It is not primarily individuals but instead mutual funds, pension funds and other institutional investors: Individuals own primarily shares in these funds. Executives are rewarded with generous salaries and generous stock options to do what's best for the shareholder. But, in the short run, is this what is best for the enterprise or the other claimants against the corporation? The recent corporate scandals have been in part the result of an overemphasis on shareholder value as the appropriate objective for corporate executives.

Shareholders can be viewed as external claimants, little different than bondholders except that they hold a riskier claim and a voting right. Corporate managers should do what is in the long run interest of the enterprise. If they do, shareholders will end up being well rewarded. Who has the most at stake in a corporation? Not the shareholder with an indirect claim through a mutual fund, but workers and managers who have firm specific capital invested in the firm. If the firm fails, they loose their jobs and often their retirement package and their health benefits.

## EVOLUTION OF THE CORPORATION

Herendeen and Hendrickson-Smith traced out the evolution of the large corporate enterprise. Until the last half of the 19th century most shares were held by small groups of investors who were typically active in the management of the firm. During the latter half of the 19th century, secondary markets for the debt and equity claims of the larger corporations developed. Secondary markets were important for several reasons: First, they allowed separation of saving and investment decisions. This meant that the optimal financial investment decision of savers was to hold a portfolio of assets that gave the optimum mix of risk and return. (See Fama.) Savers were no longer concerned primarily with the performance of individual firms. If individual firms performed poorly investors could sell the shares. Executives and managers made decisions on investment in real productive assets of the firm. Another result was the division of authority between executives (and inside shareholders) who made entrepreneurial decisions and shareholders and creditors who made financial investment decisions.

In effect, shareholders became little different than creditors except they held a riskier claim. Many of the functions of ownership passed to the corporate collective. Crucial to this development was the concept of limited liability: Shareholders could lose no more than their original investment. The development of secondary markets was crucial for the development of long-term financing, both debt and equity. This meant that claim holders could sell their claims at any time and did not have to hold them until maturity. Since stocks have infinite maturity few outside investors would hold them if there were no active secondary market. Bonds had maturities of 20, 30 or more years and also would only be held if there were active secondary markets. And the liquidity provided by secondary markets reduced the cost of long-term funds to firms.

The legal status of the corporation also evolved over time. Limited liability only works if the courts support it. Secondary markets work because of binding contractual arrangements. The most important legal breakthrough was the acceptance of the corporation as a legal entity. This meant that the corporation could own property, make legally binding contracts, issue debt and sue or be sued in courts. In the U.S. this development came in the middle of the 19th century. The result was that shareholders no longer owned the real assets of the corporation; the corporate collective owned them. Instead the shareholder owned an undefined claim against residual income and a voting right. Corporate executives, in the form of dividend policy, defined the income claim.

Another crucial development in the 20th century was the development of a professional managerial and executive class trained in the major business schools. This meant that managers and executives were no longer recruited from the ranks of shareholders but were recruited from the business schools and promoted from within or hired in the market for managers and executives. Now the separation of ownership and control went one step further: Individual managers and executives could come and go but the corporate collective with its shared values and accumulated knowledge lived on. In the modern corporation power accrues to the office, not to the individual. An individual has power and authority because he is chairman of a large corporation. When he leaves the power does not go with him, it passes to his successor. He may of course expand the power of the office while he holds it.

The organizational structure also evolved over time: from U-Form (unitary structure) to M-Form (multi-divisional structure) to J-form structure. (J for Japanese.) The M-Form structure allowed decision making to move down the chain of command so that operating decisions (output, employment and pricing decisions) could be made at plant or division levels. Top management became concerned primarily with investment and financing decisions. In J-Form there was also coordination across divisions and between firms and suppliers. Along with this was the development of accounting and budgeting systems, the development of standard operating procedures and the development of internal systems of control and coordination that allowed larger and larger organizations to be run efficiently. One of the most recent advances was the personal computer and the inter-net, which allowed almost instantaneous transmission of information and financial transactions worldwide.

## THE NATURE OF THE CORPORATE FIRM

What are the implications of this evolutionary view for the theory of the corporate firm? It is that the corporation is a social institution that has evolved over hundreds of years. What is the motive force that drives this evolutionary process? The conventional view in economics and finance is that the firm is a nexus of contracts that tie together the various participants of the firm. The firm has no interest of its own independent of its various constituents. When all contracts are optimally organized, each participant receives the marginal value of his contribution. But if this is the case are shareholders any different than other claimants? According to Jensen they are. Because they hold the residual claim they guarantee payment to the other claimants and are bearers of residual risk. Thus Jensen argues that control rights are vested in shareholders. But is this really the case? Shareholders have limited liability and thus can lose only their original investment and often in bankruptcy proceedings do no even lose that. Limited liability makes their claim little different from the claim of bondholders except that it is riskier and includes a voting right. The people with the most residual risk are workers and managers who risk losing their jobs, their retirement fund and their health benefits.

In the contracts view, it is the self-interest of individual investors, workers and managers that drive the system. But can this drive the evolution of the system that lives beyond the life of individual participants. Why should individuals be interested in the long run survival of the firm? An alternative view is the transactions cost approach of Coase and Williamson. This approach says that firms exist because some transactions can be done more cheaply within firms than in markets. Another approach is the property rights approach of Grossman and Hart. This approach says that ownership gives decision makers control rights that would be unavailable under alternative forms of organization. Bolton and Scharfstein argue that these approaches don't deal adequately with the question of separation of ownership and control because they assume that firms are owned and managed by the same person. In reality managers may control the assets of the corporation but they do not own them. Bolton and Scharfstein stress the importance of corporate headquarters in the allocation of capital and the role of internal capital markets.

Here we follow the evolution of the enterprise view or evolutionary view for short. Edith Penrose, Robin Marris, Alfred Chandler, Richard Nelson and Sydney Winter, David Teese, Herbert Simon and Paul Auerbach have put forth versions of this view. This view sees the enterprise rather than the individual as the appropriate unit of analysis for studying the evolution of the corporation. But how is the enterprise defined? Edith Penrose defined the firm (enterprise) as a bundle of factor services and an administrative structure. The bundle of factor services are determined by the assets it controls. These assets include physical assets, intangible assets such as patents and copyrights and brand names, good will (created by advertising, product promotion and reputation) and human capital of workers, managers, and executives. Many of these assets are firm specific and depend on the past history of the firm. Capital goods, specialized knowledge, brand loyalty, good will and financial assets and liabilities are accumulated over time as the firm adds to its existing stocks and as old stocks are depreciated or sold. The same is true of human assets, which are rented not owned. Workers and managers gain firm specific knowledge over time and are replaced by new workers and managers as they mature and eventually retire. The administrative structure includes a central administration that coordinates the activities of the firm, sets forth its goals and articulates its set of shared values. In addition it includes the various divisions, sub-divisions, plants and departments all tied together by the hierarchical structure of authority.

The enterprise develops an interest of its own, independent of the interest of its individual participants. This interest is imbedded in the collective memory and shared values of the organization, which is often called the corporate culture. It also includes the standard operating procedures and learned routines that guide the behavior of the firm. Top executives and the Board of Directors articulate this collective interest. However, they see themselves as representing the interest of the enterprise rather than their own interest or the interest of shareholders. The corporation evolves adaptively over time as managers, workers, creditors and suppliers find new methods of production, new products to produce, new ways to organize the production process, new methods of sales promotion, new methods of distribution, and new ways of financing that either reduce cost of any given output, increase output for any given cost or increase future output for any given investment outlay. The objective of the firm is to survive and grow but it can only do so if it has clearly articulated goals and a set of shared values.

The firms external markets give the firm autonomy: individual workers, managers, creditors, and suppliers can come and go without jeopardizing the life of the firm. The firm's internal organizational structure and its culture give the firm viability. This viability gives the firm the ability to live beyond the life of its individual participants. The firm in principle has attained perpetual life. Firms that are successful over the long run are those that have built an enduring corporate culture that has won the support and loyalty of successive generations of executives, managers, workers, suppliers and customers.

Social institutions are ways that society coordinates individual interests to group interests. (See Chapter 2 above) They rely on human nature and arise both spontaneously and as a result of human planning and design. Markets rely on the natural self-interest of individuals and, if properly organized, channel this self-interest to the public good. With all social institutions there are two basic problems that must be dealt with: First, most social institutions develop interests of their own that are separate from the interest of their constituents. General Motors has interests of its own, independent of interests of their managers, workers or shareholders. Labor unions develop interests independent of worker interests, mainly because they must make alliances with other interest groups in order to increase their lobbying power in Washington. The Department of Defense has interest of its own, independent of the interest of Congress, the President or the public. Top executives and Boards of Directors articulate these group interests. Internal control mechanism like accounting and budgeting procedures, hiring firing and promotion procedures, standard operating procedures, and the shared values of the organization ensure (in most cases) that the decisions of lower level workers and managers will be consistent with the overall objectives of the firm.

Second, social institutions must be held accountable to some broader notion of the public interest. With our political system we have the Constitution and separation of power to protect the governed from the government. The corporate system is held accountable in several ways. First, there is the Securities and Exchange Commission, which requires public accounting statements to be made available to investors. In addition there are regulations by various agencies such as the FDA, the EPA, the Federal Reserve, the Office of the Comptroller of Currency and many more depending on the industry. More generally there is the political process. In cases of gross misconduct, politicians soon see the political advantage of calling for public hearings, finding scapegoats and introducing new legislation. Within any given corporation, there is the Board of Directors, which oversees the corporation and, in principle at least, holds executives and managers accountable. And the ultimate check is the market. A corporation must generate an income stream to survive. Failure to do so leads to insolvency and ultimately bankruptcy. But things don't stop there; millions of shareholders and their political and legal representatives want to know how a large public corporation that apparently was doing well can suddenly go broke and loose money for all those investors.

## RECENT DEVELOPMENTS

Over the past thirty years maximizing short run share price has become the primary objective of corporate executives. Partly this was the result of business schools, especially MBA programs, that had drilled into future managers and executives the desirability of maximizing shareholder returns; partly it was due to the development of stock option packages that rewarded executives generously if share price increased; partly it was the result of pressure from investment bankers and mutual fund managers who have gained from rising share prices; partly it was the result of tax laws that make interest on debt tax deductible whereas dividends to shareholders are treated as part of income for both the corporation and the shareholder and are taxed at both levels. (The new tax law just passed in May 2003 reduces taxes on dividends and capital gains to a 15% rate.) Financial institutions are particularly vulnerable because they operate with much higher leverage than non-financial firms. This is partly because of the liquidity of their assets but also, at least for depository institutions; it is due to deposit insurance that removes much of the downside risk. As a result the FDIC imposes capital adequacy requirements.

During a long expansion such as the one in the 1980s or the one in the 1990s, there is a tendency for internal rates of return to rise relative to the cost of debt. This means that it is profitable for firms to increase their leverage ratios. Higher leverage increases the internal return on equity and increases share prices. Thus there are strong incentives in the system for executives to increase leverage during a boom and to contribute to an overvaluing of the companies stock. This happened both in the 1980s and in the 1990s. The problem is that when the boom ends many firms have debt structures that are no longer sustainable. When income is rising, debt service is relatively easy and asset and equity values rise to provide collateral for the debt. When income is falling, during a recession, debt service becomes difficult as it becomes a much higher proportion of income. In addition asset and equity values fall reducing the collateral that supports the debt. Enron and World Com were merely extreme cases of this phenomenon.

Many of the high tech stocks that crashed in 2000 were not accompanied by big bankruptcies. This was because the tech companies were financed mostly with new issues of equity, much of it put up by venture capital firms. The tech firms did not have many tangible assets to issue debt against. Shareholders lost a lot of money but without much debt big bankruptcies did not occur.

Also during good times corporate accounting standards deteriorate as managers and accountants attempt to put the best possible interpretation on earnings in order to impress fund managers who are the major purchasers of the stock. When profits deteriorate at the end of the boom, accountants and managers try to hide the deteriorating financial situation from fund managers in hopes of avoiding sale of the stock, falling stock prices and financial distress. Again Enron and World Com were merely the extreme cases of a very common occurrence.

Our tax laws contribute to the incentive to over-issue debt during an expansion. Interest on debt is tax-deductible on Federal corporate income tax. Dividends are treated as part of net income and are not tax-deductible expenses. So the corporation pays tax on the amount paid as dividends and then shareholders pay tax on them again as part of personal income. This has the effect of biasing corporate financing decisions toward debt rather than equity. It also means that most corporations increase equity through retained earnings rather than new issues of equity. Shareholders have been taxed lower on capital gains than on dividend income. (Up until the new tax law passed in May 2003.) In addition investment bankers have an incentive to push those stocks and bonds that they are underwriting and put pressure on their research and retail divisions to promote those stocks to their customers. This has been going on for a long time but has only become a serious issue in the last couple of years.

## CAN ACCOUNTING RULES FOOL THE MARKET?

The capital asset pricing model and other standard models in finance assumes that the market incorporates all available public information. This model implies that stock prices reflect the fundamentals of a corporation. These fundamentals include market interest rates and profit expectations. Any new information will immediately be reflected in stock prices. It has often been argued that the market sees through accounting rules and reflects the true earning power of the firm. This view has been brought into question by recent events. In hindsight it appears that many stocks, especially in the high tech sector were overvalued in the late 90s. In many cases the firms had no earnings and price reflected future earnings that would never be realized.

Companies like Enron and World Com continued to sell at high prices after current and future earnings had disappeared at least in part because accountants were able to hide the true situation of the firms. Thus, at least in the short run, the market can be fooled by incorrect or misleading accounting information. Also, at least in the short run, stock prices can be held up by unsustainable expectations. When prices are rising, no one wants to sell even if investors know that the stocks are over valued. No one wants to be the first out. But when the price does finally fall everyone gets out at once. The classic example of this was the stock market crash of 1987. However, Enron, World Com and other big bankruptcies did not occur because of bad accounting. They occurred for the same reason that bankruptcies usually occur: The companies borrowed too much against future income during the good times. When the good times ended they had debt levels that were unsustainable. Misleading accounting was a way to cover up the true situation in the futile hope that earnings would recover. When the accounting frauds were discovered share price plummeted and the companies were forced into bankruptcy. Investment bankers reinforced this process by continuing to push the stocks when they knew that earnings no longer justified the price. They did so because their companies were big underwriters for the debt and equity of the firms. They too were hoping for a miracle to bail them out.

## POSSIBLE REFORMS

What are some possible reforms that might improve the performance of the corporate sector? First, stock options for corporate executives should be reformed. Many have proposed expensing options. This is a move in the right direction but doesn't go far enough. First, it is difficult to price options. Option pricing formulas are available but is this the way to go? Another proposal is to reward executives with shares rather than options to buy shares. Options are highly leveraged and add to the volatility of share prices. Shares are much easier to expense because shares have a readily available market price. Shares could be issued with time limitations on when they could be sold. Another possibility would be to give corporate executives salaries plus bonuses based on average net corporate income over the past three or four years. This would remove the direct tie between share price and executive compensation. Another problem is the level of executive compensation. In recent years executive compensation in the US has become much higher than in Europe or Japan. Boards of directors need to take the initiative to attempt to hold the line on executive compensation. If they do not there will be political pressure for public action to limit executive salaries. These very high salaries and stock options often represent monopoly rent and may be unrelated to the productivity of the executives.

Second, what could be done about dividend policy? The Bush Administration was proposing doing away with dividend taxation at the shareholder level. This would eliminate the double taxation of dividends. What was passed by Congress and signed by the President was a reduction of both dividend and capital gain taxes at the shareholder level to a 15% rate. Unfortunately, this would leave intact the bias toward debt finance at the firm level. A better solution would have been to allow tax deductibility of dividends at the firm level. This would encourage corporations to pay higher dividends. Currently there are many corporations that pay no dividends and shareholder return is solely capital gains (or losses). This would imply raising fewer funds from retained earnings and more from new issue of stock. Alternatively, corporations could be allowed to deduct the full cost of equity, which would be dividends plus expected capital gains. This would essentially eliminate the corporate income tax. Milton Friedman and Lester Thurow have proposed eliminating the corporate income tax. It would mean that all corporate income would be taxed at the shareholder level. Another possibility would be to eliminate tax deductibility of interest (as well as dividends) at the firm level and tax corporate income fully at the firm level. This would eliminate taxation of corporate income at the shareholder level and for that reason would probably be politically unacceptable. The important thing is to remove the tax bias in favor of debt financing.

What about the accounting scandals? There has long been a conflict of interest with accounting firms that provide auditing services and also consulting and other accounting services for corporations. Ideally auditing firms should be set up as separate firms or at least as separate subsidiaries in accounting firms that would be hired by the SEC to audit corporations according to accounting standards established by the SEC. Investment banking firms should be required to separate their underwriting functions from their research and retail functions. These functions should be put in separate independent subsidiaries.

## TO WHOM ARE CORPORATE EXECUTIVES ACCOUNTABLE?

The idea that shareholders are the owners of the corporation is part of the ideology of the capitalist system. It is unlikely that this ideology will be given up easily. However, history has shown that corporations that have survived for long periods of time were those that developed a corporate culture and shared values with which their executives, managers and workers could identify. This meant that managers and executives worked for the good of the enterprise. It is probably true that in the long run maximizing shareholder value is equivalent to maximizing long run profits to the enterprise. However, in the short run the two are not equivalent: Maximizing short run share price is often inconsistent with what is in the best interest of the enterprise.

Increasing leverage during good times can run up share price. This means increasing returns to share holders by reducing the value of bondholder claims. The company buying its own shares can also increase share prices. This also has the affect of increasing leverage. Also leveraged buy-outs of the type that occurred in the 1980s run up the leverage ratio; increase share prices and decrease value to bondholders. Likewise share price can be temporarily increased or kept from falling by misleading or fraudulent accounting. And investment bankers can temporarily influence stock prices by promoting stocks through their research and retail activities. And increased leverage during a boom makes the firm vulnerable to financial distress when the boom ends.

The way to reduce these types of abuses is to convince corporate executives and managers that the best way to do what is best for shareholders in the long run is to do what is in the long run interest of the firm. To do this the present incentive system that encourages executives to concentrate on short run-share price should be eliminated. This means reform of executive compensation so that it is tied to the long run performance of the firm. It means reform of our tax laws so that debt and equity finance are treated the same. It means reform of the auditing system so that auditors can be truly independent. It means reform of the investment banking system so that investment advisors will be independent of the underwriting functions of investment banks. None of these will guarantee that we will not have another over or undervalued market. There will probably always be business cycles even with the best of monetary and fiscal policies. But these kinds of reforms could reduce the type of excesses that have occurred during the last five years and have also occurred after other long expansions such as the one in the 1980s. Many are reforms that are long overdue.

## SUMMARY

In this chapter we have looked at the evolution of the large corporation and examined how this evolution has affected the nature of the corporation. We concluded that the corporation is a legal person that owns all corporate assets. The shareholder owns a claim against the corporation; this claim is for dividends, paid at the discretion of managers, and for capital gains or losses. The shareholder also has a voting right that is valuable mainly in that that it can be sold with the stock to a group that may wish to gain control of the corporation. This claim is little different than the claim of a bondholder except that it is a riskier claim. Most individuals invest in mutual funds or pension funds. These funds in turn invest in corporate shares. The recent corporate scandals resulted in part because corporate executives had an incentive to maximize short run share price. This turned out in many cases to not be in the long run interest of the corporate enterprise. The reforms suggested are designed to align executive interest more closely with the long run interest of the enterprise.

## REVIEW QUESTIONS

Multiple Choice: Select the correct answer:

1. The productive assets of a corporation are owned by:
   a. The shareholders
   b. The bondholders
   c. The corporation as a legal entity

2. In most large corporations there is:
   a. Concentration of ownership and control
   b. Separation of ownership and control
   c. Neither of the above
3. One of the advantages of the corporate form of organization is that:
   a. Shareholders are not responsible for the debts of the corporation
   b. Shareholders are responsible for the debts of the corporation
   c. Shareholder's liability is limited to the amount of their investment

### Essays

1. Top corporate executives should attempt to maximize short run share price of the corporation. Do you agree or disagree. Explain.
2. During a business expansion, there is an incentive for corporate executives to increase leverage. Explain why.
3. List and explain some of the advantages of the corporate form of organization.

## SUGGESTED READINGS

Alchian, A. and H. Demsetz, "Production, Information Cost and Economic Organization," *American Economic Review*, 62, no. 5 (December 1972): 772–95.

Aoki, M., "Toward an Economic Model of the Japanese Firm," *Journal of Economic Literature*, 28, no. 1 (March 1990): 1–27.

Auerbach, Paul, *Competition: The Economics of Industrial Change*, Oxford: Blackwell, 1989.

Berle, Adolf A. Jr. and Gardner C. Means, *The Modern Corporation and Private Property*, Revised Edition, New York: Harcourt Brace and World, Harvest Books, 1968.

Bolton, Patrick and David S. Scharfstein, "Corporate Finance, The Theory of the Firm and Organizations," *Journal of Economic Perspectives,* 12, no. 4 (Fall 1998): 95–114.

Chandler, Alfred, "Organizational Capabilities and Economic History of the Industrial Enterprise," *Journal of Economic Perspectives,* 6, no. 3 (Summer 1992): 79–100.

Fama, Eugene, "Agency Cost and the Theory of The Firm" *Journal of Political Economy*, 88, no. 2 (April 1980): 302–25.

Friedman, Milton, *Capitalism and Freedom*, (Chicago: Phoenix Books, University of Chicago Press, 1962).

Grossman, Sanford and Oliver Hart, "The Costs and Benefits of Ownership: A Theory of Vertical and Lateral Integration," *Journal of Political Economy,* (August

1986): 691–719. Galbraith, John Kenneth, *The New Industrial State,* Boston: Houghton Mifflin, 1967.

Hart, Oliver, *Firms, Contracts and Financial Structure*, Oxford: Oxford University Press, 1995.

Herendeen, James B., *The Economics of The Corporate Economy*, New York: Dunellen, 1975.

Herendeen, James B. and Janet Hendrickson-Smith, "The Evolution of the Corporate Enterprise: From Sea-Going Ventures to Leveraged Buyouts," *Pennsylvania Economic Review,* 2, no. 1 (Spring 1992): 17–22.

Jenson, Michael C. and William Meckling, "Theory of the Firm: Managerial Behavior, Agency Cost and Ownership Structure," *Journal of Financial Economics,* (1976): 305–60.

Marris, Robin, *The Economic Theory of 'Managerial' Capitalism*, New York: The Free Press of Glencoe, 1964.

Miller, Arthur Selwyn, "The Legal Foundations of the Corporate State," *Journal of Economic Issues,* (March 1972): 59–79.

Minsky, Hyman, P., *Can "It" Happen Again?* Armonk, N. Y.: M. E. Sharp, Inc., 1982.

Nelson, Richard and Sydney Winters, *An Evolutionary Theory of Economic Change*, Cambridge: Harvard University Press: 1982.

North, Douglas, "Institutions," *Journal of Economic Perspectives,* 5, no. 1 (Winter 1991): 97–112.

Penrose, Edith, *Theory of the Growth of the Firm,* Oxford: Blackwell, 1959.

Shiller, Robert J., *Irrational Exuberance,* Princeton: Princeton University Press, 2000.

Simon, Herbert, "Organizations and Markets," *Journal of Economic Perspectives,* 5, no. 2 (Spring, 1991): 25–44.

Teese, David, "The Dynamics of Industrial Capitalism: Perspectives on Alfred Chandler's 'Scale and Scope'," *Journal of Economic Literature*, 31, no. 1 (March 1993): 199–225.

Thurow, Lester, *The Zero Sum Society,* New York: Penguin Books, 1981.

Williamson, Oliver J, "Transactions Cost Economic: The Governance of Contractual Relations," *Journal of Law and Economics,* 22, (1979), 233–271.

*Part III*

# MACROECONOMIC ISSUES

# *Chapter Fifteen*

# Measuring Economic Activity

## NATIONAL INCOME AND NATIONAL PRODUCT

Macroeconomic Analysis developed in the 1930s along with the development of national income accounting. National income accounting gave us a way to measure economic activity. It was based on certain key accounting concepts. First, was that we could add up aggregate production if we had a common measuring rod. That measuring rod was money. We can't add up tons of steel and bushels of wheat, and legal contracts drawn by lawyers. We can however add up the value of steel production, the value of wheat production and the value of the services produced by lawyers. However, to avoid double counting we must subtract out at each level the value of goods or services purchased from other firms. For the steel producer the value of iron ore and other produced inputs; for the wheat farmer the value of purchased seed, fertilizer and gasoline; for the law firm the value of new law books, the cost of advertising his services, etc. When this is done we have left for each productive unit its income generated or its value added. As we saw in Chapter 7, this value added is equal to wage and salary income, rental income, interest income and profits (or net income of enterprises). In other words value added is equal to the income generated by the firm (or other productive units). Added up for all productive units we have value added for the economy.

Gross value added for the economy we call gross domestic product (GDP). Net domestic product (NDP) is gross domestic product minus capital consumption allowance, which is primarily depreciation of business and government capital goods. Adding to this net income receipts from the rest of the world gives net national product (NNP). This in principle should equal net value added or national income. Net national product adjusted for statistical discrepancy is net value added for the economy. Statistical discrepancy is an error term that takes into account the different sums that you get when you add up the income side of the accounts and the product or output side of the accounts. The measurements (actually estimates) of income generated and net output produced are far from perfect and cannot be expected to add up exactly.

The other important concept is that value added must equal the value of all final goods. Final goods are goods consumed (personal consumption expenditures), goods added to the stock of capital goods of business or government (business plus government investment), government purchases of non-capital goods and services (including wages and salaries of government employees), and goods exported minus goods imported (net exports). Thus we have four basic equalities of national income accounting. National income equals national output equals the value of all final goods and service produced equals the sum of value added by all productive units.

If national income equals national output, then growth in national income equals growth of national output. Also, if national income equals national output, then national income per capita must equal national output per capita and national income per worker must equal national output per worker. And, likewise, growth in output per capita must equal growth in income per capita; and growth in output per worker must equal growth of income per worker. Realize that these accounting identities only hold for aggregate output and income.

For all kinds of reasons individual incomes can be more or less than individual output. However, if one person has income exceeding output, then some other person must have income that is less than output. The same is true for growth in income per capita or growth in income per worker. Any individual's income can grow faster or slower than the individual's output. A primary reason that per worker or per capita income and output does not have to be equal is taxes and transfers. But, there are also lots of other reasons. For per capita incomes we are looking at incomes and output for all persons. Some of these will not yet be in the work force and other will be retired and will have left the work force. And when we look at income and output per worker, it is very difficult to impute output to individual workers and therefore difficult to say whether any individual's income is equal to that individual's output.

The intuition of national income and national product is that all income must be generated by output. If we look at individual countries the same ideas hold. A country can only have high income per worker if it has high output per worker. For a poor country to become a rich country it must have growth in output per worker in order to have growth in income per worker. Redistributing incomes does not change these relations. If aggregate income doesn't grow, redistribution only takes income from some groups and gives it to others. The country is no richer than before and it may actually be poorer if redistribution takes income from high productivity individuals and gives it to low productivity individuals. And if a poor country wants to catch up to rich countries it must grow faster for a sustained period of time. For forty years after World War II Western Europe and Japan grew faster than the U.S. That allowed them to catch up to the U.S. so that by the end of the eighties their per capita incomes were roughly equal to per capita incomes in the US. Since then their growth rates have slowed and during the nineties were less than the growth rates of the U.S. South Korea was a poor country at the end of the 1950s but by growing very fast has become a relatively rich country by the beginning of the 21st Century. The same is true of several other Southeastern Asian Countries. We will examine in a later chapter why some countries succeed in growing and others do not.

## THE SECTOR RECEIPTS AND EXPENDITURE TABLE

A convenient way to look at aggregate income and aggregate output is with a Sector Receipts and Expenditure Table. The national income accounts divide the economy into four sectors. These are the Household Sector, which is comprised of all families and individuals; the Business Sector, which is comprised of all firms; the Government Sector, which includes Federal, State and Local Government units; and the Foreign Sector that includes net transactions between the US and the rest of the world. On the receipts side we have final receipts for each sector. On the expenditure side we have final expenditure for each sector. The difference between receipts and expenditures for each sector is that sectors net saving or net borrowing. Realize that these are flows of receipts or expenditure over a period of time, usually one year.

For the Household Sector final receipts are disposable income. This is national income minus taxes and minus business retained earnings and plus transfers. On the expenditure side is household consumption expenditures (both durable and non-durable.) The difference between disposable income and consumption expenditure is household saving. This is the net accumulation of financial assets by households. It is the current period accumulation of financial assets minus any new issue of debt. Individual households may be net borrowers or net savers but the household sector as a whole is normally a net saving sector. For the business sector final receipts are business-retained earnings. All other business receipts are paid out as expenses in the form of wages and salaries, rental expense, interest expense, and dividends paid to shareholders or taxes paid to government. Expenses for goods and services purchased from other firms cancel out for the aggregate economy. (With the exception of the purchase of capital goods.)

On the expenditure side, for the Business Sector we have gross investment in new capital goods, including changes in inventories. Final spending for business is spending for new capital goods or spending to increase future production. The difference between business retained earnings and business investment spending is the business sector deficit. The other way of looking at this is that the business sector finances its new investment in two ways: one, out of internal funds or retained earnings; and two, by issuing new debt or issuing new shares of stock.

For the Government Sector final receipts are net taxes or taxes minus transfers. Transfers are deducted because they show up as part of the final income of the people that receive them. Remember that transfers were part of disposable income of households and are spent or saved by household. These are tax receipts for all government; Federal, State and Local. Final expenditures for government are government expenditures for goods and services. Again transfers are omitted because they are not spent by government but rather by the recipients, mostly households. Spending on goods and services is made up of two primary categories: government purchases which would include purchases of defense goods, purchases of office supplies for government, rent for government buildings, etc., and wages and salaries of government employees (including military employees). The hiring of government employees is treated as the purchase of a service. The difference between government receipt (net taxes), and government expenditures (the purchase of goods and services), is the government deficit (or surplus). Realize that this is for all government and therefore is not the same as the Federal deficit that we discussed in Chapter 3.

For the foreign sector final receipts is often referred to as net foreign transfers. It is income paid to foreign recipients by US payers (primarily interest and dividends paid on US Securities held by foreigners and government transfers to foreigners) minus any payments of a similar nature paid to US recipients by foreigners. On the expenditure side is net exports. Exports are the sale of goods and services to foreigners by the US. Imports are the purchase of goods and services from foreigners by the US. Thus net exports are the value of exports minus the value of imports. This number is also referred to as the trade balance. For the last twenty years or so the US has been running a trade deficit; we have been importing, in dollar terms, more than we export. The difference between net foreign receipts and net exports (which for the US is negative) is net foreign saving (if it is positive) or net foreign borrowing if it is negative. Because our trade deficit exceeds foreign receipt, this number has been positive for the last 20 or so years. This means that we are a net importer of funds from the rest of the world. The negative of this figure is often called the current account deficit. We will discuss the foreign sector in much more detail in chapter 20.

The sum of all final receipts for the four sectors gives us gross aggregate income. The sum of all expenditures is called gross domestic product (or gross aggregate expenditures). Our accounting identities require the two sides to be equal and in the accounts they are except for a small statistical discrepancy. So for the aggregate economy receipts minus expenditures must equal zero. This means that the sum of the deficits and surpluses must also be zero. The net saving of the household and foreign sectors must equal the net borrowing of the government sector and the business sector.

Table 15.1 gives the Receipts and Expenditures Table for the US economy for For 2006 GDP (gross domestic product) was equal to 13,322 billion dollars. GDI (gross domestic income) was the same. Disposable income was 9598 billion dollars, about 72% of the total. Consumption was 9347 billion dollars or about 70% of the total. Saving is disposable income minus consumption or 251 billion dollars. This was about 2% of gross income. Saving, recall, is the net accumulation of financial assets during the year. For the business sector, gross retained-earnings were 1,361 billion dollars or about 10% of GDP. Business investment in capital goods and inventories was 2235 billion dollars or about 17% of GDP. The difference is the business sector deficit or the net amount of borrowing in 2006 by the business sector.

Net tax receipts for all government was 2298 billion dollars or about 17% of GDP. Realize that this is net of transfers, most of which show up as part of disposable income. Government expenditures on goods and services were 2,542 billion or about 19% of GDP. Again this figure is net of government transfers most of which would be spent or saved by households. The government deficit was −244 billion dollars or about 2% of GDP. Realize that this is the combined deficit of all government and if not the same as the federal deficit. This is the net amount borrowed by the government sector.

For the Foreign Sector (rest of world or ROW), net income paid to the foreign sector was 65 billion dollars or less than 1% of GDP. This is the difference between what we pay to the ROW and what they pay to us. On the expenditure side net exports of goods and services are exports minus imports. This was –802 billion dollars. This is what is called the trade deficit. Exports are about 10% of GDP. Imports are about 16% of GDP. Net exports are about 6% of GDP and are negative. The US has been running a trade deficit for about 20 years. Net foreign saving is net imports of funds from abroad. It is net foreign transfers minus net exports. (Subtracting a minus number gives a plus number.)

**Table 15.1. Final Receipts, Final Expenditures and Net Saving or Borrowing by Sector for the Aggregate U.S. Economy, Billions of Dollars, 2006 (Third Quarter, Annual Rate)**

| *Sector* | *Final Receipts* | *Final Expenditures* | *Deficit (−) or Surplus (+)* |
|---|---|---|---|
| Households or Persons | Disposable Income<br>9,598 | Personal Consumption<br>9,347 | Personal Saving<br>251 |
| Deficit Enterprises | Gross Retained Earnings<br>1361 | Gross Investment<br>223 | Net Business Deficit<br>−874 |
| Government | New Tax Receipts<br>2,298 | Spending on Goods and Services<br>2,542 | Government Deficit<br>−244 |
| Rest of the World | Net Foreign Trans.<br>65 | Net Exports<br>−802 | Net Foreign Saving<br>867 |
| Total Economy | Gross Domestic Income<br>13,322 | Gross Domestic Product<br>13,322 | 0 |

*Source: Economic Report of the President, February 2007.* (Numbers have been rounded)

What the table shows is that the saving of households and the import of funds from abroad finance the net deficits of the business sector and the government sector. This has been the case for most of the last 20 years. The exception was the last few years of the 1990s when the government sector was running net surpluses and thus was briefly a net saving sector. The receipts side adds up to gross domestic income. The expenditure side adds up to gross domestic product. Since the two are equal the difference is zero. Or in terms of the last column, the sum of the deficits and surpluses are zero. Net saving has to equal net borrowing. Every financial asset is an asset for its holder and a liability for its issuer.

## NOMINAL AND REAL GDP

For any given year GDP figures can be interpreted as the gross value of output for the economy. However, as we move from year to year, GDP grows (except during a recession) for two reasons: first output grows as we produce more goods and services and second, the general level of prices grows as we experience inflation. The problem is to separate out the two affects. The way this is done is first to develop a price index appropriate to the final goods of GDP. This index, in ratio form, is the ratio of what GDP is worth today to what the same quantity of goods and services would have been worth in some base year (at base year prices). That ratio multiplied by 100, gives the price index for that year. Doing this for every year gives us a series of price indexes. In the base year the ratio is always 1.0 and the index is always 100. GDP in current prices for each year is called nominal GDP. GDP in base year prices is called real GDP. Because it is measured with a constant set of prices, it can be taken to represent a measure of output (or real income).

To obtain real GDP from nominal GDP we divide the nominal GDP for each year by the price ratio for the same year. The price ratio is the price index divided by 100, or the index on a base of 1.0. Thus in the base year real and nominal GDP are always the same. When the price ratio is greater than one, real GDP will be less than nominal GDP. When the price ratio is less than one, as it usually is in years prior to the base year, real GDP will be greater than nominal GDP. The logic of the procedure can demonstrated with a simple equation. Let $P_t$ represent the price ratio for year t and $Q_t$ represent real GDP for year t, then:

$$(1)\ Q_t = P_tQ_t/P_t.$$

What we observe each year is nominal GDP ($P_tQ_t$). If we have accurately constructed our price index then $P_t$ in the numerator and $P_t$ in the denominator are in principle equal and cancel out giving us real GDP on both sides.

## RATES OF GROWTH OF OUTPUT AND OF PRICES

We have seen above that measuring output in constant prices allows us a common unit for comparing output over time. By converting these common units to rates of change we can see how much output and prices grow over time. From equation (1) we saw that $P_tQ_t$ was nominal output. The percent change in $P_tQ_t$ is given by:

(2) % change in $(P_tQ_t)$ per unit of time = % change in $P_t$ + % change in $Q_t$

What this tells us is that over time nominal output can grow for two reasons. Output can grow as a result of additional production or the general lever of prices can grow as a result of inflation. The % change in $Q_t$ is the (change in $Q_t/Q_t$)(100). The % change in $P_t$ is the (change in $P_t$)/$P_t$)(100). The relationship only holds exactly when we have continuous rates of change. When we measure output and price changes in discrete units (say year to year) the relationship is only approximately true.

This is important because it allows us to measure how much of the growth in nominal output is due to inflation and how much is due to additional production and thus additional real income. If only prices increase we are no better off. We have the same output measured in higher prices. If only output increases, we have more production and more real income. In most years both grow and what are important is how much of the growth reflects output growth and how much reflects price level growth

However if the work force grows we do not know whether output per worker has grown. This requires another identity.

(3) $Q_t = (q_t)(N_t)$ where

$N_t$ is the number of workers during period t and $q_t = Q_t/N_t$ is output per worker. What this says is that total output is equal to output per worker times the number of workers. If we convert this to percent rates of change over time we have:

(4) % change in $Q_t$ = % change in $q_t$ + % change in $N_t$.

What this says is that real output can grow for two reasons. Output per worker can grow and the number of workers can grow. Again this identity only holds approximately with discrete changes in either variable. By subtracting $N_t$from both sides we have:

(5) % change in $Q_t$ − % change in $N_t$ = % change in $q_t$.

The percent change in output minus the percent change in the number of workers equals the percent change in output per worker. Since total output must equal total income we can also write this as.

(6) % change in $Y_t$ − % change in $N_t$ = % change in $q_t$, where $Y_t$ = real income.

The percent change in real income per worker is equal to the percent change in real output per worker. And:

(7) $(P_tY_t)/N_t$= Nominal income per worker. Expressed as percent changes over time we have:

(8) % change in $P_t$ + % change $Y_t$ − % change in $N_t$ = % change in nominal income per worker or:

The growth in real income per worker plus the rate of inflation is equal to the growth of nominal income per worker.

## SUMMARY

In this chapter we have summarized the major ideas of national income accounting. Aggregate output is output generated by the economy in a given time period, usually a quarter or a year. The sector receipts and expenditure table allows us to look at final receipts and final expenses for the major sectors of the economy. The difference between receipts and expenditures for each sector gives the sectors net saving or net borrowing (if negative). The sum of these deficits and surpluses for the total economy must be zero; total new borrowing must equal total new lending.

Real national output is output measured in constant prices. Nominal aggregate output is output measured in current prices. When we measure output in constant prices we can interpret it as a measure of production that can be compared from year because the general level of prices is being held constant. When we calculate growth rates we see that growth of nominal output is equal to growth of real output plus growth of prices. This allows us, on a year-to-year basis, to show how much growth of GDP was due to growth of output and how much was due to increases in the general level of prices. Also, national income equals national output and growth in national income equals growth of national output. Growth of average output per worker equals growth average income per worker. All of these accounting relationships are very convenient because they give us an accounting framework on which to build a macroeconomic theory of the determinants of aggregate output (and its growth rate), the level and rate of unemployment, the general level of prices (and the rate of inflation), and the general level of interest rates. It is to that task that we turn in the next chapter.

## REVIEW QUESTIONS

Multiple Choice: Select the correct answer:

1. Real GDP is:
   a. Nominal GDP times the price level.
   b. Nominal GDP divided by the price level.
   c. Nominal GDP minus the price level.
2. Growth of real output is equal to:
   a. Growth of nominal output minus growth of prices.
   b. Growth of nominal output plus growth of prices.
   c. Nominal output divided by the price level.
3. Value added is:
   a. Sales minus cost of goods purchased.
   b. After-tax net income of firms.
   c. Sales plus cost goods purchased.
   d. None of the above.
4. Growth of real output is equal to:
   a. Growth of output per worker minus growth of the work force.
   b. Growth of output per worker plus growth of the work force.
   c. Growth of output per worker times growth of the work force

   Nominal GDP in 2002 was 10,400 billion dollars. Nominal GDP in 2003 was about 11,000 billion dollars. The price index was 103 in 2002 and 105 in 2003:
5. What real GDP for 2002?
   a. 10,097 billion
   b. 10,712 billion
   c. 101.96 billion
   d. 107.12 billion
6. What was real GDP for 2003?
   a. 104.76 billion
   b. 10,476 billion
   c. 11,550 billion
   d. 115.50 billion
7. What was the growth rate of real GDP from 2002–2003?
   a. .0375%%
   b. 1.057%
   c. 3.75%
   d. 5.76%
8. What was the percent rate of inflation from 2002 to 2003?
   a. 5.76%

b. 1.94%
c. 1.057%
d. 1.094%

9. What was the % rate of growth of nominal GDP from 2002 to 2003?
a. 1.94%
b. 1.057%
c. 5.76%
d. 3.75%

## Essays

1. Distinguish between nominal and real GDP and the growth rates of nominal GDP, real GDP, and the price level. What does each measure? Why are these measures important?
2. The growth of nominal GDP is approximately equal to the growth of real GDP plus the growth of prices. Give an intuitive explanation of why this is so.
3. For the aggregate economy growth of income per worker is equal to growth of output per worker. Why do we expect this to be true?

## SUGGESTED READINGS

Budd, Edward C., "National Income and Product," In Herendeen, James B., Editor, *Modern Political Economy: Ideas and Issues*, Englewood Cliff, N.J.: Prentice Hall 1968, 80–85.

Burton, Maureen and Raymond Lombra, *The Financial System and the Economy*, 3rd ed., (Mason, Oh: 2003), Chapter 4.

Dornbusch, Rudiger and Stanley Fisher, *Macro Economics*, 6th ed. (New York: McGraw-Hill, 1994), Chapter 2.

## *Chapter Sixteen*

# Aggregate Supply and Demand

## INTRODUCTION

The aggregate supply and demand model is the primary macro model in economics. It uses the accounting concepts developed in the last chapter to develop an aggregate model to determine real output and the price level for the economy and it includes policy variables that can be used to analyze how government policy can influence the level of output, the price level, the level of interest rates and the rate of unemployment.

## AGGREGATE DEMAND

Nominal aggregate demand is the expenditure side of the Receipts-Expenditure Table developed in the previous chapter. Recall that aggregate expenditure is the sum of final expenditure by the four sectors of the economy. This is consumption expenditure on goods and services by households plus investment expenditure on new capital goods by firms plus government expenditure on goods and services plus net exports of goods and services to the foreign sector (exports minus imports). As we saw in the previous chapter real aggregate demand is nominal demand divided by the price level (in ratio form). The question is, does real aggregate demand vary with the price level? It does if we assume that the money stock is given in nominal terms. If we lower the price level a given nominal money supply will buy more goods and services. If we raise the price level, a given nominal money stock will buy less goods and services. Think of it at the individual level. If you have $3,000 in your checking account and prices increase your $3,000 will buy less goods and services. If prices fall your $3,000 will buy more goods and services. Also if US prices fall relative to foreign prices net exports will rise and this will also increase aggregate demand. This could result if foreign price and the exchange rate are given. If US prices with foreign prices given, net exports will fall.

Two real aggregate demand curves are shown in figure 16.1. Each traces out the increase in real output demanded as the price level falls. To move from one demand curve to the other we must assume that one of the determinants of aggregate demand has changed.

The question is what determines the level of aggregate demand at any given price level? For an answer we must look at what determines the components of aggregate demand. First what about consumption? The theory of consumption says that consumption depends on three primary things: Disposable income, interest rates and wealth. Disposable income is the most important, especially in the short run. Most households spend a high portion of their income on consumption and save the rest. For individual households saving may be positive or negative, depending on whether, in the current period, they are net savers or net borrowers. But the household sector as a whole it is a net saving sector. Recall that disposable income is income after taxes but including transfers. Thus the government has the means to influence disposable income and thus consumption. Congress and the President through fiscal (or budget) policy determine both taxes and spending at the Federal

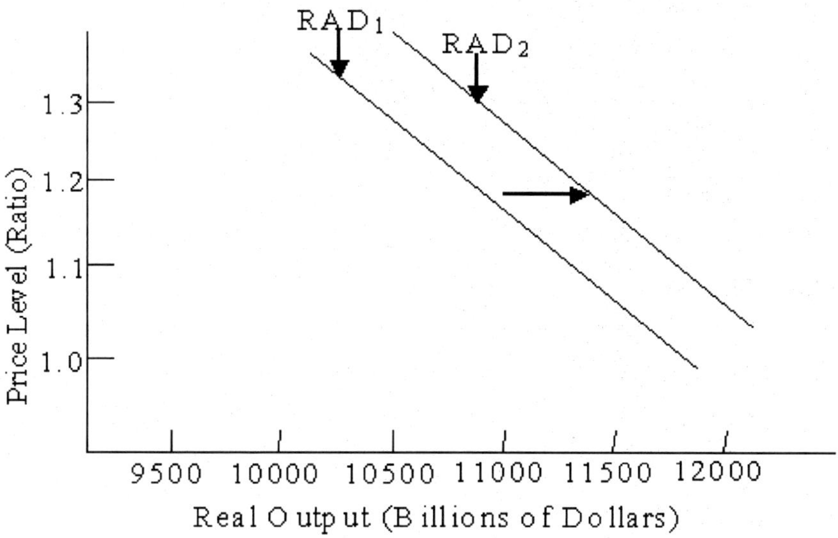


**Figure 16.1. Real Aggregate Demand**

level. An increase in tax rates will decrease disposable income and decrease consumption and aggregate demand. A decrease in tax rates will increase disposable income and increase aggregate demand. This assumes that government spending policy has remained the same. An increase in transfer payments (which may be viewed as negative taxes) would also increase consumption and aggregate demand and a decrease in transfers will decrease consumption and decrease demand. However, transfers are treated as entitlements and are usually not changed to affect aggregate demand.

Second, how does government spending affect demand? Recall that government spending is one of the components of aggregate demand. An increase in government spending of, say, a billion dollars will, in the current period, increase demand by a billion dollars (assuming no offsetting increase in taxes). And a decrease in spending will decrease demand by an equivalent amount. In successive periods there may be further increases, or decreases, due to multiplier effects. Multiplier effects occur when the initial spending is re-spent by the recipients. The size of the multiplier effects depends mainly on the rate government taxes additional income and the rate that households save additional income. Other components of demand have similar multiplier effects.

The third determinant of demand is monetary policy. Monetary policy is conducted by the Federal Reserve System (the FED) and works primarily through its effect on interest rates, the money supply and credit availability. With an expansionary monetary policy, the FED buys Federal Government Securities. This increases reserves in the banking system and decreases short-term interest rates. Lower interest rates will encourage banks to increase lending and businesses and household to increase borrowing. This will cause increased spending especially for consumer durable goods and business investment in new capital goods and thus increase aggregate demand. Increased borrowing will increase checkable deposits and the money supply as households and businesses deposit the proceeds of their loans. The money supply is made up of checkable deposits of the public plus currency in circulation. If the Fed sells securities it has the opposite effect. Bank reserves are decreased, interest rates are increased and banks are forced to cut back on lending as households and firms cut back on borrowing. And a cut back on borrowing leads to a cut back on checkable deposits and thus the money supply. And a cut back on borrowing leads to a cut back of consumer and business spending which reduces aggregate demand.

The last major determinant of aggregate demand is the international value of the dollar. If the dollar rises in value it means that US goods become more expensive relative to foreign goods. This will decrease our exports and increase our imports or decrease net exports and thus decrease aggregate demand. A fall in the value of the dollar will have the opposite effect. US goods become cheaper relative to foreign goods. This will increase our exports and decrease our imports or increase net exports and thus increase aggregate demand. These are short run results. In the long run, rising inflation may offset the effects of a falling dollar; falling inflation may offset the effect of a rising dollar. Also realize that a change in the exchange rate shifts the aggregate demand curve right or left. A change in the price level, given the exchange rate, moves us along a given aggregate demand curve.

## AGGREGATE SUPPLY

Aggregate supply depends on decisions of producers as to how much goods and service to produce and to offer for sale. Real aggregate supply is supply measured in constant dollars. This is our measure of production. How do firms respond to an increase or decrease in the general level of prices? If all prices and costs moved together we would have to say that there would be no effect. In other words if all prices and costs rose by 10 percent, real output would not change as there would be no incentive to increase output. This is what is assumed with long run supply. To get a short run supply curve, we must assume that not all prices move together. There are two primary ways to get this result. One is to assume that prices increase relative to wage and material costs. Wages are less flexible than prices in the short run. And many raw material prices are determined in world markets and are relatively independent of domestic prices. Thus when prices increase relative to costs there is an incentive for firms to expand output. This gives us an up-sloping relation between the price level and real output supplied. If prices decrease relative to wages and raw material prices, firms have an incentive to contract output.

The other approach is to assume that price expectations are given in the short run. When prices increase relative to what had been expected at the beginning of the period, firms have an incentive to expand output and we also get an up-sloping short run supply curve. If prices fall relative to what had been expected at the beginning of the period, firms have an incentive to contract output. The two approaches are similar in that price expectations depend in part on wage contracts and raw material prices. This approach assumes that when expected prices equal realized prices, output is at its normal or long run equilibrium level. Normal output acts as a shifter of the short run supply curve.

Figure 16.2 shows two short run aggregate supply curves. They plot the price level against real output supplied. Movement along either supply curve tells how supply changes in the short run as the price level rises. A shift from

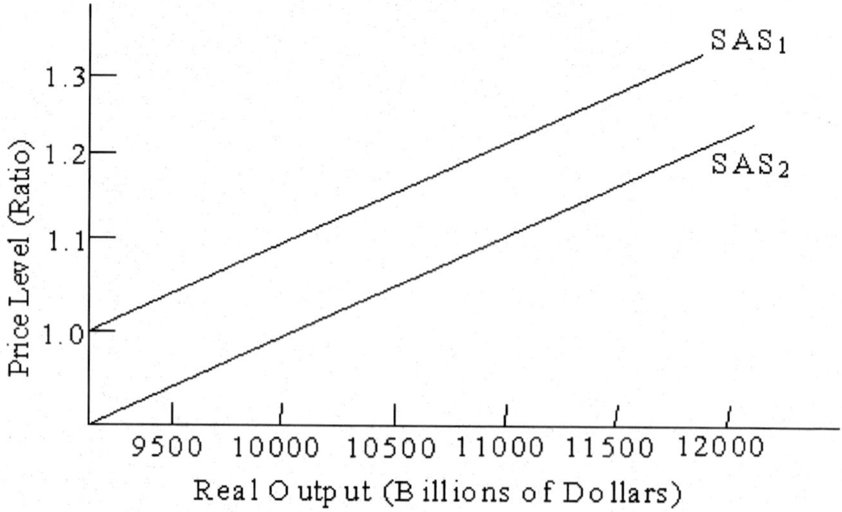


**Figure 16.2. Short Run Real Aggregate Supply**

$RAS_1$ to $RAS_2$ shows what happens if we change one of the determinants of supply, given the price level. A decrease in price expectations would shift the supply curve right. An increase in normal output would also shift the supply curve right. The convenience of the price expectations approach is that it gives us a simply way to relate short run and long run supply. The model says that when price expectations are realized, that is, when realized prices equal expected prices, that output will be at its normal or trend value. If realized prices exceed expected prices, then firms will have an incentive to expand output and output will be above the normal level. When realized prices are below what had been expected, firms will have an incentive to contract output and output will be below normal. When output is above normal we are in an economic expansion. When output is below normal we are in an economic contraction. Output above or below normal, are short run solutions that require expectations to not be realized. In the long run, if prices are greater than expected, then price expectations will have to rise. If they are less than expected, then price expectations will have to fall. This gives us a model of the economy where output will fluctuate around normal output. These fluctuations we call the business cycle.

Figure 16.3 shows the relation between short run and long run aggregate supply. The long run supply curve is vertical in the static or no growth model. This assumes that we have a given normal work force, a given normal capital stock and a given normal level of productivity as measured by output per worker. The short run supply curve crosses the long run supply

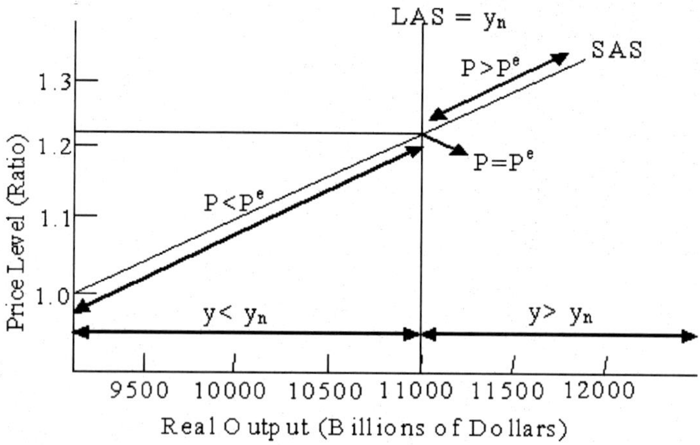


**Figure 16.3. Short Run and Long Run Real Aggregate Supply**

curve where price expectations are realized. This is at price of 1.24 with normal output of 11,000 billion dollars. At normal or trend output realized prices equal expected prices. At less than normal output realized prices, along the supply curve will be less than expected prices, which are given along any given supply curve. In other words, if prices are less than expected firms will reduce output. When prices are greater than expected, output will be above normal; firms will expand output. When price expectations are realized output will be at the normal output and this is always on the long run supply curve.

However, what determines normal output and how does normal output change over time? Normal output depends on the economies production possibilities. These are determined at any point in time by the labor force, the stock of capital goods (including knowledge), productivity of labor and capital goods and on the existing organization of the production process. We discussed these when we discussed production possibilities in Chapter 2. In other words normal output is a point on the economies production possibility curve. The mix of output implied by that point depends on the past history of the economy. What concerns us here is what causes normal output to grow over time. Normal output grows over time because of growth of its determinants: The labor force grows as new workers enter the work force in excess to retiring workers leaving the work force. This requires growth in the population, which for the US economy is about one percent per year. As we discussed in Chapter 2, the labor force also may grows as a result changes in labor force participation rates. The biggest change in the last 50 years has been the increased labor force participation by women.

The capital stock grows as firms invest in new productive capacity and new techniques of production. Productivity grows because workers joining the work force have new skills and existing worker acquire new skills. And firms, when they add capacity, add capital goods that embody the latest available economically feasible technology. Thus output per worker grows both because workers become more productive but also because they are being combined with more productive capital goods. Also labor and capital productivity may rise as firms and society find more efficient way of organizing the production process. All of these factors determine the rate at which normal (or trend) output grows over time. For the U.S. economy trend output grows at about 3.5% per year: One percent due to population growth and two and one half percent due to productivity growth.

## SHIFTERS OF AGGREGATE DEMAND

Aggregate demand grows over time for several reasons. First, consumption grows over time as disposable income grows as new workers enter the employed work force. Second, government spending grows each year but at varying rates depending on current fiscal policy and the state of the economy. Government tax revenues also grow over time depending on current tax policy and the state of the economy. And tax policy affects both disposable income of households and retained income of firms that in turn affect demand. Also changes in income expectations of households and profit expectations of firms will affect spending by households and firms and thus also affect demand over time. And net exports will grow over time depending on growth of domestic income and growth of foreign income and on the level of exchange rates.

## SHIFTERS OF AGGREGATE SUPPLY

As we discussed above long run aggregate supply grows over time with growth of the work force, growth of the capital stock, growth of productivity and with development of new ways to organize the production process. When looked at over time, this gives us an up-sloping path of normal output. The percentage slope of this path is the long run trend growth of output for the economy. However as we saw above short run supply can deviate from its long run trend. In the simple model described above a change in the expected level of prices can shift the short run supply curve left or right. In a more general sense, changes in wage rate or raw material costs can shift the supply curve. Intersections of short run supply with demand can be above or below normal output. However in the long run price expectations must rise or fall to give equilibrium on the long run output path where expected prices equal realized prices and where output is at its normal level. Or, alternatively, wage and material cost must rise or fall so that markets clear at normal output.

However the speed with which these adjustments come about may be too slow to be politically acceptable. When output is below normal, unemployment will be above normal. Monetary or fiscal policy may be used (not always successfully) to nudge it back toward the trend level. We call this trend level, normal output. This normal output grows over time for the reasons we discussed above. This normal growth is equal to the normal growth of output per worker plus normal growth of the work force. Output per worker grows as workers become more productive and as they are combined with more productive capital goods and more productive ways of organizing production.

In figure 16.4 we show shifting demand and shifting short run supply to show how output can cycle around normal output. At point A we have $SAS_1$ intersecting $RAD_1$at \$11,000 billion of real output and price level of 1.24 on the long run supply curve. If demand shifts to $RAD_2$ say as a result of an expansionary monetary policy the short run result is at point B where $RAD_2$ intersects the $RAS_1$ at about \$11,300 of real output with price level of 1.25. In the short run the supply curve does not shift, because expected prices adjust slower than realized prices. However in the long run price expectations have to adjust to equal realized prices. The supply curve shifts left to $SAS_2$ where

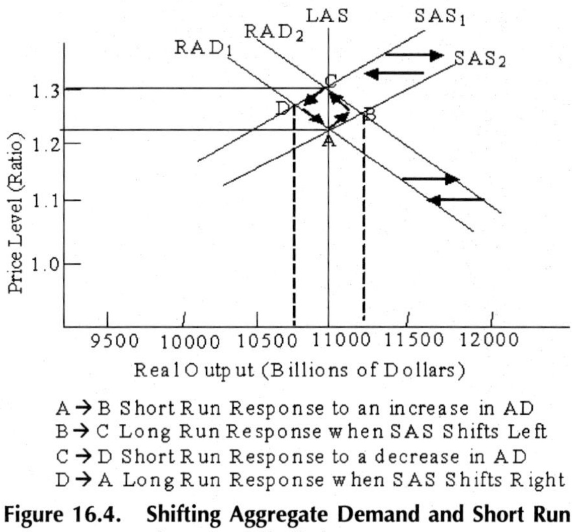


**Figure 16.4. Shifting Aggregate Demand and Short Run Aggregate Supply and Cyclical Short Run Output**

it intersects demand on the long run supply curve with real output of $11,000 billion and price level of 1.3. However, if the FED tightens monetary policy to combat the rising price level, real aggregate demand could shift back to $RAD_1$ and short run equilibrium would be at point D where the new demand curve (in this case the original demand curve) intersects $RAS_2$. Real output is now $10,700 billion and the price level is at 1.26. In the long run the supply curve will shift down to intersect the demand curve on the long run supply curve at $11,000 billion of real output with price level of 1.24. We are right back where we started. Real output cycles around normal output but real output returns to normal output in the long run. This adjustment process assumes that shits in supply lag shifts in demand. Price expectations are given in the current period but can change in the next period.

## THE PATH OF OUTPUT THROUGH TIME

Over time normal output grows as the work force grows, as the capital stock grows, as output per worker grows and as the way production is organized changes. This gives us a rising trend of output (and income) over time. Fluctuations around the trend path of output represent the business cycle. Output may be above or below trend because aggregate demand and short run aggregate supply may intersect off the trend path. And adjustments back to the trend path take time. During an expansion output rises above normal. Over time excess capacity develops and firms have to cut back on production. As firms cut output, incomes fall as workers are laid off and profits fall. Firms reduce investment in new capacity and households cut back on purchases of housing, autos, and other household capital goods. The FED lowers interest rates to attempt to spur the economy out of recession. Congress and the President may cut taxes to further attempt to spur the economy. However we will start by assuming that normal output is constant over time.

Figure 16.5 plots real output from figure 16.4 against time. A' corresponds to point A in Figure 16.4. Real output is at its trend value of 11,000 billion dollars. Point B' corresponds to point B in figure 16.4. Real out is above normal at 11,300 billion. Point C' corresponds to point C in figure 16.4 real output is back at its trend value. Point D' corresponds to point D in the previous figure. Real output is back at its trend value of 11,000 billion. By connecting points A', B', C' and D' with a curved line we get the depiction of a business cycle. From A' to B' output is expanding. From B' to D' output is contracting. From D' to A" output is expanding. Realize that we are dealing with a no growth economy. Trend output is 11,000 billion.

Growth of trend output is zero. During the expansion phases output growth is positive. During the contraction phase output is growing at a negative rate.

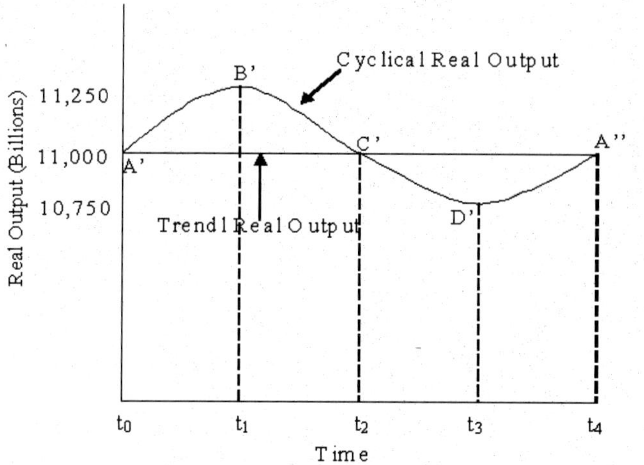


**Figure 16.5. Path of Output over Time: Long Run Real Output Constant**

From A' to B' average growth is (300/11,000)(100) = 2.7 percent. From B' to C' output growth is (-300/11,000)(100) = −2.7%. From C' to D' Growth is (−300/11,000)(100) = −2.7%. From D' to A" growth is (300/11,000)(100) = 2.7%. The growth rate is positive, then negative, then positive as output cycles around trend output that has zero growth. Realize that output is moving through time. Each successive short run output in figure 16.4 and 16.5 represents successive points in time. For simplicity we can assume that the time periods are one year. In this example demand is shifted by changes in monetary policy. Short run supply is shifted as expected prices adjust to equal realized prices. Demand could also be shifted by changes in fiscal policy or changes in the value of the dollar. Changing price expectations could be driven by changes in wage rates or changes in raw material prices.

Figure 16.6 shows shifting long run supply and shifting demand over time. Points A and B represent two long run equilibriums. Long run supply shifts as normal output grows due to growth of the work force, growth of the capital stock and growth of output per worker. Demand grows over time as consumption grows as business investment grows, as government spending grows and as net exports grow. With price expectations given, the short run supply curve will shift right by the same amount as the long run supply curve and the price level will remain constant. In the short run, output can be greater or less that normal but now will be fluctuating around normal output with a rising trend.

This is shown in figure 16.7. Normal or trend output is rising over time as the long run supply curve in figure 16.6 shifts right over time. Points A, B, C and D represent short run solutions as demand and short run supply intersect first below normal output, then at normal output, then above normal output

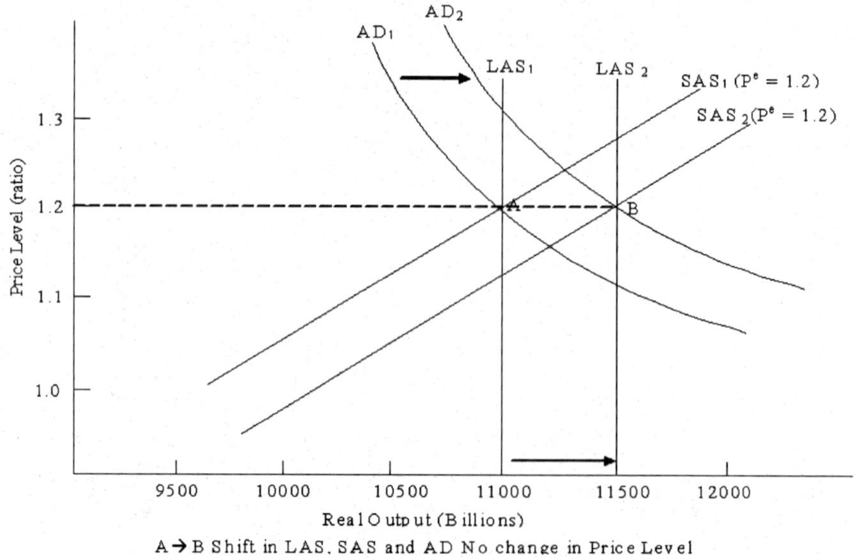


**Figure 16.6. Shifting Long Run Aggregate Supply and Demand**

and last at normal output. The curved line connecting these points represents the path of output over time. During the expansion, cyclical output growth is above trend or normal growth. From point B to point D trend growth is about (600)/11,300)(100) = 5.3%. If this represents two years, then annual trend growth is about 2.6%.From point A to point B average cyclical growth is (600/10,700)(100) = 5.6%. From B to C it is (500/11,300) = 4.4% From C to D it is (100/11,800)(100) = 0.8%. Again we assume that the time periods are one year. The point is that during an expansion output growth must exceed trend growth. During a contraction, output growth must be less than trend growth. When the two lines cross, cyclical growth is equal to trend growth.

## SUMMARY

In this chapter we have discussed aggregate demand and supply. Aggregate demand represents total final expenditure for the economy. The components of final spending are spending on goods and services by households (consumption), spending on new capital goods by firms (business investment), spending by government for goods and services, including new capital goods (government spending) and net spending on US goods by the rest of the world (net exports). Aggregate demand is negatively related to the general level of prices as lower prices increase real purchasing power for any given nominal money stock and because if US prices fall relative to foreign prices export demand

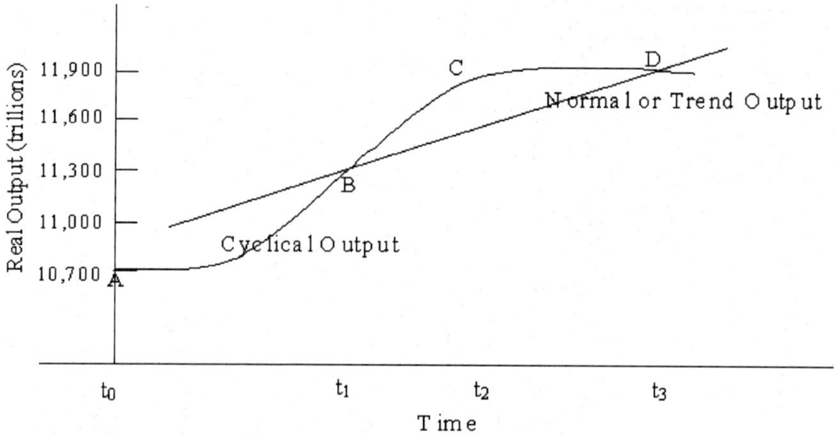


**Figure 16.7. The Path of Output over Time: Dynamic Model**

will rise. Demand shifts over time as consumption grow, as government spending increases, as tax policies change and as net exports grow or contract. Long run aggregate supply represents normal output. It grows over time as the work force grows, as the stock of capital increases and as the productivity of both workers and capital goods increases. Short run supply can deviate from long run supply because output can be above normal during an expansion or below normal during a contraction. The intersection of short run supply and demand at output above or below normal gives us the business cycle. We will discuss the causes of the business cycle in more detail in chapter 17.

## REVIEW QUESTIONS

Multiple Choice: Select the correct answer:

1. An increase in disposable income, with interest rates and wealth given, will:
   a. Increase consumption and decrease saving.
   b. Increase consumption and increase saving.
   c. Decrease consumption and decrease saving.
   d. Decrease consumption and increase saving.
2. The sale of government securities by the Central Bank will:
   a. Increase bank reserves and decrease interest rate.
   b. Decrease bank reserves and increase interest rates.
   c. Decrease bank reserves and decrease interest rates.
   d. Increase bank reserves and increase interest rates.

3. Business investment in new capital goods will increase if:
   a. Interest rates increase.
   b. Interest rates decrease.
   c. Profit expectations decrease
4. The short run aggregate supply curve is up sloping with respect to the price level because:
   a. Firms expand output when prices increase relative to what was expected.
   b. Firms expand output when prices decrease relative to what was expected.
   c. Higher prices decrease real purchasing power.
   d. Higher prices increase real purchasing power.
5. When output is less than normal we expect unemployment rate to be:
   a. Greater than normal.
   b. Less than normal.
   c. The normal rate.
6. For a given nominal growth in aggregate demand:
   a. Higher real growth will mean higher inflation.
   b. Higher real growth will mean lower inflation.
   c. Neither of the above.

**Essays**

1. During a recovery output must grow faster than normal output to bring about recovery and reduce unemployment. Explain why.
2. What are the main shifters of aggregate demand over time? What are the main shifters of short run aggregate supply? What are the main shifters of long run aggregate supply over time?

## SUGGESTED READINGS

Burton, Maureen and Raymond Lombra, *The Financial System and the Economy: Principles of Money and Banking*, 3rd ed. Mason, Ohio: Thompson-Southwestern, Chapter 22.

Dornbusch, Rudiger and Stanley Fisher, *Macroeconomics.* 6th ed., New York, McGraw-Hill, 1994, Chapter 7.

# *Chapter Seventeen*

# Business Cycles

## DEPRESSION AND RECESSION

Economists often talk about recessions and depressions. What is the difference between them? A recession is a temporary fall in output usually lasting from one to three years. To be officially called a recession there needs to be at least two quarters of negative growth. This means aggregate real output must actually fall for two quarters. During a recession we expect unemployment to rise above normal. We can also have slowdowns (growth recessions) when output growth falls below normal but we don't have negative growth. In other words, if trend output growth is 3.5% per year and growth drops to 1% per year that would be a growth recession. Output is still growing but at a rate below normal. Assuming this continued for a year or two, we would expect unemployment to rise above normal. During the expansion phase of a business cycle we expect output to grow at above the normal rate, otherwise we would not recover. During the expansion unemployment will fall and toward the end of the expansion will fall below normal or trend unemployment. Expansions last from three years to seven or eight years. During an expansion growth will be above normal. During the early stages of the expansion growth may be 5% or 6% per year.

A depression is a prolonged fall in output when there is also a breakdown of the financial system. The great Depression of the 1930s lasted ten years and was accompanied with a severe breakdown of the financial system. Others countries experienced similar depressions during the 1920s and 1930s.

## THE GREAT DEPRESSION

The Great Depression was a traumatic experience for the US. Unemployment hit 25% at its peak in 1933 and 20% at its second peak in 1937. For agriculture and many small businesses there was massive underemployment. The stock market crashed in 1929, hit bottom in 1933 but did not really recover until after World War II. Between 1929 and 1933 some 9000 banks went broke out of a total of about 25,000: more than a third of all the banks in the country. The depression started in mid 1929 before the stock market crash. The stock market crash came in October of 1929.

What were the causes of the Great Depression? Seventy years later economists do not completely agree. However a consensus view has emerged in the last 10 years or so. During World War I many European Countries had been forced to leave the Gold Standard as inflation had accelerated during the War. In the twenties most of them tried to return to the Gold Standard at the pre-World War I prices of gold. This was only possible with severe deflation and resulting high unemployment. By the end of the twenties and early thirties most had been forced to devalue their currencies by raising their official price of gold. The US, which had suffered much less during World War I, remained at the pre World War I price of gold throughout the twenties. Unfortunately that left the dollar overvalued by the end of the twenties when recession hit the US. An overvalued dollar makes US exports more expensive to the rest of the world and makes imports less expensive.

The Hoover Administration refused to consider devaluing the dollar and, to make matters worse; Congress passed the Smoot-Hawley Tariff in 1930. This restricted imports and made it difficult for other countries to export to us and thus earn dollars to buy our goods. In 1931, England and the Commonwealth Countries devalued, leaving the US as one of the major holdouts from devaluation. From 1931 to 1933 commodity prices continued to fall and banks continued to fail as the country sank into severe depression. If the US had not passed the Smoot–Hawley Tariff and had devalued in 1931 when England did, the severity of the Great depression would likely have been much less.

When President Roosevelt came in, in 1933, he allowed the dollar to float and then reset its price at $35.00 per ounce of gold in early 1934, up from $20.67 per ounce. The devaluation and other New Deal programs brought some relief. But with the world in recession the devaluation by itself could not increase export demand or domestic demand enough to revive the economy. Finally, World War II brought us out of the Great Depression.

## RECENT RECESSIONS

Since World War II, there have been several mild recessions but not another severe Depression like the one of the 1930s. We will look at the record since 1970. First we will look at the data in time series form. Figure 17.1 plots real GDP in 2000 dollars from 1970 to 2004. The percentage slopes of the real GDP and trend GDP represent percentage growth rates. Contractions and expansions are indicated. There was a brief contraction in 1969–70. In the seventies there were two brief expansions: 1971–73 and 1976–79. There was a recession in 1974–75 and again in 1979–80. There was a partial recovery in 1980 and then a contraction in 1981–82. We have combined these two recessions into one from 1979–1982. This was followed by a long expansion from 1982–1989. There was a brief recession in 1990–91 then a long expansion from 1992–2000. In 2001 2002 there was a mild contraction then recovery from 2003–2005. The trend line shows GDP corrected for the business cycle. Trend GDP was increasing at a declining percentage rate from 1970 until about 1992. Then the percentage trend turned up and has been rising since.

In figure 17.2 are plotted the year to year growth rates of real GDP over the same period. They represent the percentage rates of change of the data in the

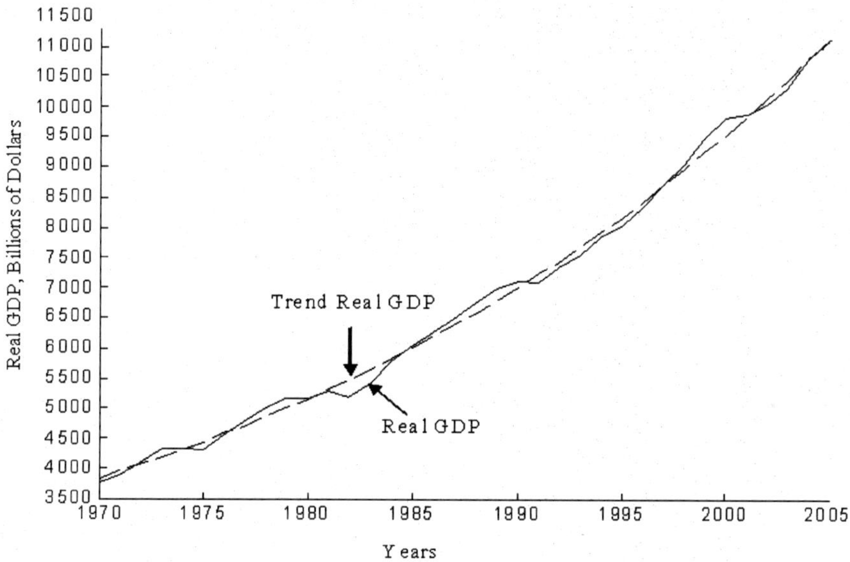


Source: Economic Report of the President, 2006

**Figure 17.1. Annual Real GDP Over Time; Trend And Cyclical, 1970–2005**

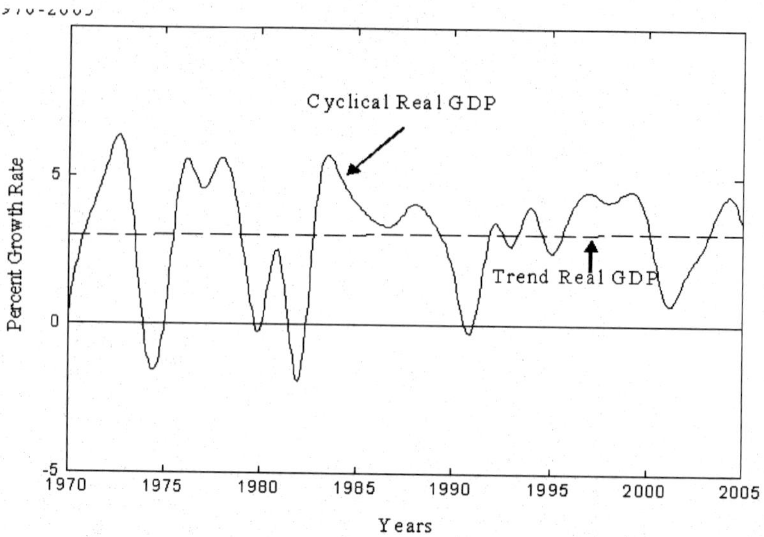


**Figure 17.2. Year to Year Growth Rate of Real GDP: over Time; Trend and Cyclical, 1970–2005**

previous figure. This figure shows the business cycle in growth rates of GDP rather than levels of GDP. The expansions represent periods of relatively high growth. The contractions represent periods of declining growth usually turning negative at the bottom of the contraction. In this diagram we have indicated each recession. Each long expansion corresponds roughly to a two-term presidency of the same party: Kennedy-Johnson in the sixties; Reagan in the eighties; Clinton in the nineties. Nixon-Ford in the late sixties and early seventies were also of the same party but Ford was serving out Nixon's term after he resigned from office.

In figure 17.3 we show the growth rate of productivity as measured by output per worker hour. Notice that it roughly follows the same pattern as the growth rate of output except the trend and the cycles are at a lower growth rate for any given year. The difference between the two for either the trend or the cyclical data is the growth of the work force that is about one percent per year. The cycle does not mean that workers work harder during an expansion and less hard during a contraction. Instead it reflects the fact that output varies more over the cycle more than employment does. When output growth rises faster than employment growth, average growth of output per worker will rise. When output growth decline faster than employment growth average growth of output per worker will decline. The key identity is that the growth of output is equal to the growth of output per worker plus the growth of the work force. This is only approximately true in figures 17.3 because produc-

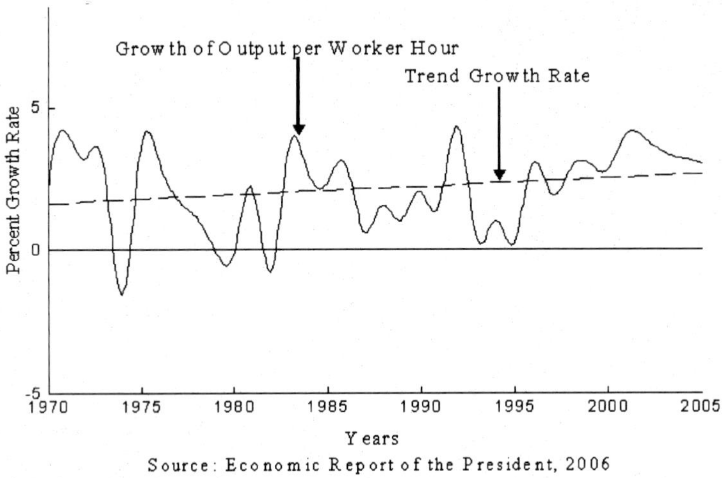


**Figure 17.3. Year to Year Growth Rate of Output per Worker Hour; Trend and Cyclical, 1970–2005**

tivity is measured in output per worker hour not output per worker. But number of workers and number of worker hours will move together.

Figure 17.4 shows the civilian unemployment rate and its trend for the years 1970 through 2005. Note that the unemployment rate moves inverse to the business cycle. When output is above trend, unemployment will normally be below trend. Cyclical unemployment follows the business cycle but in an inverse manner. However trend unemployment has also been quite variable, it declined in the 60s increased in the 70s and early eighties and has declined since. Why did trend unemployment increase in the 70s and early eighties, Probably for two primary reasons. First these are the years that the baby boom generation hit the labor force. With relatively slow growth in the 70s and early 80s, this was bound to push up trend unemployment. Second this was also the period of rapid increase in labor force participation rates for women. This also tended to push up trend unemployment.

Now let us look at these expansions and contractions in more detail. Although our Figures start with 1970, we will look briefly at the sixties to give some background for the more recent years. There was a mild recession in 1960–61 at about the time that the Kennedy Administration came into office. On the recommendation of his economic advisors, especially Walter Heller, Chairman of the Council of Economic Advisors, President Kennedy recommended a tax cut to stimulate aggregate demand. This was the first time that a tax cut had been proposed to spur aggregate demand. The tax cut was finally passed in 1964, after the Kennedy assassination, under President Johnson. By

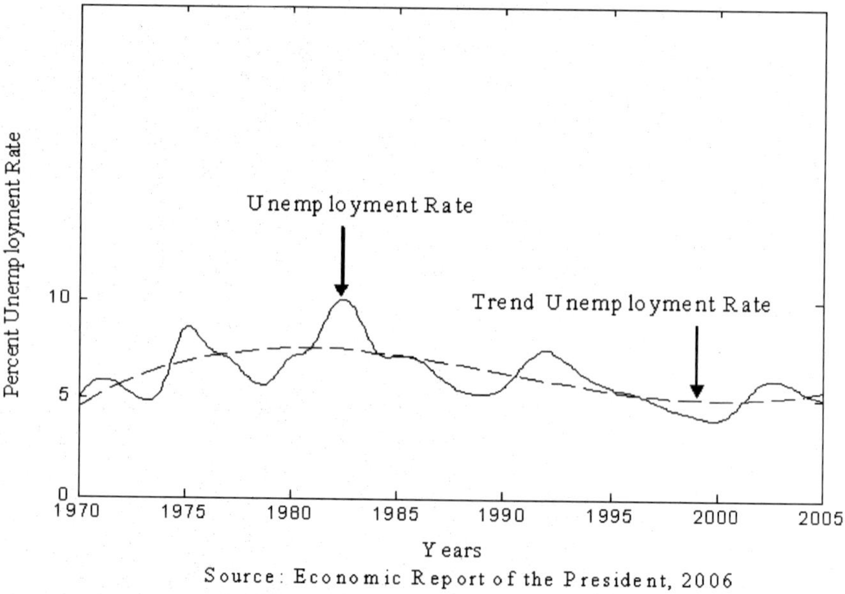


**Figure 17.4. Annual Unemployment and Trend Unemployment, 1970–2005**

then the economy was recovering and continued to expand as the tax cut took affect. Then in 1965 the US entered the Viet-Nam War and defense expenditures continued to expand the economy in 1966, 67 and 68.

In 1969 the Nixon Administration came into office and war expenditures began to taper off as the US tried to negotiate a truce in the War. Inflation had accelerated in 1965–69. The FED under Chairman Arthur Burns tightened monetary policy in 1969 and the economy entered a mild recession in late 1969 and 1970. By mid 1971, the Nixon Administration decided that a recovery in 1972 was crucial for the Administration in order to ensure reelection of the President. In August of 1971 President Nixon announced his "New Economic Policy." The key features were a proposed tax cut, a decision to no longer supply gold to the rest of the world at the official price of $35 per oz., the price that had been established in 1934 under President Roosevelt, and the establishment of wage price guidelines to help contain inflation.

The dollar was allowed to float for a year or so. An attempt was made to reestablish fixed exchange rates at about a ten percent devaluation of the dollar. That attempt failed and in 1973 the US officially decided to let the dollar float. This marked the end of the gold standard and the end of Breton-Woods, the International Monetary Agreement that had been adopted after World War II. And in affect it marked the official beginning of the dollar standard. The dollar replaced gold as the international reserve currency. Other countries could choose to peg their currencies to the dollar or could allow them to float against the dollar. We will return to this issue in a later chapter. In the short run the Nixon policies were a great success. By mid 1972 inflation was down, unemployment was down and real growth of GDP was up. President Nixon was re-elected with 60% of the vote.

Unfortunately for President Nixon, the good times didn't last long. By 1973 the falling dollar contributed to a sharp increase in commodity prices, and inflation accelerated. The wage-price guideline could no longer contain retail prices, when wholesale prices were accelerating rapidly, and had to be abandoned. In late 1973 the Arab-Israeli War brought an embargo of oil to the west by the recently formed OPEC Oil Cartel. The price of crude oil went from about $2.50 a barrel to about $14.00 a barrel in a matter of months. Gasoline price shot up in the winter of 1974 and inflation accelerated further.

In the mean time, President Nixon became embroiled in the Watergate Scandal and in the summer of 1974 was forced out of office. Gerald Ford, President Nixon's Vice President became President. Belatedly the FED started tightening in late 1974, inflation fell and the dollar rose in 1975 and 76. Jimmy Carter became President in January of 1977. Unfortunately his appointment of Chairman of the FED (G. William Miller) was not a wise one. Easy monetary policy allowed the dollar to fall and inflation again accelerated. Then in 1979 the Iranian Revolution led to a return of oil shortages. Gasoline prices again shot up and inflation accelerated further. President Carter appointed Paul Volcker Chairman of the FED in the spring of 1979 and by mid year he had announced new policies for the FED. The FED would no longer attempt to target short-term interest rates but would instead target Bank Reserves and growth of the money supply. Short-term interest rates soon shot up to 15% and the economy entered a short recession in late 79 and early 80. 1980 was an election year with President Carter running against challenger, Ronald Reagan. The FED eased and the economy briefly recovered in late 80.

Ronald Reagan was elected and took office in January of 1981. President Reagan and his supporters had announced their intention of asking for a major cut in marginal tax rates and in asking for major increases in defense spending. The inflation of the 70s and early eighties had pushed much of the middle class into much higher tax brackets so there was wide support for tax relief. The Fed viewed the Reagan policies as highly inflationary and quickly tightened monetary policy in early 1981 and kept it tight for a year and a half. Short-term interest rates rose to nearly 20%, the economy entered a sharp recession and unemployment peaked at over 10% in 1982; a post World War II record. In the meantime the dollar had started rising in 1980 and continued to rise until late 1985. The rising dollar contributed to falling prices for internationally traded commodities. Prices of agricultural commodities, of oil, of gold, of silver, and other basic commodities fell sharply offsetting their big rises in the 70s. The recession in combination with the rising value of the dollar and falling commodity prices allowed inflation to fall rapidly from about 12% in 1981 to about 3% in 1986.

The FED started easing in August of 1982 and by 1983 and 1984 the economy was recovering quickly. The easier monetary policy was reinforced by the tax cuts and increased defense spending. Inflation remained low during the recovery in part because of the strong dollar. The dollar remained strong in part because US real interest rates remained high relative to real interest rates in Western Europe, England and Japan. The strong dollar meant depressed demand for US exports and cheap imports. This restricted the ability of US firms to increase prices and restricted the ability of US unions to win wage gains. The recovery was briefly threatened in October of 1987 when we experienced a sharp collapse of the stock market. The market had become overvalued and had started falling in mid 87. When the Fed hinted at a modest tightening the bubble burst and the market dropped by about 30% in a matter of days. The Fed acted quickly to provide liquidity to New York banks, which in turn provided liquidity to the big Wall Street brokerage firms who were hard hit by the collapse. The market gradually recovered and the economy continued to grow. What helped sustain the recovery was the falling dollar from 1986–90. This brought relief to agriculture and other export oriented industries that had been extremely depressed during the first two-thirds of the eighties.

The boom ended in 1989 with the end of the Cold War. Defense industries in Southern California and New England were hit first. Inflation was rising, partly due to the falling dollar and the FED pushed up short-term interest rates throughout 1989 and by the spring of 1990 the economy was in recession. The recession was relatively mild but the recovery was slow. President Bush had been elected in 1988 and took office in January of 1989. The war in Kuwait occurred in late 1990 and early 1991. By 1992 when President Bush was running for reelection against challenger Bill Clinton the economy was growing but not fast enough to reduce unemployment. The recovery, though on its way, did not come fast enough to save President Bush. Clinton won with his slogan "It's the economy stupid."

The economy continued to grow for eight years under President Clinton. Partly the growth was driven by the technology revolution in the computer, computer software, and inter-net and telecommunications industries. Partly it was the result of good fiscal and monetary policies under the leadership of Robert Ruben, Secretary of Treasury and Alan Greenspan, Chairman of the Federal Reserve Board. The Federal government budget deficit had increased during the eighties and remained high in the early nineties. In the later half of the nineties, the deficit declined and during 1998, 1999 and 2000 there were small surpluses. The reduction of the deficit was partly due to the strong economy that increased tax revenues, it was partly due to spending restraint by Congress and it was partly due to changed accounting rules that separated government spending into current and capital expenditure. Capital expenditures by government were no longer part of the current account budget and this reduced the current account deficit. By the end of the nineties policy makers and politicians were predicting surpluses for the next ten years and Congress was wondering how it would spend all of this money. Forgetting, no doubt, that if they spent it there would no longer be surpluses.

2000 was an election year and George Bush the son of the earlier President defeated Al Gore in a disputed election. During 2000 the FED had been pushing up interest rates to slow the economy. The stock market had become seriously overvalued, especially in the high tech sector. By August of 2000 the Federal Funds Rate had risen to six and one half percent and the Fed ended its increases. The economy slowed and started moving into recession. By the spring of 2001 the economy was in recession and the stock market had crashed. The Fed moved quickly in mid-2001 to bring interest rates down and continued to lower them until the spring of 2003 when the Federal Funds rate was at one percent, the lowest rate in 40 years. In mid 2004 they again started pushing up short-term interest rates.

In the fall of 2001, the US was hit by the 9-11 attacks on New York City and Washington, DC, and the economy was soon on a war footing. The surplus quickly disappeared: Killed by falling tax revenues as a result of the recession and falling stock prices and increased expenditures for the war in Afghanistan, then the War in Iraq and for Homeland Security. The tax cuts of 2002 and 2003, although designed to spur the economy, also added to the deficits in the short run. Although the recession occurred in 2001 and the economy started growing again in 2002, growth remained below trend until the latter half of 2003. This meant that the economy was not growing fast enough to reduce unemployment. Growth has to be above trend during a recovery in order for unemployment to fall. And unemployment lags growth by six months or so. This is because in the early stages of recovery firms rely on existing worker and don't start hiring new workers until they are relatively sure the recovery will continue. Finally in the latter half of 2003 growth exceeded trend and by the end of the year unemployment started falling. The recovery continued in 2004 and 2005.

The Fed had kept the Federal Funds rate at 1% for a year and one half. This means that real short-term interest rates were negative as the inflation rate was about one and one half or two percent. The real rate is the interest rate minus the inflation rate. This is the first time that the short-term real rate has been negative since the 1970s. The international value of the dollar had been falling for about a year and in 2004 was down about ten percent from the beginning of 2003. Part of the reason that the dollar was falling was that real short-term interest rates in the US were lower than real short-term interest rates in Europe, Great Britain or Japan. In Japan short-term interest rates are near zero but inflation had been negative for some time (prices had been falling.) As a result real rates were above nominal rates. The other reason that the dollar was falling was the large US trade deficit. As long as the dollar remained strong other countries were glad to have dollars to invest in the US or to hold as transaction balances. With the dollar falling, other countries were less willing to hold dollars or to invest in the US and as they trade their dollars for euros, yen or pounds, the dollar falls even more. And as the dollar falls commodity prices had started to rise. In 2004, agricultural prices were rising for the first time in nearly 10 years. By mid-2004, the FED started raising short-term interest rates. By mid 2005 the dollar had strengthened and inflationary pressures appeared to be moderating but were still being pushed up by high oil prices.

## CAUSES OF THE BUSINESS CYCLE

There are at lest three different views of the Business Cycle among economists. One view is that the economy is basically stable and will adjust to shocks to supply or demand relatively quickly. Attempts by government to stabilize the cycle will usually just make things worse. The Government should maintain a stable monetary environment targeting a long run inflation rate and then just stay out of the way. This is essentially the view of the Chicago School and their followers and is called the New Classical View. Second there is the Neo-Keynesian View that believes that the economy is prone to business cycles and although these cycles may self adjust in the long run, that this adjustment process is costly in terms of high unemployment and foregone output. Therefore the Government should actively attempt to stabilize the economy, preferably with monetary policy but also with fiscal policy if necessary.

A third view is that the economy is inherently unstable. We had business cycles long before we had active stabilization policy. But since we have had active policy we have added another source of instability. This is because government policy may be stabilizing or destabilizing depending on the circumstances. The War in Vietnam led to rising prices in the late 60s, but this probably could have been prevented with higher taxes or more restrictive monetary policy. The problem was that neither was politically acceptable at the time. President Nixon's "New Economic Policy" gave us low inflation and recovery in 1972 and ensured his reelection. But when inflation accelerated in 1973, it helped ensure his removal from office. President Bush in 1991 was planning his reelection in 1992. At the time his advisors thought that expansionary monetary policy by the FED would ensure a strong economy for him in 1992. Unfortunately for President Bush, the recovery was slow and the public still viewed the economy as in recession and President Bush was defeated. When politicians manipulate the economy for electoral purposes it is called a political business cycle. Although politician attempt to manipulate the economy for political purposes, they often fail.

Economists often view the business cycle as resulting from shocks to supply or demand. Shocks to demand can include unanticipated changes in monetary policy or fiscal policy. It may also include unanticipated changes in the international value of the dollar or unanticipated increases or decreases in profit expectations of firms or income expectations of households. Supply shocks include unanticipated changes in raw material prices, unanticipated changes in wage rates or unanticipated changes in inflationary expectations. Changes in raw material prices or inflationary expectations may be due to unanticipated changes in the value of the dollar. If the dollar falls that will increase the price of imports and increase the demand for exports that will also increase the price of exports. This is especially true of imports or exports like basic raw materials that are traded in international markets.

A second type of supply side shock is the adjustments of capacity and capacity utilization. During an expansion demand grows and firms respond by investing in new productive capacity. Households respond by adding new capacity in the form of housing and consumer durable goods. As the expansion continues, demand continues to grow and investment spending adds to demand growth. But on the supply side, investment adds to the capital stock and capacity grows. At the end of an expansion interest rates will rise both because of rising demand for funds and because the FED will push up short rates to slow the expansion. When the expansion ends firms will reduce investment in new capacity and households will also reduce investment in consumer durables and housing. As demand falls firms will develop excess capacity and this will tend to depress prices, especially of basic commodities. With falling demand and falling profits, firms will reduce employment and this will further slow the economy. Getting a recovery started again can be difficult. Firms have excess capacity and little incentive to invest. Households have reduced income expectations and are reluctant to purchase durables. And both firms and households may be faced with debt loads taken on during the expansion that prevent them from borrowing during the early stages of recovery. Thus expansions and contractions are a cumulative process. They may start with an initial shock to the system but once started feed on their own momentum. An expansion may continue until chocked off by rising raw material price or rising interest rates or both. A contraction may continue until lower interest rates and falling commodity prices to again start the cycle of expansion.

## SUMMARY

Over time the economy expands and contracts around a long-run trend path that we call normal output. Expansions can last from two to eight years. Contractions usually last two to three years. The Great Depression of the thirties lasted 10 years and involved a breakdown of the monetary and financial system. Since World War II we have had relatively mild recessions and expansions. Recessions have usually not lasted more than one to three years, mostly because the FED moves quickly to lower interest rates and bring about recovery. Recoveries have varied from two or three years to eight years. The length of the recovery depends on how long the economy can expand without developing shortages in some crucial areas of the economy and on the rate of growth in productivity. Faster productivity growth allows the economy to expand at a faster rate without hitting capacity constraints.

## REVIEW QUESTIONS

Multiple Choice: Select the correct answer:

1. During an expansion cyclical real output will grow:
   a. Faster than trend real output
   b. Slower than trend real output
   c. Same rate as trend real.
2. During a contraction cyclical real output will grow:
   a. Faster than trend real output
   b. Slower than trend real output
   c. At the same rate as trend real output
3. Normally expansions are:
   a. Longer than contractions
   b. Shorter than contractions
   c. About the same length as contractions

## Essays

1. Discuss the expansions of the 1980s and the 1990s. How did they differ in terms of the key variables that appeared to be driving the expansions.
2. Explain how the state of the economy helped President Clinton to survive impeachment proceedings. How did the state of the economy contribute to President Nixon's inability to survive when faced with impeachment proceedings?
3. Discuss the major factors that cause the business cycle. Distinguish between supply side shifters and demand side shifters. How are the factors that affect cyclical output different from the factors that affect trend output.

## SUGGESTED READINGS

De Long, J. Bradford, "Introduction to the Symposium on Business Cycles," *The Journal of Economic Perspectives*, 13, no. 2 (Spring 1999): 19–22.

Herendeen, James B. *The Economics of the Corporate Economy*, (Dunellen Publishing Company, 1975): 187–204; 237–40.

Mankiw, N. Gregory, "Real Business Cycles: A Keynesian Perspective," *The Journal of Economic Perspectives*, 3, no. 3 (Summer 1989): 79–90.

Plosser, Charles I. "Understanding Real Business Cycles," *The Journal of Economic Perspectives*, 3, no. 3 (Summer 1989): 51–77.

Romer, Christina D. "Changes in Business Cycles: Evidence and Explanations" *Journal of Economic Perspectives*, 13, no. 2 (Spring, 1999): 23–44.

Schumpeter, Joseph A. *Business Cycles: A Theoretic, Historical and statistical analysis of the Capitalist Process*, Abridged Paperback Edition, (York, McGraw-Hill, 1964, First Edition, 1939): Chapter 3.

Williams, Raburn McFetridge, *The Politics of Boom and Bust in Twentieth-Century America:A Macroeconomic History*, Minneapolis/St Paul, West Publishing Co., 1994, Chapters 20–27.

Zarnowitz, Victor, "The Theory and History Behind Business Cycles" *The Journal of Economic Perspectives*, 13, no. 2 (Spring 1999): 69–90.

# *Chapter Eighteen*

# The Federal Reserve System and the Money Supply Process

## INTRODUCTION

The Federal Reserve System (The FED) was established in 1913. The US had had a National Bank in its early day but the Second National Bank's Charter was not renewed in the 1830s. These National Banks were not really Central Banks, as we think of them today. The country did without a Central Bank until 1913. However, there had been periodic banking panics throughout the 19th Century. The most recent had been in 1907. The System was designed in part after the Bank of England and was intended to avoid banking panics by providing an "elastic currency." The FED would do this by discounting (buying) commercial paper of banks and short-term securities of the Federal Government. After World War II, The Fed went to buying or selling government securities as its primary policy tool.

## ORGANIZATIONAL STRUCTURE

### Regional Banks

The FED has 12 Regional Banks where all banking functions are carried out. These are in New York, Boston, Philadelphia, Richmond, Atlanta, Chicago, Cleveland, Denver, Dallas, Minneapolis, Saint Louis and San Francisco. They are concentrated in the eastern part of the country because that was where the population was in 1913. No new banks have been created but there have been several branch banks added. Each Bank has a President, elected by its Member Banks subject to the approval of the Chairman of the Federal Reserve Board.

## The Board of Governors

The Board of Governors is the governing body for the Federal Reserve System. It is made up of seven members appointed by the President and approved by the Senate. The members are appointed for 14-year staggered terms: a term expiring every two years. If a member resigns before his/her 14-year term is up, a new member is appointed to complete the un-expired term. The member is then eligible to serve another complete 14-year term. If a member is appointed and serves his full 14-year term then he is not eligible for another term. The reason for the long and staggered terms is so that no one President gets to appoint too many members. However members often do not serve their full terms.

The President with approval of the Senate appoints one member Chairman. The Chairman serves a four-year term, roughly consistent with the term of the President. He can be reappointed as long as he remains a member of the board. Alan Greenspan held the office for 18 years, retiring at the end of 2005. He was originally appointed to serve out an un-expired term. The vice chairman also serves for a four-year term. The Current chairman is Ben Bernanke, recently appointed by President Bush.

## The Federal Open Market Committee (FOMC)

The Federal Open Market Committee, or FOMC as it is usually referred to, is made up of the seven board members plus the 12 regional Presidents of the Federal Reserve Banks. The voting members of the FOMC are the seven Board Members plus five of the 12 Regional Presidents. The President of the New York Reserve Bank is a permanent voting member. The other four voting members rotate among the other 11 Regional Presidents. The New York President is a permanent voting member because the New York Fed is where open market operations are actually carried out. The reason for allowing only five regional Presidents to vote at any one time was to ensure that the Board (if it voted together) would always have a majority. This was to ensure that monetary policy decisions would remain in Washington. Congress added this provision when the system was reformed in the mid 1930s. The FOMC meets eight times a year in Washington and decides on the stance of monetary policy for the next six weeks. The Government Securities Trading Desk at the New York Federal Reserve Bank then carries out its directives.

## FUNCTIONS OF THE FED

### The FED Has Four Primary Functions

*(1) The Conduct of Monetary Policy*

Probably the most important function of the FED is to conduct the nations monetary policy. As we will see below, monetary policy involves targeting short-term interest rates, targeting the growth of the money supply and targeting the long run inflation rate, all with the purpose of stabilizing the economy over the business cycle and controlling the rate of inflation.

*(2) The Regulation of the Banking System*

The Fed shares regulatory authority over the Banking System with two other regulatory agencies: The Federal Deposit Insurance Corporation (FDIC), and The Office of Comptroller of Currency (OCC). The FDIC is the agency that runs the Deposit Insurance System. Checkable deposits, saving accounts and small (under $100,000) certificate of deposits are insured by the Federal Government up to $100,000 per account per depositor. The FDIC's regulatory authority is to ensure the soundness of Banks and Thrifts (Saving Banks and Saving and Loan Associations). Credit Unions are regulated by a separate agency, the National Credit Union Administration and are insured by the National Credit Union Share Insurance Association.

The OCC (Office of Comptroller of Currency) is the agency that charters all National Banks, and as such has regulatory authority over all National Banks. The US has what is called a dual Banking System. There are National Banks, chartered by the Federal Government, and State Banks, chartered by the State Governments. National Banks are required to belong to the Federal Reserve System. State Banks may be members but are not required to be. Banks can chose whether to be State Chartered Banks or Federally Chartered Banks. If they choose to be State Chartered, they can also choose whether to be members of the Federal Reserve System. Nationally Chartered banks have as their primary regulatory agency the OCC. State Chartered Banks that are members of The FED have as their primary regulator the FED. State Chartered Banks that are not members of the FED have as their primary regulator the FDIC. Bank holding companies have the FED as their primary regulator. (These are companies that own several banks as well as investment banks and insurance companies.) Since 1980 all Banks, Thrifts and Credit Unions have been required to hold reserves at the FED.

*(3) Lender of Last Resort*

The FED stands ready to supply liquidity to the banking system in case of a financial crisis that might risk the safety of the system. It does this primarily through Open Market Operations (OMOs) that will be discussed below.

*(4) Bank for banks and for government*

Only the Federal Government, commercial banks, and banks for Thrifts and Credit Unions and foreign Central Banks can hold deposits at the FED. The FED also keeps balances at Foreign Central Banks. These are necessary for International transactions between governments and for foreign exchange transactions. The US treasury keeps most of its cash balances at the FED.

## POLICY TOOLS OF THE FED

### Open Market Operations (OMOs)

Open market operations are the buying and selling of Federal Government Securities by the FED. When the FED buys government securities, it pays for them by checks drawn on the FED. These checks are deposited by security dealers to their accounts at commercial banks The banks in turn clear the checks by depositing them to their accounts at the FED where they increase reserve balances at the FED. Banks can in turn lend out any excess reserves. This process is described in more detail in the next chapter. The net result is that the increase in the supply of reserves pushes down short-term interest rates. Lower short-term interest rates encourage borrowers, both businesses and households, to borrow more and spend more. And as loan proceeds are deposited, checkable deposits increase and the money supply increases. As we saw in Chapter 16, increased borrowing and spending, increases aggregate demand.

When the FED sells securities, we have the same process in reverse. The security dealers pay for the securities with checks drawn on their accounts at commercial banks. For the banks this means a reduction in reserves. The reduced supply of reserves will push up short-term interest rates as banks compete to get reserves to meet their reserve requirements. Higher interest rates will discourage borrowing by households and businesses. As loans are cut back, deposits will also fall and the money supply will fall. The reduced borrowing and spending will reduce aggregate demand. Realize that we are talking about a static system; in reality the FED rarely tries to reduce the money supply. Instead it uses open market operations to cause the money supply to grow at slower or faster rates, depending on its current policy stance.

### Reserve Requirements

The FED sets reserve requirements for the banking system. Currently these are at 10%. Banks can count as reserves deposits at the FED and vault cash. These reserves must equal 10% of outstanding checkable deposits of banks with the public. If banks are short of reserves they can borrow reserves in the Federal Funds Market. The Federal Funds Market is a very short-term market (overnight or one to two days). Banks with excess reserves can lend in the Federal Funds Market. It is a temporary place for funds until banks can increase (or decrease) loans or buy (or sell) government securities. The Fed rarely changes reserve requirements. They have been at 10% since 1996. They were at 12% from 1981 until 1996. Instead their primary function is to reinforce OMOs by forcing banks into the market, either to get reserves or to get rid of reserves. The FED pays no interest on reserve balances so banks have an incentive to get rid of excess unless interest rates are very low.

### The Discount Rate and Lending Policy

The discount rate is the rate the FED charges banks that borrow directly from the FED. It is an administered rate rather than a market rate like the Federal Funds Rate. However the FED sets it close to the Federal Funds rate target. Up until recently, it was set a little below the Federal Funds rate target, usually a quarter of a percentage point below. Recently the FED has set it a quarter to a half of a percentage point above the Federal funds rate target. This has converted it to a penalty rate in order to discourage banks from borrowing from the FED. The Fed has always discouraged banks from borrowing from the FED. Loans are usually only for emergency situations when banks have temporary liquidity problems. Bank loans are only a very small proportion of FED assets. In general The FED prefers that banks meet their reserve needs in the Federal Funds Market. For short-term borrowing banks also rely on the commercial paper market. For capital funds, banks rely on the bond market and shareholder equity. Issuing checkable and non-checkable deposits raises the majority of their funds.

## INDEPENDENCE OF THE FED

The Fed is set up as an independent government entity in order to free it from the day-to-day pressures of the political process. Its independence comes from three sources:

### (1) The FED is Independent by Statute

Governors have 14-year staggered terms to keep too many members from being appointed by any one President. The Board and FOMC have the authority to act on monetary and regulatory issues without having to consult with Congress, the President or the Secretary of Treasury. Although not required by law the Chairman does meet regularly with the Secretary of Treasury. However unlike the Supreme Court, the FED is not independent by the Constitution, but by act of Congress. Congress could remove this independence but is highly unlikely to do so.

### (2) The FED is Independent by Budget Process

Unlike most government agencies it does not have to go to Congress for appropriations. The FED earns interest on its holdings of Federal Government securities. These comprise about 88% of its assets. Its two primarily liabilities are currency in circulation and reserve deposits of banks. It pays no interest on either. Therefore the FED is a very profitable operation. It is required by law to pay back to the treasury any income over and above its necessary expenses. But having its own source of funding reinforces its independence.

### (3) The FED is Independent by Custom and Tradition

We have a long tradition of an independent FED Any attempt by Congress or the President to remove or limit that independence would likely be opposed by the financial community and by the public.

Why is the FED independent? The FED is independent so that it will not be subject to political pressures in its conduct of monetary and regulatory policy. This allows the FED to act as a check on Congress and the President in their conduct of fiscal policy. Congress can run large deficits but the FED does not have to finance them. During the 1980s we had large Federal deficits but we had declining inflation. The reason was that the FED did not monetize these rising deficits by buying government securities beyond what was necessary to allow the economy to grow with declining inflation. Much of the debt was sold to the public and to foreigners. In countries that do not have independent central banks or that do not have well-developed markets for government debt, central banks often have to buy rising government debt and the result is increasing inflation.

Should the FED be independent? Many of the critics of an independent FED say that it is inconsistent with a democratic society to have a central bank that is not accountable to the political process. This oversimplifies the issue. The FED is only independent in the short run. Congress can remove its independence if it abuses its power. Its independence is often very convenient for Congress and the President because the FED can be a convenient scapegoat that gives them political cover when unpopular decisions have to be made. In the early eighties the sharply rising interest rates were very unpopular and politicians and interest groups complained loudly. But when inflation came down and the economy recovered these same politicians were glad to say that "they" brought down inflation. Ultimately, it is a political question as to whether to have an independent Central Bank. In the US we have made that political decision and so have many other countries. Evidence seems to show that countries with independent Central Banks have lower inflation than countries that do not have independent Central Banks.

## LIMITS ON THE ABILITY OF BANKS TO CREATE DEPOSITS

Banks are limited in their ability to create deposits by four primary things. First, they are limited by the demand for loans by the public. Banks need to be able to expand loans to expand deposits. They can also buy government securities, but this is usually much less profitable than expanding loans. Second, banks are limited by the cost of funds. The short-run cost of funds is the Federal Funds Rate that is under the control of the Federal Reserve. Banks can only expand loans and deposits if it is profitable to do so. The FED can make it unprofitable by pushing up the Federal Funds Rate. Or it can make it more profitable by pushing down the Federal Funds Rate. Third, banks are constrained by reserve requirement that are set by the FED. These reinforce its open market operations that target the Federal Funds Rate. Last, banks are constrained by the demand for currency. Currency acts as a drain on reserves. If the public holds its cash in the form of currency rather than checkable deposits, it deprives the banks of reserves that could be used as the basis of more loans.

To summarize, banks only make loans and issue deposits if it is profitable for them to do so. The Fed targets the Federal Funds rate that determines the short term cost of funds but also influences the long-term cost of funds. The FED also sets reserve requirements that reinforce its ability to set the cost of funds. The public determines the demand for loans and the demand for currency.

## LIMITS ON THE FED'S ABILITY TO CREATE RESERVES

The FED is not constrained by the same things that constrain banks. The FED is a government agency. Its purpose is not to make a profit but to conduct the nations monetary and bank regulatory policies. It has no reserve requirements, although it has to hold a certain amount of reserves, as would any other bank. The FED's primary sources of funds are issuing currency and issuing bank reserve deposits. It pays no interest on currency and also is prohibited by law from paying interest on bank reserves. Therefore the FED is not constrained as are bank by cost of funds. It makes very few loans but holds primarily government securities. It does not buy securities directly from the treasury but instead buys (or sells) them on the open market.

Given these factors, what does limit the FED's ability to issue reserves and thus expand the money supply? First, the FED is limited by its own policy rules and objectives. It is responsible for the nations monetary policy: It targets the Federal Funds Rate in the short run. Over longer periods it targets the inflation rate and targets the growth of the monetary base and the money supply. The monetary base is currency in circulation (outside the banking system) plus reserve deposits of banks. The money supply is currency in circulation plus checkable deposits of the public.

Second, the FED is constrained by the political process. It may be independent but it can read the election returns. It knows that Congress and the President could remove or limit its independence if it abuses its powers.

Third, domestic and international financial markets limit the FED. Although the FED doesn't target stock or bond prices, it still watches them very closely. Likewise it doesn't target the international value of the dollar. But if the dollar falls (or rises) too much, the FED will feel compelled to act, usually in cooperation with the Treasury Department, and other major Central Banks.

## SUMMARY

The FED serves as the nations Central Bank. It is responsible for conducting the nations monetary policy and regulating the banking system. It shares regulatory powers with the Office of Comptroller of Currency and the Federal Deposit Insurance Corporation. The FED's primary policy tool is open market operations. This involves the buy or selling of government securities on the open market. When the Fed buys securities it has the effect of lowering the Federal Funds Rate and allowing the banking system to expand loans and deposits. This allows an expansion of the money supply. When the FED sells government securities, it has the effect of raising the Federal Funds Rate and encouraging the banking system to contract loans and deposits. This has the effect of contracting the money supply. The FED's short run policy target is the Federal Funds Rate. The FED's primary long run objective is the inflation rate. In the shorter run the Fed is also concerned with output and employment over the business cycle.

The FED is also concerned with the international value of the dollar. It usually intervenes only is the dollar becomes seriously overvalued or seriously undervalued in terms of purchasing power parity. (We discuss purchasing power parity in a chapter 20.) The FED's independence means that it can act quickly when policy change is needed. However the FED's policy actions affect the economy only with lags that are not too predictable. It takes about a year for a change in FED policy to affect output, about a year and one half to affect the inflation rate of final goods. Its affect on short-term interest rates is very quick. Its affect on long-term rates is slower and less predictable.

## REVIEW QUESTIONS

Multiple Choice: Select the correct answer:

1. The purchase of government securities by the FED will:
   a. Increase bank reserves and increase interest rates
   b. Decrease bank reserves and decrease interest rates
   c. Increase bank reserves and decrease interest rate
   d. Decrease bank reserves and increase interest rates
2. The sale of government securities by the FED will:
   a. Increase bank reserves and increase interest rates
   b. Increase bank reserves and decrease interest rates
   c. Decrease bank reserves and decrease interest rates
   d. Decrease bank reserves and increase interest rates
3. Which of the following is not a function of the Federal Reserve:
   a. Determination of tax and spending policy for the government
   b. Bank for banks and the Federal Government.
   c. Lender of last resort
   d. Conduct of monetary policy
4. Open market operations are:
   a. The purchase or sale of government securities by commercial banks.
   b. The purchase or sale of government securities by the Federal Reserve.
   c. The borrowing of reserves by banks from the Central Bank.

### Essays

1. Explain how the Fed is independent and why the Fed is independent.
2. What limits the ability of banks to expand deposits and the money supply? What limits the FED's ability to expand the monetary base? Why does the FED face different limits than banks?

## SUGGESTED READINGS

Burton, Maureen and Raymond Lombra, *The Financial System and the Economy: Principles of Money and Banking*, 3rd ed. Mason, Oh: Thompson-Southwestern, 2003, Chapters 5, 21, 24, 25–27.

Dornbusch, Rudiger and Stanley Fisher, *Macro Economics*, 6th ed. New York, McGraw-Hill, 1994: Chapter 15

Tucker, Irving, *Economics Today*, 3rd ed. Mason, Ohio, Thompson-Southwestern: Chapter 24–26.

# *Chapter Nineteen*

# Macroeconomic Policy: Stabilization, Growth and Inflation

## MEASURING THE HEALTH OF THE ECONOMY

A doctor measures the health of a patient by looking at key variables and comparing them to their normal values. For example the doctor may take your temperature. If it is above normal it implies a fever and then the doctor can look for the source of the fever. The doctor may take your weight and compare it with normal weight for a person of your height and body build. He then may recommend a weight loss program. He may take an EKG to record your heartbeat to see is it is normal. He may take your blood pressure to see is it is normal.

An economist looking at the macro economy does something very similar. He looks at certain key variables such as the unemployment rate, the inflation rate, the growth rate of trend real GDP, the growth rate of trend output per worker, and the international value of the dollar. He compares each of these variables to their normal or target values to measure the health of the economy. If normal unemployment were 5.5%, then an unemployment rate of say 7% would imply a recession. An unemployment rate of four percent would imply an expansion. If target inflation is one percent per year and inflation is at six percent a year it means that the FED is missing its inflation target and that a change in policy is called for. If trend growth of real GDP is 2% per year and the target is 3.5% per year then a change in growth policy may be called for. If trend growth of output per worker is 1% per year and the target is 2.5% per year then policies to increase trend productivity growth might be called for. If the dollar is over valued relative to other major currencies then a policy to lower the value of the dollar might be called for.

## STABILIZATION POLICY

Stabilization policy involves policy to attempt to stabilize the fluctuations of real GDP around trend. This involves attempting to reduce output growth above trend during an expansion and attempting to reduce the reduction of growth below trend. As we pointed out in the previous chapter, government policy does not always succeed in stabilizing the economy and may at times make the fluctuations greater. The primary ways that government can stabilize the economy is through fiscal and monetary policy.

### Fiscal Policy

Fiscal policy involves changes in government spending or in taxes designed to stabilize the economy. With spending policy unchanged, a cut in taxes will spur the economy by increasing disposable income of households and retained earnings of business. Households will spend most of the increase in disposable income on additional consumption. Businesses will spend most of any increase in retained earnings on business investment for new capital goods. An increase in spending by government (with tax policy unchanged) adds directly to aggregate demand. With either a tax cut or a spending increase we expect, over time, multiplier affects as the original increase in income is re-spent. The size of the multiplier will depend on how much of the additional income is saved and how much is taxed away by government. The spending multiplier is estimated to be a little over two.

This means that an increase in government spending by one billion dollars will ultimately increase demand by over two billion dollars. The tax multiplier is somewhat smaller because taxes work indirectly through disposable income and retained earnings. Thus a one billion dollar tax cut would involve a somewhat smaller multiplier effect. Also the magnitude of the multiplier effect will depend on how much interest rates change. With an expansionary fiscal policy, with no change in monetary policy, interest rates are expected to rise because of the increase in demand for funds as the economy expands. This increase in interest rates will be expected to dampen the multiplier affect of any given change in spending or taxes.

If spending is cut or taxes increased we call this a contractionary fiscal policy. A contractionary fiscal policy will also have multiplier effects. In other words a spending cut of a billion dollars might ultimately lead to a total reduction of demand of over two billion dollars. A tax increase will also have multiplier effects, but the tax multiplier is somewhat smaller than the spending multiplier.

The problem with fiscal policy is that it must be determined through the political processes. The appropriate committees of congress must first approve a tax cut or spending increase. The committees are lobbied by interest groups who are interested in who gets the tax cut or who gets the spending increase; There is no such thing as an across the board spending increase. Much of spending is already mandated by entitlements, so the battle is always over a small share of the total budget. The same is true with a tax cut. The tax interest groups lobby the tax writing committees to preserve or extend their particular tax benefit. Congress cannot just raise or lower taxes; it must seek a consensus among the interest groups that will also be more or less acceptable to the electorate. After passing the committees the bills must be passed by the full Senate and House. It must then go to a Conference Committee to work out differences between the bills of the two houses. If both Houses of Congress then pass this compromise, it goes to the President. If he signs it, it becomes law. If he vetoes the bill it takes a two-thirds vote of both houses to override. This seldom happens. The point is that the political process is long and drawn out and by the time a bill is passed the need may no longer be there. Thus fiscal policy has declined in importance as a primary stabilization tool over the last twenty years. Instead the emphasis of fiscal policy has become more oriented toward long-term growth.

## MONETARY POLICY

The Federal Reserve System conducts monetary policy. The primary policy tool of the FED is Open Market Operations (OMOs). This involves buying or selling of Federal Government Securities on the open market by the FED's trading desk at the New York Federal Reserve Bank. The trading desk is under the direction of the Federal Open Market Committee.

When the FED buys government securities it pays for them with checks drawn on the FED. It buys them from licensed government security dealers on Wall Street. The security dealers in turn deposit the checks to their accounts at commercial banks. The banks in turn clear the checks by depositing them to their accounts at the New York Federal Reserve Bank. The bank must only keep 10% of these new funds as reserves. The rest can be loaned out or used to buy securities. The proceeds of the loans will be deposited to the banking system and 90% can be re-loaned by the next bank. However, how much is re-deposited and re-loaned will actually be much less than 90% because the public will hold part of any new funds as currency. The banking system cannot make loans against currency held by the public, only against reserves created by the FED and against reserves created by loans to the public. When the FED sells securities to security dealers we have the same process in reverse. The security dealers pay for the securities by writing a check on their banking accounts at commercial banks. This reduces bank reserves and forces banks to cut back on loans. A cut back on loans means a cut back on deposits. And if the public holds fewer deposits it will likely also hold less currency.

The process described above is often called the multiplier model of deposit expansion. But what motivates this process? What motivates it is the behavior of the FED, the banking system and the public. When the FED buys securities, it increases the supply of reserves of the banking system. This means some banks will now have excess reserves. Remember they are only required to have reserves equal to 10% of outstanding checkable deposits. The FED pays no interest on bank reserves. Banks with excess reserves can lend them in the Federal Funds market but the excess supply of reserves will force down the Federal Funds Rate, the rate that the Fed targets for monetary policy. The FED does not directly set the Federal Funds Rate. Instead it increases or decreases the supply of reserves in order to force down or force up the Federal Funds Rate. Thus the Federal Funds Rate is a market-determined rate where the FED essentially controls the supply of funds in the market.

The banking system and the public determine the demand for funds. A fall in the Federal Funds Rate will encourage banks to lower loan and deposit rates. Because loan rates are less flexible than deposit rates, a fall in the Federal Funds rate will widen the margin on loans and encourage banks to expand loans. Lower loan rates will encourage households and businesses to increase borrowing, an increase in borrowing will increase deposits as borrowers deposit the proceeds of loans to their accounts and as the money is spent, it gets re-deposited to other accounts. As deposits grow, the money supply grows. As households and businesses spend the funds borrowed it increases aggregate demand and increases GDP as supply responds to the increased demand.

When the FED tightens monetary policy it sells government securities. Security dealers pay for these securities with checks drawn on their accounts at commercial banks. This has the effect of reducing reserves of the banking system at the Fed and forces up the Federal Funds rate as banks with deficit reserves are forced to borrow reserves from the Federal Funds market. This bids up the Federal Funds rate. This is the marginal cost of short-term funds to the banking system. Banks are forced to increase loan and deposit rates. Because deposit rates are more flexible than loan rates, the margin between loan and deposit rates narrows. This encourages banks to cut back on loans, that in turn cuts back deposits created by loans and cuts back on the money supply. Higher interest rates and restrictions on availability of funds will force firms and households to cut back on borrowing.

Unfortunately the system works better at slowing the economy than it does at expanding the economy. If the FED is willing to push interest rates high enough it can bring the economy to a halt. It has done so several times: 1974–75, 1981–82, 1989–90, and 2000–2001. Getting the economy moving again is more difficult. The reason is that even though the Fed can bring down short term interest rates it cannot force households and businesses to borrow. In a recession businesses and households are often over burdened with debt from the previous expansion. They are interested in paying off debt, not taking on more debt. The recoveries of 1991–92 and 2002–03 were slow in part for this reason. The recovery of 1983–84 was very rapid. The reason probably was that fiscal policy was very expansive. The Reagan tax cuts and defense spending increases were already in place when the Fed started easing in late 1982.

In 1992–93 there was no comparable fiscal expansion. In fact the Clinton administration raised taxes in 1993. This may have slowed the recovery some but it set the stage for the long recovery of the 90s because it allowed the FED to follow a basically low interest rate policy through out the rest of the decade. The Bush Administration has faced a very different situation in the early 2000s. The tax cuts of 2002 and 2003 were mostly cuts in future taxes and did not start having their effect until late 2003, two years after the recession. Unfortunately the recession, the war in Afghanistan and Iraq, and the tax cuts have left us with a large Federal Budget Deficit that will probably be with us for the next ten years.

## THE MIX OF FISCAL AND MONETARY POLICY

We have just been discussing the interrelation between fiscal and monetary policy. In this section we will do this in a more formal manner. Since fiscal policy is a slow and cumbersome process in terms of enactment whereas the FED can act quickly once it decides a policy change is needed, we will look at how the FED responds to a change in fiscal policy. We will discuss four primary cases:

### No Accommodation

No accommodation is the textbook case of independence of fiscal and monetary policy. If, for example, the Congress and President pass a tax cut, this assumes that monetary policy remains unchanged. In this case there would be an increase in the government deficit and we would expect interest rates to rise. The higher interest rates would reduce the expansionary effect of the tax cut. An increase in government spending would have a similar effect. With no change in taxes, the budget deficit would increase and interest rates would increase and the expansionary effect of the spending increase would be dampened. With a restrictive fiscal policy we would have the opposite effect. A tax increase or a spending cut would reduce the budget deficit and interest rates would fall. This would have the effect of reducing the contraction effect of the fiscal policy. During the eighties, after 84, the FED did not accommodate the large budget deficits, interest rates remained high throughout the rest of the eighties. If the Fed had accommodated the deficits we would have had much higher inflation. Instead, inflation declined throughout most of the decade.

## Partial Accommodation

Partial accommodation is when the FED partially accommodates a change in fiscal policy. An expansionary fiscal policy would be matched with some expansion of monetary policy. Interest rates would still rise but not by as much as would have been the case with no accommodation. Likewise with a contractionary fiscal policy, interest rates would fall but not by as much as in the case of no accommodation.

## Full Accommodation

With full accommodation the FED would fully accommodate any change in fiscal policy. This would mean that any increase in the budget deficit would be fully purchased by the FED. An expansionary fiscal policy would be reinforced by the expansionary monetary policy. Any decrease in the deficit would be accompanied by an equivalent sale of government securities by the FED. This would reinforce any restrictive effect of fiscal policy. We had approximately full accommodation during World War II as the FED held interest rates constant in the face of big increases in government deficits with an agreement with the Treasury to support the price of government securities. Also during 2002 and 2003, the FED was holding short term interest rates constant, despite tax cuts and increases in government spending that have increased the deficit. It has done this to bring about a recovery from the 2001 recession. In mid 2004 the FED stated raising the Federal Funds Rate target by a quarter of a percentage point at each meeting of the FOMC. This policy has continued through early 2006.

## Reverse Accommodation

Reverse accommodation is when the FED moves in the opposite direction as fiscal policy. An expansionary fiscal policy would be met by a contractionary monetary policy. A contractionary fiscal policy would be met with an expansionary monetary policy. In 1981 and 1982, tax cuts and spending increases were turning fiscal policy expansionary. However the FED remained very restrictive until August of 1982 and kept the economy in a rather severe recession. They did this to bring down the high inflation that had developed in the late 70s and continued in the early eighties. Also, in the nineties, Federal deficits were declining at least in part due to a relatively restrictive fiscal policy. This allowed the FED to follow a relatively expansionary monetary policy that kept interest rates low and helped maintain the long expansion between 1993 and 2000.

## GROWTH POLICY

Growth Policy involves policy to attempt to increase the trend growth rate of real output of the economy. As we saw above, stabilization policy is concerned with stabilizing the fluctuations of real GDP around the trend path. Growth policy is aimed at increasing the growth rate of trend GDP. What can government do to increase trend growth. We will stick primarily to Macro policies. Macro policies can take three primary forms:

### The Mix of Government Spending

Government spending takes many forms. Spending on education, on agriculture, on national defense, on transfers and many more. Some of these expenditures are growth generating and others are not. First, it is useful to separate spending into current and capital spending. Current spending is spending for goods or services that are used during the current period: Fuel, electricity and office supplies for government offices, salaries for government employees, munitions, fuel and food and salaries for the military. Transfers are primarily redistribution of income from one group of taxpayers to another. Most are from the working to the non-working; the primary examples being Social Security and Medicare. Most transfers would go for current spending, not capital spending. Capital spending is spending for goods or services that are expected to give a flow of services or of income in future periods. Examples would be spending on new transportation systems such as the construction of the Interstate Highway System in the 1950s, 1960s, and 1970s. Spending to build new schools, airports, water and sewer system would be also be examples. Or spending to development a new missile defense system. These types of spending are often called spending for social overhead capital.

Is social overhead capital spending growth generating? Some probably is and some may not be. National defense may be necessary, but is it growth generating? The Soviet Union collapsed in part because it was devoting too high a proportion of its GDP to national defense during the cold war. However there may be spin-offs from defense spending to the private economy. The computer and radar were both developed during World War II primarily for military purposes but both were great innovations for the private sector after the War. There is little doubt that government subsidies to the railroads and later to highways and to education were growth generating expenditures.

## The Structure of Taxes

In recent years tax cuts have become the primary fiscal policy for growth, at least among many Republicans. The Kennedy-Johnson tax cut passed in 1964 was designed to stabilize the economy, not to increase long run growth. With the Reagan tax cuts in 1981–83, the goal was explicitly growth. The rationale was that a cut in marginal tax rates would stimulate business investment, spur household durable spending, and induce workers to increase the supply of labor by increasing the after tax reward to labor. The tax reform act of 1986 was also oriented toward growth by reducing marginal rates and simplifying the tax code. Whether-or-not the tax cuts of the eighties actually increased trend growth is still debatable. We had a long expansion in the eighties but it doesn't appear that trend growth increased much until the nineties.

## The Size of the Deficit and Interest Rate Policy

The other way that fiscal policy can affect growth is through the size of the budget deficit. Other things equal, a larger government deficit, as a share of GDP, will imply higher interest rates. The reason is that if the FED monetizes the deficit, and the debt is growing faster than GDP, it will lead to rising inflation. In the eighties the rising deficits did not lead to rising inflation because the FED kept real interest rates high. In the nineties the falling deficits allowed the FED to keep real interest rates low. We had something that many Keynesians thought could not happen: high growth despite falling government budget deficits. The growth was driven by low interest rates and private sector investment. And although trend real growth had been declining in the seventies and early eighties, by the nineties, the trend appeared to be rising again.

### Regulation and Deregulation

Although not strictly a macro policy, deregulation has also been viewed by many as a way of increasing growth. Regulations that limit competition in various ways, that regulate price or output, restrict freedom of labor markets and so on may have growth restricting effects. The US economy went though a period of deregulation during the late 1970s and 1980s. Airlines were deregulated, trucking was deregulated and depository institutions (banks, thrifts and credit unions) were partially deregulated. In the 1990s we saw further deregulation of the Financial Services Industry (commercial banks, investment banks and insurance companies) and partial deregulation of agriculture. Whether these deregulations actually increased growth is difficult to say. However during the 1990s the US economy grew much faster than the economies of Western Europe and Japan that were, in general, much more regulated than the US economy.

## INFLATION POLICY

We have discussed monetary policy above but the primary emphasis was on stabilization. The FED has two primary objectives: Stabilizing the economy over the business cycle and controlling the inflation rate. Most economists would argue that the primary goal of the FED should be targeting a long run inflation rate. The secondary goal should be stabilization. Some economists believe that the FED should just concentrate on inflation and let stabilization take care of itself. A third possible target for the FED is the international value of the dollar. Normally the FED concentrates on the first two and lets the dollar take care of itself. However, when the dollar falls too much or rises too much, the FED then feels compelled to act, normally in cooperation with the Treasury Department. The problem is that there may be conflicts between the three goals. If the FED is too expansionary during a recovery it may lead to rising inflation and the FED ends up missing its inflation target. Or if the FED keeps interest rates low to bring about a recovery it may lead to a falling dollar, and a falling dollar may contribute to rising inflation. Thus the FED follows a precarious path of trying to maintain balance between its three primary objectives with only one primary policy tool: the ability, within limits, to set short-term interest rates.

In the short run the FED can influence interest rates, real output, and the price level (or rate of inflation). In the long run most economists believe that monetary policy only affects the inflation rate. The reason is that in the long run output and unemployment fluctuate around their normal or trend levels pretty much independent of the trend inflation rate. In the 1970s we had relatively high inflation and relatively low growth of output. Figure 19.1 gives the inflation rate as measured by the consumer price index (CPI) and the short-term interest rate as measured by the annual average six-month treasury-bill rate. Note that inflation exceeded interest rates in the mid 70s and late 70s and again in the early 2000s. Figure 19.2 shows the realized real short-term interest rate for the same period. The real rate is the interest rate minus the inflation rate. It is the difference between the two series in figure 19.1. Note that the real interest rate was negative from 73–76 and from 77–80. It was again negative from 2002–2005. It was abnormally high during the first two thirds of the eighties and again in the late nineties.

Unemployment remained relatively high throughout the 1970s and early 1980s. (For unemployment rates see figure 17.4) During the rest of the eighties and during the nineties, after 92, we had low inflation and relatively high growth. (For growth rates see figure 17.2.)And unemployment declined during both expansions. The theory behind this long run relation is the idea that if all prices and wages rise together at the same rate, there is no incentive for firms to change output. In the short run relative prices change over the business cycle, allowing output and employment changes. In the long run prices adjust back to their normal relationship. This is called the neutrality proposition and says that in the long run monetary policy is neutral with respect to real output, employment and real (inflation adjusted) interest rates. It says

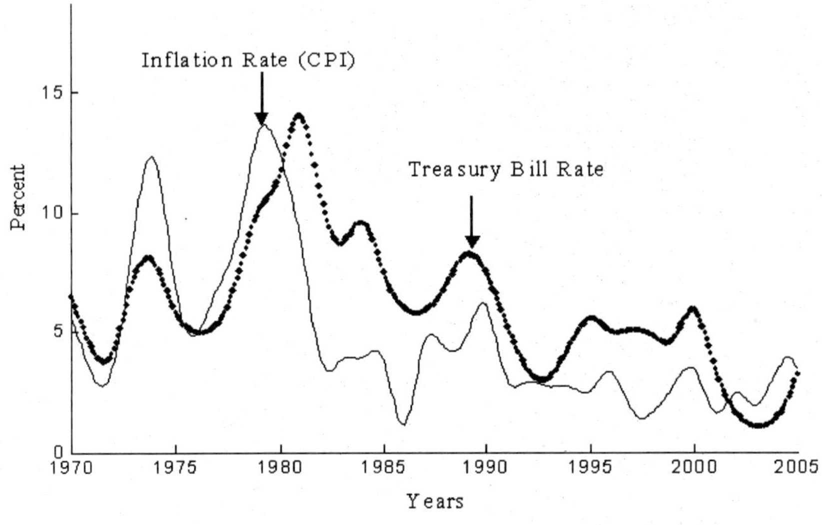


Source: Economic Report of the President, 2006

**Figure 19.1. Annual Short-Term Interest Rate and Inflation Rate, 1970–2005**

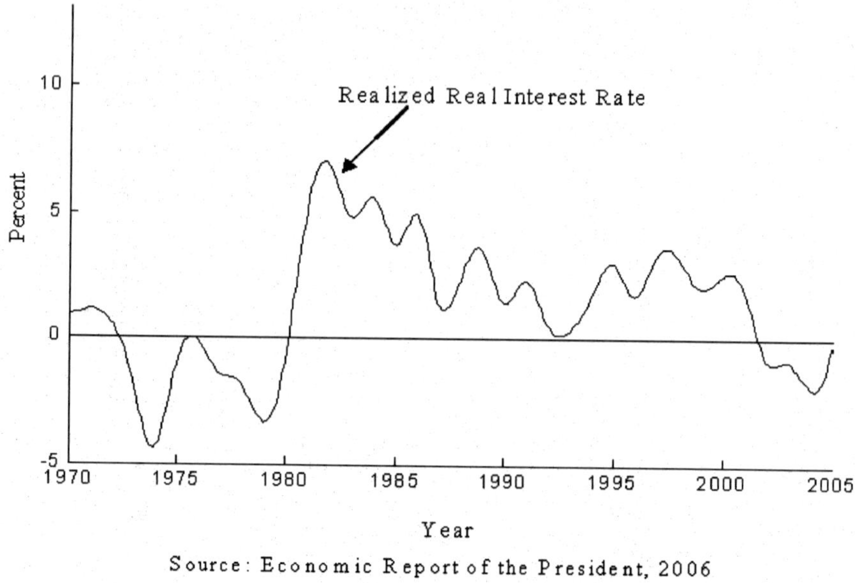


**Figure 19.2. Short-Term Realized Real Interest Rate, 1970–2005**

that in the long run monetary policy affects only the inflation rate. We live in the short run, long run theories only tell us the direction we may be headed.

## SUMMARY

In this chapter we have discussed macro economic policy. The three primary types of macro policy are stabilization policy, growth policy, and inflation policy. Stabilization policy involves policy to stabilize fluctuations of output around normal or trend output. Growth policy is policy designed to increase the long-run trend growth rate. Inflation policy is policy designed to choose and target a trend inflation rate. Fiscal policy can be used to attempt to stabilize the economy. The problem is that fiscal policy is slow to enact, as it has to go through the political process. As a result in the last twenty years monetary policy has come to be the primary stabilization tool. Fiscal policy is still used but its primary emphasis has been on long-term growth. What is important for both stabilization and growth is the mix of fiscal and monetary policy. During the eighties we had relatively restrictive monetary policy in that real interest rates were substantially above normal. This was accompanied with a relatively expansive fiscal policy in that there were relatively large federal budget deficits throughout the decade. During the nineties we had the opposite mix. Budget deficits declined and turned to surpluses by the end of the decade. This allowed relatively low interest rates, which were an important spur to private investment. These relatively low interest rates did not lead to inflation because high growth led to supply side expansion and because the dollar remained relatively strong which also acted as a deterrent to inflation.

## REVIEW QUESTIONS

Multiple Choice: Select the correct answer:

1. An accommodative monetary policy means that an expansionary fiscal policy will be met with:
   a. A contractionary monetary policy.
   b. An expansionary monetary policy.
   c. No change in monetary policy.
   d. None of the above.
2. Business investment in new capital goods will decrease if:
   a. Interest rates increase.
   b. Interest rates decrease.
   c. Profit expectations increase.
3. The aggregate demand curve is down sloping because:
   a. Falling prices increase real purchasing power
   b. Rising prices increase real purchasing power.
   c. Firms expand output when prices increase relative to expected prices.
   d. Firms expand output when prices decrease relative to expected prices.
4. A policy of reverse accommodation by the FED requires that an expansionary fiscal policy be met with:
   a. A contractionary monetary policy.
   b. An expansionary monetary policy.
   c. No change in monetary policy.
5. For the aggregate economy, growth in real income per worker requires:
   a. Growth of the price level
   b. Growth of output per worker.
   c. Growth of the work force.
6. An accommodative monetary policy requires that an expansionary fiscal policy be met with:
   a. A decrease in reserves by the FED.
   b. An increase in reserves by the FED.
   c. No change in reserves by the FED.

### Essays

1. Discuss the primary ways that fiscal policy can affect the trend growth rate of real GDP. Explain.
2. Explain how a major tax cut will likely affect real output, the price level, interest rates and the size of the government budget deficit. Assume that monetary policy remains unchanged.
3. Explain how a major tax cut will likely affect real output, the price level, interest rates and the size of the government budget deficit. Assume that monetary policy remains unchanged.

## SUGGESTED READINGS

Burton, Maureen and Raymond Lombra, *The Financial System and the Economy: Principles of Money and Banking*, 3rd ed., Mason, Ohio, Thompson-Southwestern, 2003: Chapters 22, 22.

Sachs, Jeffrey and Felipe B. Larrain, *Macroeconomics in the Global Economy*, Englewood Cliffs, NJ: Prentice Hall, 1993, Chapters 12–14.

Tucker, Irvin B., *Survey of Economics*, 3rd ed., Mason, Ohio: Thompson-Southwestern, 2003 Chapters 24, 25, and 26.

Williams, Raburn McFetridge, *The Politics of Boom and Bust in Twentieth-Century America:A Macroeconomic History*, Minneapolis/St Paul, West Publishing Co., 1994, Chapters 20–27.

## *Chapter Twenty*

# The US and the Rest of the World: Money Markets, Goods Markets and Financial Markets

### WHY IS THE FOREIGN SECTOR IMPORTANT?

The foreign sector is important to the US economy for several reasons. First, net exports are a component of aggregate demand. An increase in net exports increases demand and a decrease in net exports decreases demand. Net exports are only about four or five percent of GDP and have been negative for the last 20 years. That means that they have been a drag on demand. However, along with our trade deficit has come a large import of funds from abroad. This has helped keep interest rates low and has led to substantial investment in real productive capacity in the US by foreign firms. This of course could change if the dollar weakens against other major currencies.

Also the price of exports and imports affects domestic prices. When the price of feed grains and food grains increased during the 1970s, it wasn't just exported grains whose price increased but the price of all grains, domestic and exported and the price of all products to which grains were a major input: livestock products, cereals, pastas and many more. Likewise with the increase in oil prices in the 1970s, oil prices increased worldwide. And the price of electricity, of coal, of plastics, and other goods that used oil as an input or that were substitutes for oil also increased. An export booms, resulting from high world demand, a falling international value of the dollar and easy US monetary policy drove the inflation of the 1970s.

Also US interest rates and foreign rates are inter-related through international financial markets. This is especially true of long-term rates but as we will see below rates also depend on rates of change of exchange rates. Short-term rates are more under the control of Central Bankers of the major countries or currency blocks.

## THE CIRCULAR FLOW OF GOODS AND SERVICES, FINANCIAL ASSETS AND MONEY BETWEEN THE U.S. AND THE REST OF THE WORLD

For convenience, economists often think of a two-country world: the US and the rest of the world (often referred to as ROW). The US and the rest of the world add up to the world economy. There are three primary types of flows between the US and ROW: flows of goods and services, flows of financial assets (capital funds) and flows of money or foreign exchange. These are shown in figure 20.1, a Circular Flow Diagram between the US and the Rest of the World.

### Flows of Goods and Services

These are shown at the top of the Circular Flow Diagram. We export goods and services to the ROW. They import goods and services from us. A fundamental accounting identity is that our exports (measured in dollars) to ROW must equal the ROW imports to us (also measured in dollars, or in foreign currency corrected by the exchange rate). Also we import goods and services from the ROW. They export goods and services to us. Again their exports measured in dollars must equal our imports measured in dollars. (We see below how to convert dollar values to foreign currency values). However our exports need not equal our imports. If the dollar value of exports exceeds the dollar value of imports then we have a trade surplus and the ROW has a trade deficit with us of equal (but negative) value. If our imports exceed our exports

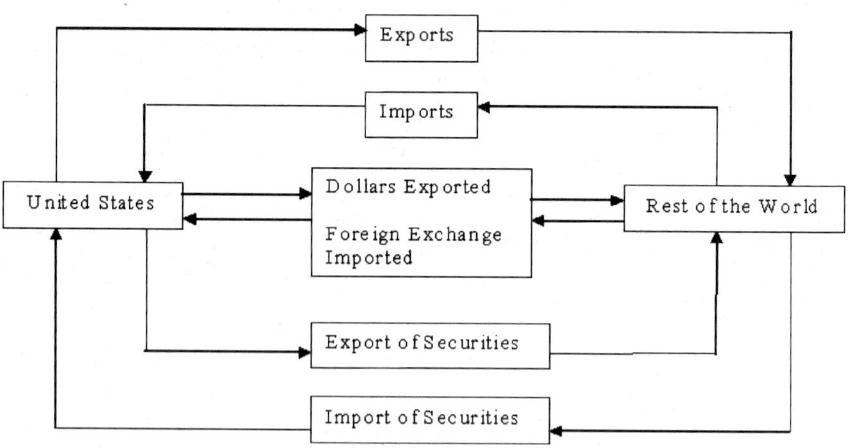


**Figure 20.1. Flow of Goods, Securities and Money; US and the Rest of the World**

in dollar values then we have a trade deficit. The ROW has a trade surplus of equal value in dollars. The US has been running a trade deficit with the rest of the world for close to 20 years.

Relative prices of goods and services are determined in the goods markets. Since prices of each country are in its own currency, to compare prices we must convert to a common currency.The relative price of a US good compared to a comparable foreign good is the US price divided by dollar price of the foreign good. The dollar price of the foreign good is the foreign currency price divided by the exchange rate where the exchange rate is the foreign currency price of one dollar.

## Flows of Financial Assets (or Liabilities)

These are shown in the bottom half of Figure 20.1. If we run a trade deficit it means that we pay more dollars to other countries to buy their goods and services than they pay foreign currencies to us (in dollar values) to buy our goods and services. We, in effect, become an importer of funds from the ROW. They use their excess dollars to buy financial assets issued by the US or to make direct investment in the US, say by building an auto plant here, or to accumulate dollars for transactions purposes or for store of value purposes. Dollars are usually considered a safe store of value and a ready means of exchange because most countries or businesses or individuals worldwide accept them. Flows of financial assets are considered the capital account. (Here we mean capital funds, not capital goods.)

In financial markets, relative interest rates are determined. The interest rate ratio is the ratio of the dollar yield on US securities to the dollar yield on foreign securities of comparable risk and maturity. The dollar yield on foreign securities is the foreign interest rates plus the rate of change in the exchange rate between the dollar and the foreign currency. If the rate of change of the exchange rate is positive it means the dollar is rising in value relative to the foreign currency.

## Flows of Money (or Foreign Exchange)

These are shown in the center of Figure 20.1. We export dollars to acquire (or import) foreign currencies in order to purchase foreign goods and services or foreign financial assets or foreign real assets. The ROW imports dollars (or exports foreign currencies) in order to buy our goods and services, our financial assets and our real assets. If we export more dollars than we import foreign currencies (in dollar terms) we have a positive balance of payments. If we import more foreign currencies (in dollar term) than we export dollars we have a negative balance of payments. The foreign exchange market is where exchange rates are determined. Currency flows are considered the balance of payments account. Our trade deficit is mostly offset by a capital account surplus. We are a net exporter of financial assets, or looked at the other way we are a net importer of funds. However, the trade deficit will only equal the capital account surplus if the balance of payments happens to be zero. The balance of payments is the difference between the two accounts. It is the difference between our export of dollars and our import of foreign currencies (valued in dollars).

## UNDERSTANDING EXCHANGE RATES

The exchange rate is the rate at which you can exchange one currency for another. If you go to Europe for vacation, you must convert your dollars to euros. The current rate is about $0.85 per Euro. Alternatively, 1/0.85 = 1.18. It takes 1.18 euros to buy 1.00 dollar. Shortly after the Euro was first issued the ratio was about 1.00. One dollar was equal to one Euro. In the early years of the Euro, say 2002, the Euro had fallen to about 0.80 dollars, or 1.25 euros per dollar. During 2003 and early 2004 the dollar was falling relative to the euro (or the euro was rising relative to the dollar) and the rate in the winter of 2004 was about 1.25 dollars per Euro. What difference does it make what the exchange rate is? Assuming domestic prices in Europe and in the US stay the same, if the dollar increases relative to the euro it means that US goods and services have gotten more expensive relative to European goods and services. It takes more euros to buy one dollar, and therefore more euros to buy any given quantity of US goods. Alternatively, if the dollar falls relative to the euro, and domestic prices in the US and Europe remain the same it means that US goods have become cheaper relative to comparable European goods. It now takes fewer euros to buy a given quantity of dollars and therefore a given quantity of US goods. If we look at the Yen something comparable has happened. It now takes about 115 yen to buy one dollar. Alternatively, one Yen costs 1/115 or $0.0087, a little less than one cent. In 2004 the yen was about 105 per dollar or one yen cost 1/105 or 0.0095 dollars, about one cent. The point is that the Yen price of dollars has risen in 2006. Again, if domestic prices haven't changed, it means that US goods have become more expensive to Japanese buyers. Or, alternatively, Japanese goods have become less expensive to American buyers.

Figure 20.2 shows the supply and demand for dollars relative to the Euro. On the vertical axis is the Euro price of dollars. This tells how many euros it takes to buy one dollar. The demand curve is the demand for dollars by the

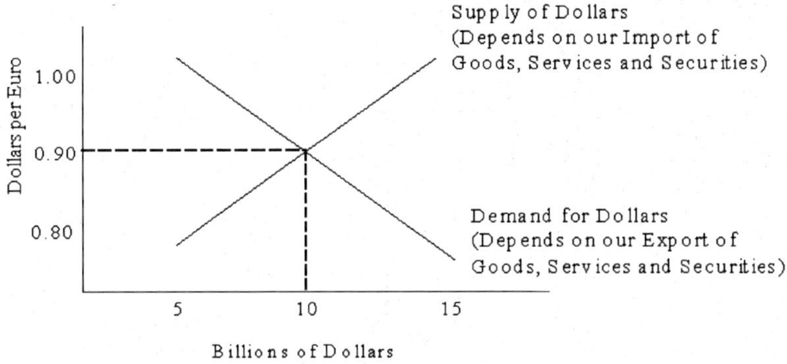


**Figure 20.2. Exchange Rate and the Supply and Demand for Dollars in Terms of Euros**

European Community and depends on their demand for our goods, services and securities as well as their demand for dollars as a reserve currency. In other words demand for dollars depends on our export of goods, services, securities and currency. As the exchange rate falls the price dollar of US goods, services and securities fall relative to the dollar price of European goods, services and securities. This gives us the downward sloping demand for dollars. The supply curve depends on our supply of dollars to the Euro Community. We supply dollars in order to get Euros to buy European goods, services or securities. This depends on our import of their goods, services, and securities. As the exchange rises the dollar price o European goods falls and we will demand more imports and supply more dollars to get euros to pay for them. In figure 21.2 the supply of dollar to the European Community is equal to the demand for dollars by the European community at 0.90 euros per dollar. Or alternatively, the dollar price of a euro is 1/0.90 = 1.11. It costs $1.11 to buy one Euro. The quantity of dollars demanded and supplied at that price is 10 million dollars. The numbers are purely illustrative.

Given the exchange rate, the primary thing that increases our exports is an increase in European income relative to US income. Also given the exchange rate the primary thing that increases our import is an increase in US income relative to European income. One reason our trade deficit has persisted is that for the last twenty years US income has been growing faster than income in Europe and Japan.

The other major factor that affects the exchange rate between the dollar and the Euro is the monetary polices of the US and of the European community. If we keep US real interest rates high relative to European real interest rates it will strengthen the dollar by increasing the demand for US securities. If we allow our real interest rates to be low relative to European real interest rates, it will weaken the dollar buy increasing our demand for European securities.

## PURCHASING POWER PARITY

Purchasing power parity exists when the dollar price of US goods equals the dollar price of comparable foreign goods. We express this in ratio form as:

(1) The price of US goods/(price of foreign goods/exchange rate) = 1 or
(2) The price of US goods = the price of foreign goods/exchange rate.

When the purchasing power ratio is equal to one we have purchasing power parity. This is a form of the law of one price. It says that the same goods should sell for the same price in different markets. When the ratio is greater than one, the dollar price of US goods is greater than the dollar price of foreign goods. When this is the case, for goods in general, we say that the dollar is overvalued (or the foreign currency is under valued). At the current exchange rate US goods are more expensive than comparable foreign goods. If the purchasing power ratio is less than one for goods in general then we say the dollar is undervalued (or the foreign currency is overvalued). To do this for goods in general we have to compare comparable bundles of goods for each country. And we would have to use price indexes for each countries goods. And ideally we would want to look at tradable goods only, since we do not expect that the prices of goods that are not tradable across countries to be equalized.

Let us take a simple example for an individual good. Suppose a Ford Taurus costs 25,000 dollars and a Volkswagen Passant costs 25,000 euros and the exchange rate is one then 25,000 dollars/(25,000 euros/1) = 1.00. We make the perhaps heroic assumption that the two cars are comparable. At an exchange rate of 1.0 we have purchasing power parity. If the euro falls (the dollar rises) to 1.25 euros per dollar then if the domestic prices have not changed the purchasing power ratio is 25,000 dollars/(25,000 euros/1.25) = 1.25. The dollar price of the VW is now $20,000 and the Ford is still $25,000. The price of the VW has fallen relative to the price of the Ford.

If instead the euro rises relative to the dollar (the dollar falls) say to 0.80 euros per dollar then the price ratio will be 25,000 dollars/(25,000 euros/0.80) = 0.8. The dollar price of the VW is now $31,250. The dollar price of the Taurus is still $25,000. The point is, that changes in exchange rates changes the relative price of goods. If the dollar rises in value it makes US goods more expensive to other countries. When the dollar falls it makes US goods less expensive to other countries.

For goods in general we would look at an index of the value of the dollar. We would look at how the dollar changed relative to other major currencies. As with a price index, the index is on a base of 100 for a selected base year. If the index rises, the dollar rises in value relative to the other major currencies. The annual percent rate of change in the index will measure the change in the value of the dollar. If the change is positive, the dollar is rising. If it is negative, the dollar is falling.

Realize of course that the purchasing power ratio can change if the relative prices of goods change, as well as from changes in exchanges in rates. If productivity in auto production is higher in the US than in Germany, then we would expect over time for the price of US cars to fall relative to the price of German cars, at any given exchange rate.

Purchasing power parity can also be expressed as rates of change in prices and exchange rates over time. This is called dynamic purchasing power parity. Expressing equation (2) above as rates of change over time (say per year) we have:

(3) The percent change in US prices = the percent change in foreign prices − the percent change in the value of the dollar, or:
(4) The percent rate change in the value of the dollar = the percent change in foreign prices − the percent change in US prices.

If foreign prices are rising faster that US prices, then purchasing power parity requires that the dollar be rising. If US prices are rising faster than foreign prices then purchasing power parity requires that the dollar be falling.

Realize that purchasing power parity rarely holds exactly, either in the form of levels of prices or in the form of rates of change of prices. It probably comes closest to holding for basic commodities that are highly standardized and that are traded in international markets. Wheat, corn, soybeans, gold, silver and crude oil might be examples. For differentiated products like automobiles, or computers it will hold much less well. For many products tariffs, export subsidies, and import quotas keep purchasing power parity from holding. And for all goods there will be differences due to transportation and distribution costs. And for non-tradable goods purchasing power parity will not necessarily hold.

What is important is that the purchasing power parity relation tells us the directions that we can expect prices to change when exchange rates change. In the 1970s US prices were raising faster than prices for some of our major trading partners, in particular Europe and Japan. At the same time the dollar fell relative to these other major currencies. Did rising prices cause the dollar to fall, or did the falling dollar cause prices to rise: Probably a little of both.

For basic commodities, the price change came simultaneously with the falling dollar. For final goods price changes lagged the falling dollar by at least a year. Thus changes in exchange rates can be taken to be a leading indicator as to the direction of change in final goods prices. It will be more important for countries where exports and imports are a large share of GDP. It will be less important for countries where exports and imports are a relatively small share of GDP.

For the US exports run about 12 percent of GDP and imports run about 15 percent of GDP. In the 1970s, inflation was driven by high demand for exports and a falling dollar. This could not have occurred if the FED had been willing to push interest rates higher and slowed money growth sooner. In the eighties we had the opposite situation. Decisive action by the FED in 1981–82 slowed the economy and led to a rising dollar that continued to rise until late 1985. At the same time basic commodity prices in the US collapsed, both due to falling world demand and the rising dollar. The sharp fall in commodity prices made possible the sudden decline in inflation that occurred between 1983 and 1986.

Recently (2003–2005) the dollar had been falling and commodity prices had been rising. If the FED had continued to keep short-term interest rates low (one percent Federal Funds Rate target) we could expect an increase in inflation in a year or so. When the dollar falls, to move toward purchasing power parity, either US prices must rise or prices in the rest of the world must fall. Likely there will be some of both. Japan has seen falling prices for a decade, partially due to its overvalued currency. Starting in mid 2004 the FED started pushing up short-term interest rates and has continued to do so in 2005 and early 2006. But rising inflation has kept real short term interest rates negative through 2005. They are probably slightly positive in mid 2006.

## INTEREST RATE PARITY

Interest rate parity says that the dollar yield on US securities should equal the dollar yield on comparable foreign securities. In ratio form this is expressed as:

(5) The US interest rate/(the foreign interest rate − the rate of change in the value of the dollar) = 1.0, or

(6) The US interest rate = the foreign interest rate − the rate of change in the value of the dollar.

If the ratio given by equation (5) is greater than one, the dollar yield on US securities is greater than the dollar yield on foreign securities. If the ratio is less than one the dollar yield on US securities is less than the dollar yield on foreign securities. The dollar yield on foreign securities is the foreign interest rate minus the rate of appreciation of the dollar. We subtract the rate of appreciation of the dollar because it represents how much foreign securities are deprecating in value relative to US securities. If the US interest rate is 6% and the dollar is appreciating at three percent per year then the foreign rate is 9% to give interest rate parity. If US interest rates are 6% and the dollar is depreciating at 3% per year then the foreign rate would have to be 3% to have interest rate parity. If we have dynamic purchasing power parity and interest rate parity, we can derive another fundamental relation:

(7) The US interest rate − the US inflation rate = the foreign interest rate − the foreign inflation rate.

This relation says that real interest rates will be equalized across countries. For each country the real interest rate is the nominal rate minus the inflation rate. If US interest rates are 6% and US inflation is 3% then the US real rate is 3%. If the foreign interest rate is 9% and foreign inflation is 6% then the foreign real rate is also equal to 3% and equal to the US real rate.

Realize that interest rate parity only holds approximately for securities of similar risk and maturity. It comes closer to holding on long-term securities traded in international markets. Short-term securities are strongly influenced, at least in the short run, by central banks in their pursuit of monetary policy. Like purchasing power parity, interest rate parity is primarily important because it tells us the direction that interest rates will change when there are changes in inflation rates or exchange rates. If inflation in the US rises relative to other countries, we can expect nominal interest rates to rise in order to keep real rates from falling. Likewise, a rise in inflation in the US relative to other countries will mean that the dollar will likely fall to bring us back toward purchasing power parity.

## EXCHANGE RATES AND TRADE

There is a basic contradiction in using exchange rate policy to promote trade. First to attract foreign funds a country needs a strong currency. But to encourage exports a country needs a weak currency. When countries allow their currencies to become overvalued it attracts foreign funds. But when foreign investors realize that the country can't defend the overvalued currency, the funds flow out and the country is forced to devalue. With devaluation and a weakened currency, exports will rise at least in the short run. But over the longer term devaluation usually leads to higher inflation and the initial gains are lost as the price of exports rise back toward purchasing power parity. The US has not been exempt from these problems. In the seventies when the dollar fell we had an export boom, especially in the raw material industries. But along with the falling dollar came rising inflation. At the end of the seventies and beginning of the eighties, the FED tightened, the dollar rose and inflation came down. Those same industries that had a boom in the seventies, now suffered a severe recession in the first two thirds of the eighties. In the late eighties the dollar fell and the export industries recovered. Figure 20.3 shows the index of the real value of the dollar from 1973–2004. The real value is the index of the nominal value adjusted for changes in the consumer price indexes. The dollar fell sharply in the seventies. Our series starts in 1973 when the dollar was allowed to float. Estimates of the real value in 1970 put it at about 120. (See Herendeen and Hallberg.)

During the first two thirds eighties the dollar remained strong, and US inflation fell. The US economy enjoyed a long expansion, despite a substantial

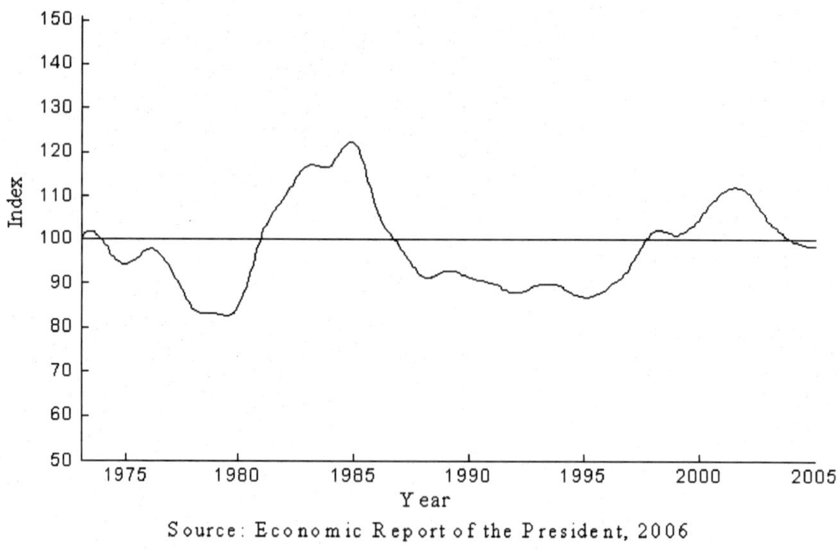


**Figure 20.3. Index of the Real Value of the Dollar, 1973–2005**

trade deficit and budget deficits. The dollar fell in the late eighties and stayed at an index of about 90 from 1988–1995. We had a long expansion in the nineties. The dollar was strong in the latter nineties until about 2001. During 2003–2005 the dollar was falling with the implicit approval of the Bush Administration. The hope was that the cheaper dollar would lead to a reduction of the U.S. trade deficit. It did not happened. Although exports increased some, imports increased even faster. Imports rose mainly because of growth of US income as we have recovered from the recession. The problem is that commodity prices have been rising and this is likely to feed through to higher inflation. The FED has been increasing interest rates in 2005 and 2006 but rising inflation has kept real interest rates very low.

## PURCHASING POWER PARITY AS A GUIDE TO POLICY

When the US moved to flexible exchange rates in the seventies, most economists did not anticipate the highly volatile exchange rates that we have experienced over the last thirty years. This volatility affects the US economy through its effect on aggregate demand and its effect on inflation. It also affects other countries, especially those that are major trading partners and/or countries that have tied their currencies to the dollar. This problem is compounded by the fact that the dollar is the major international currency. Other countries use dollars as reserves against which they issue their own currencies and as store of value and transactions balances for use in international exchange.

Before 1973, when the dollar was allowed to float, each country in the international monetary system had a fixed price for gold that was used as international reserves. By having a fixed price of gold they also had fixed exchange rates with each other. This was known as a fixed exchange rate system. For the system to work countries had to maintain roughly the same rates of inflation. If one country had a higher rate of inflation over a sustained period of time, its currency, at the official rate, would become overvalued and eventually it would be forced to devalue. The International Monetary Fund was responsible for helping countries defend their currencies by lending them reserves, or when devaluation became inevitable, they would help engineer the devaluation and lend funds to defend the new exchange rate. The problem was that most countries were unable or unwilling to maintain comparable rates of inflation and the system broke down in the late sixties and early seventies when US inflation exceeded inflation in Western Europe and Japan and the US decided to no longer maintain the fixed dollar price of gold of $35.00 per ounce. We essentially went off the gold standard and allowed the dollar to float, i.e., find its own value in the market for international exchange.

Since then we have been on what might be called a dollar standard but with a mixed system for determining exchange rates. Some countries peg their currencies to the dollar; other countries allow their currencies to float against the dollar. To defend a pegged currency, if the currency is falling, a country can buy its currency on the open market using its reserve currency, usually dollars. It can also push up domestic interest rates and tighten domestic monetary policy. The problem is that most smaller countries and often even larger countries do not have enough reserves to defend their currency once the markets have decided that a currency is overvalued. Even borrowing from the IMF usually cannot prevent devaluation. If a countries currency peg is too low, so that the currency, at the official rate is undervalued, then the country must sell its currency on the open market, accumulating reserves(usually of dollars) in exchange. At the same time it can lower interest rates to encourage the currency to fall. Most attempts to peg currencies in the last 30 years have failed. Most economists believe that individual countries should allow their currencies to float and defend their currencies through domestic monetary policy. In other words control the domestic inflation rate and the countries exchange rate will be relatively stable in the market.

This policy might work for small countries, but what about major currencies like the Dollar, the Euro or the Yen. U.S. inflation has been relatively stable over the past twenty years (since 1985). The index of the value of the dollar has varied greatly but its trend has remained about constant at an index of about 100. (See figure 20.3 above.) These fluctuations lead to shifts in import and export prices that affect not only the US but also other countries. The sharp rise in the dollar relative to the yen in 1995–1998 contributed to the Southeast Asia Crisis of 1997–98. This was because these countries were pegging to the dollar and when the dollar went up relative to the Yen and other currencies their currencies did too and became overvalued. These countries experienced financial crisis as funds flowed out of the countries and they were forced to devalue and suffered severe recessions. The crisis eased when the FED lowered interest rates three times in late 1998, and the dollar fell back to a more reasonable level at least temporarily.

The view of some economists is that the FED in cooperation with the Treasury and major Central Banks should consider a policy of attempting to maintain approximate purchasing power parity between the dollar and the other major currencies, especially the yen and the euro. It would do this by targeting a stable index of the value of the dollar. The target might be 100 (this is about the trend value in figure 20.3) if this was determined to be a value that gave approximate purchasing power parity with the other major currencies. This would be a long run target. The index could rise or fall within predetermined limits. In the short run, however if the index fell below the predetermined limit, the Fed would increase short-term interest rates and sell foreign currencies (buy dollars) to attempt to strengthen the dollar. If the index rose above its predetermined limit, the FED would lower short-term interest rates and sell dollars in order to weaken the dollar. Selling dollars would involve buying foreign exchange. For maximum affect the FED should not sterilize the foreign exchange purchases or sales. In other words purchases of foreign exchange should not be offset by sales of US government securities by the FED. Sales of foreign exchange should not be offset by purchases of US government securities by the FED.

Would this mean is that domestic stability would be sacrificed for international stability? In most cases there is probably not a conflict. A stable dollar will keep US inflation from accelerating or decelerating. Thus this policy is not necessarily inconsistent with targeting a long run inflation rate. A stable dollar would also likely help stabilize the US business cycle. The FED could still use monetary policy to stabilize over the business cycle but would keep as its primary objective the international value of the dollar in terms of stable purchasing power. This does not mean fixed exchange rates. Individual rates would still be allowed to change as long as the index of the value of the dollar remained relatively stable. This system would only work if coordinated with the monetary and exchange rate policies of the other major countries or currency blocks. The US, the European Community, Japan and, in time, China would have to agree that maintaining stable international purchasing power for their currencies.

In the past 25 years the index of the value of the dollar has varied much more than the inflation rate. However if we look at prices of internationally traded commodities we would see that they have varied about as much as the value of the dollar but in an inverse relation. A stable dollar and stable commodity prices would likely also mean a stable inflation rate. In the past a strong dollar has helped keep inflation in check. A falling dollar as in the seventies contributed to rising inflation.

Fiscal policy could be used to supplement monetary policy to help maintain the stability of the domestic economy. Higher interest rates to strengthen the dollar could be supplemented with a tax cut to offset the depressing effect of higher interest rates. Or if lower interest rates were called for to weaken the dollar, it could be supplemented with a tax increase to offset the expansionary effects of lower interest rates. Unfortunately, this would require more coordination of fiscal and monetary policy than we currently have. In the immediate future putting more emphasis on the value of the dollar is unlikely. The incoming chairman of the FED, Ben Bernanke, is a supporter of inflation targeting. The FED is likely to continue either implicitly or explicitly to put primary emphasis on the inflation rate.

## SUMMARY

With domestic trade we have one currency and essentially no barriers to trade between states. With foreign trade there are exchange rate problems because most countries have their own currency. Some countries peg their currencies to the dollar and others allow their currencies to float against the dollar. The dollar has floated since 1973. The criterion for judging exchange rate policy is purchasing power parity. Purchasing power parity say that the dollar price of a US good should equal the dollar price of a comparable foreign good. The dollar price of a foreign good is the foreign price divided by the exchange rate.

## REVIEW QUESTIONS

Multiple Choice: Select the correct answer:

1. If U.S. inflation is greater than ROW inflation we expect he dollar to:
   a. Appreciate
   b. Depreciate
   c. Not change
2. A decrease in the value of the dollar relative to other currencies will lead to:
   a. A decrease in US net exports and a decrease in US prices.
   b. An increase in US net exports and an increase in US prices.
   c. An increase in US net exports and a decrease in US prices.
   d. A decrease in US net exports and an increase in US prices.
3. The real interest rate is:
   a. The nominal rate divided by the price level
   b. The nominal rate times the price level.
   c. The nominal rate minus the inflation rate.
   d. The nominal rate plus inflation rate.
4. The nominal interest rate is:
   a. The real rate divided by the price level.
   b. The real rate times the price level.

   c. The real rate minus the inflation rate.
   d. The real rate plus inflation rate.
5. Under fixed exchange rates, to maintain purchasing power parity US inflation would have to:
   a. Be greater than ROW inflation.
   b. Approximately equal ROW inflation.
   c. Be less than ROW inflation.
6. A decrease in US real interest rates relative to ROW real interest rates will:
   a. Strengthen the value of the dollar.
   b. Weaken the value of the dollar.
   c. Not change the value of the dollar.
7. The dollar is undervalued when the dollar price of US goods is
   a. Less than the dollar price of comparable foreign goods.
   b. Greater than the dollar price of comparable foreign goods.
   c. Equal to the dollar price of comparable foreign goods.
8. An undervalued dollar is equivalent to:
   a. A tax on US imports and a subsidy to US exports.
   b. A subsidy to US imports and a tax on US exports.
   c. Neither of the above.
9. A depreciation of the dollar leads to:
   a. Increased yield on US securities held by foreigners.
   b. Decreased yield on US securities held by foreigners.
   c. No effect on the yield on US securities held by foreigners.

### Essays

1. What is purchasing power parity? Why is it a good criterion for judging exchange rate policy? Explain.
2. The US has run large trade deficits for the last 20 years. Despite these deficits the US dollar has remained a strong international currency for most of these 20 years. Why have trade deficits not led to a weakening dollar? Explain.

## SUGGESTED READINGS

Eichengreen, Barry, *Gold Fetters*, Oxford: Oxford University Press, 1992.

Herendeen, James B. and Milton Hallberg, "What Drives Agricultural Cycles," *Challenge: The Magazine of Economic Affairs*," 40, no. 1 (January-February, 1997), 72–86.

McKinnon, Ronald, "Monetary and Exchange Rate Policies for International Financial Stability: A Proposal," *Journal of Economic Perspectives*, 2, no. 1 (Winter, 1988): 83–103.

Olson, Mancur, "The Case for Liberalizing Markets: Interview with Mancur Olson, Jr.," *Challenge: The Magazine of Economic Affairs*, 40, no. 5 (September/October, 1997): 59–79.

Sachs, Jeffrey and Felipe B. Larrain, *Macroeconomics in the Global Economy*, Englewood Cliffs: Prentice Hall, 1993, Chapters 10, 13,14.

Salvatore, Dominick, *International Economics*, Fourth Edition, New York, Macmillan, 1993.

Williamson, John, "Comment on McKinnon's Monetary Rule," *Journal of Economic Perspectives*, 2, no. 1 (Winter 1988): 113–19.

*Chapter Twenty-One*

# The Role of Financial Markets

## THE ROLE OF FINANCE IN THE ECONOMIC SYSTEM

### Micro Finance and Macro Finance

Micro finance deals with financial decisions of firms and households regarding decisions to save (and invest in financial assets) and decisions to borrow. Both households and firms must finance their economic activity. They do this in two primary ways: either from internally generated funds or from externally generated funds. Internally generated funds come from having current receipts exceed current expenditure for goods and services. When that is the case a spending unit is a net saver or surplus spending unit. If the spending unit spends more in the current period on goods and services than current receipts during the period it is a net borrower or deficit spending unit. Financial markets and financial intermediaries allocate funds from net savers to net borrowers. Macro finance deals with finance at the aggregate level: with the determinants of the general level of interest rates and with the aggregate supply and demand for funds. Macro finance may deal with an individual country such as the U.S. or with the world economy.

Financial markets may be local, regional, national or international in scope. At the local, regional and national level financial markets in the U.S. are well integrated and usually well functioning. This is because we all use the same currency, and all accept the same set of rules. At the international level financial markets may function less well because different countries have different currencies with all of the problems of exchange rates that we discussed in the previous chapter. They also may have different sets of rules regarding regulations of financial markets; regarding rights and enforceability of contracts; regarding property rights and regarding bankruptcy and loan renegotiation procedures.

Between the developed countries there are generalized accepted rules that most countries adhere to. Among the developing countries and former communist block countries, financial markets are much less well developed and have varying sets of rules.

## DIRECT AND INDIRECT FINANCE

Direct finance is when the original saver has a claim against a final borrower. If you as an individual own a bond issued by General Motors, your claim represents direct finance. You may buy the bond though a broker and the broker may take a commission for his services but your claim is still against General Motors. If instead you buy a mutual fund, the mutual fund may own bonds or stock in General Motors as well as many other corporations. This is indirect finance. You have a claim against the mutual fund; the mutual fund in turn has a claim against General Motors. Direct finance is finance through the financial markets. Indirect finance is finance through financial intermediaries. Direct finance can take many forms: There are money markets that deal in very short-term financial assets: Examples would be the federal funds market, the commercial paper market and the treasury bills market. Long-term markets would include the stock market and the bond market. Intermediate term markets would include the market for treasury notes or for notes of large corporations.

Indirect finance includes several major types. First there are Depository Institutions. These institutions issue checkable deposits and make loans and are required to hold reserves with the FED. These include commercial banks, savings and loan associations, savings banks and credit unions. Second, there are contract type intermediaries. These include primarily insurance companies and pension funds. Insurance companies raise funds by selling various types of insurance policies (such as life insurance). The funds raised are primarily in the form of premiums paid on the policies by the purchaser (owner) of the policy. The insurance company in turn invests the funds in stocks, bonds, mortgages, real estate or other types of income earning assets. It must keep enough liquid assets to pay out claims when they come due. Pension funds collect funds from their members or the member's employers during the workers earning years. These funds are invested in financial assets such as stocks, bonds, mutual funds, mortgages or other financial assets. When workers retire the pension fund must pay out pensions according to the terms of the retirement plan.

Third, there are investment type intermediaries. These are mostly various types of mutual funds. Mutual funds invest in various types of financial assets to offer to investors various mixes of risk and return through diversification that the average individual investor could not achieve for himself/herself through direct investment.

Fourth there are finance companies. These are similar to depository institutions but they do not issue deposits, either checkable or non-checkable. Instead they raise their funds primarily from borrowing either in the financial markets or from banks. In addition they raise capital from their shareholders and from internally generated funds. They in turn lend the funds to households or to firms.

Last there are other institutions that are either government run or government related. The Federal Housing Administration that insures loans of financial institutions to mostly low-income households. The Farm Credit Administration makes loans to farmers, (See chapter 9). Fanny Mae and Freddy Mac buy mortgages from financial institutions to create an active secondary market for mortgages. They fund their purchases by selling securities in the financial markets. Although technically independent, these agencies have implicit government backing and most investors believe that in case of financial distress, the government would come to the rescue. In the 1980s, the Farm Credit System was insolvent as a result of a seven-year recession in agriculture. Congress came to the rescue to bail the system out. Recently Fanny Mae and Freddy Mac have come under criticism in the press and in Congress for having financial arrangements that might pose too much risk for creditors and shareholders.

## PRIMARY MARKETS AND SECONDARY MARKETS

Primary markets are markets for new issues of securities. These markets are often private placement for new companies and the organized markets for new issues of established companies. Secondary markets are markets where existing issues are traded. The same market, say the New York Stock Exchange may sell both new issues and existing issues, just like a car dealer may sell both new cars and used cars. However the bulk of the trading in both the stock market and the bond market is in existing issues.

## WHY ARE SECONDARY MARKETS IMPORTANT?

Secondary markets are important for several reasons. First they convert relatively illiquid assets into relatively liquid assets. Very few people would be willing to hold long-term bonds of 20 or 30 years if there were no secondary market for bonds. Without a secondary market an investor would have to hold the bond to maturity to get his money or find a private buyer that would be willing to buy it. Few investors would be willing to do this unless the interest reward was very high. The same is true of stocks. Stocks have infinite maturity. There is no promise by the issuer to repay principle at some future date. Instead to cash in a stock you must sell it in the secondary market. Mortgages are similar to bonds; without a secondary market they would be difficult to sell.

Second, secondary markets are important because they reduce the cost of funds to borrowers, especially long-term borrowers. This is directly the result of the increased liquidity mentioned above. As long as investors know that they can sell the security at any time (with of course risk of possible capital loss or capital gain), the investor is willing to hold the security at a much lower interest rate or yield. Countries that do not have well developed secondary markets have much higher cost of long-term funds and therefore much greater difficulty making profitable long-term investments in real assets.

Third, secondary markets allow for the separation of ownership and control. Corporations are, in principle. owned by millions of shareholders, often indirectly through mutual funds: Top executives and the Board of Directors control the corporations. Without secondary markets this separation would be impossible.

Fourth secondary markets make possible the separation of saving and investing decisions. Millions of individual financial investors make the saving decisions; corporate executives make the investing decisions. Here we mean investing in real productive assets.

Fifth, secondary markets make possible a market for corporate control. This market involves acquisitions, mergers, takeovers and leveraged buy-outs and works primarily through investment bankers and specialized firms that exist to buy and sell other firms.

Sixth, secondary markets are important in the pricing of assets. Because of secondary markets it is easy to determine what firms are worth (or at least what the market thinks they are worth). This is very valuable information for professional investors, for investment bankers and specialists in the market for corporate control.

In order for secondary markets to develop and offer low cost long-term funds to borrowers it is also necessary to have low and stable inflation and relatively stable exchange rates. Without stable exchange rates, in terms of purchasing power parity, it is difficult to have low and stable inflation, especially for smaller countries that have relatively high imports and exports. And without low and stable inflation it is difficult to have secondary markets for long-term funds.

## THE PRICING OF FINANCIAL ASSETS

The financial markets determine the prices and yields on financial assets. The yields represent the current yield to investors. The price represents the present value of the expected income stream from the financial asset. For a bond the price depends on the coupon rate, the market discount rate and the maturity of the bond. The coupon rate is the interest rate promised on the face value of the bond. The coupon rate is usually a fixed rate. The face value is usually $1000; if the coupon rate is 10 percent, then the bond promises investors $100 per year until maturity when the principle and final years interest are paid. As market interest rates change the value of the bond will change. If market interest rates are 10% for bonds of comparable risk and maturity then the price should equal the face value of $1000. If interest rates have risen since the bond was issued, then its price will have to fall until the yield on the bond is approximately equal to the yield on new bonds. If the price falls to $950 the current yield will be (100/950)(100) = 10.5%. The yield to maturity will also depend on the number of years to maturity and whether the bond was purchased at greater or less than its par value. If interest rates on securities of similar risk and maturity fall after the bond is issued its price will rise so that its yield is comparable to the yield on new bonds. If the price rises to $1050 then the current yield is (100/1050)(100) = 9.5%. The longer the maturity of the bond, the greater the price changes for any given change in interest rates.

Thus, if interest rates are volatile, long-term bond prices will also be volatile. If the FED changes short rates this will also change expected future short rates that in turn will effect long rates and thus bond prices. Currently the Federal Funds rate target is 5%. If later this year (2006) the FED raises the Federal Funds rate target, then bond prices will likely fall. How much they fall will depend in part on whether the FED is expected to keep raising short rates. Thus the general rule is that bond prices move inversely to market interest rates and the longer the maturity the greater the price change for any given change in interest rates.

Stock prices follow the same principle except that the income stream that is discounted is much less certain. The price of a stock is the discounted value of the expected stream of future dividends. Dividends are an allocation out of net income to be paid to shareholders. The top management of the corporation determines how much dividends are paid. They may decide to pay no dividends. This can be the case for two primary reasons. First they may pay no dividends because they have very profitable investment opportunities within the firm. Microsoft, for example, paid no dividends until the last few years. It now pays a relatively low dividend. Firms with high-expected growth usually pay out a very small share of income or none at all. The other reason for not paying dividends is because the firm is having financial difficulties and can't afford to pay dividends. Normally firms keep dividends at a relatively stable percent of the book value of the firm's equity. This means that dividends tend to vary much less than net income but they grow over time as the firm adds to it equity by reinvesting part of net income.

The price of a stock is the discounted value of the current period dividend plus the discounted value of the expected capital gain. An increase in the discount rate will decrease the price of the stock. A decrease in the discount rate will increase the price of the stock. The expected capital gain represents expected future profits. An increase in expected future profits will increase the price of the stock. A decrease in expected future profits will decrease the price of the stock. So stock prices are affected negatively by the discount rate and positively by expected profits and one may offset the other or one may reinforce the other. The realized yield on a stock to shareholders is the current dividend yield plus the realized capital gain. The dividend yield is the current dividend divided by the price at the beginning of the period. The realized capital gain is the change in price during the period divided by the price at the beginning of the period. Both ratios must be multiplied by 100 to convert the yields to percentage rates. The yield to the shareholder represents the cost of equity funds to the firm.

The price earnings ratio is the ratio of current price per share divided by current earnings per share. A high price earnings ratio implies a high expected future growth rate. A low price earnings ratio implies a low expected growth rate. The inverse of the price earnings ratio is the earnings-price ratio. This number times 100 is the percent earnings yield. This number will not usually be the same as the yield to shareholders described above. For example if the P-E ratio were 20 the earnings yield would only be 5%. A shareholder would not hold a stock that was only yielding 5% unless he expected positive capital gains. But the correct total yield is the dividend yield (which is net of retained funds) plus the capital gain.

The stock market can become overvalued when investors become overconfident about expected future profits. In the late nineties technology and inter-net stocks with little or no current earnings were selling at very high prices based on inflated expectations about future profits. When it became apparent that these expected profits were not going to be realized, the stock prices fell.

## DETERMINANTS OF BUSINESS INVESTMENT IN EARNING ASSETS

Firms invest in earning assets in order to expand capacity to meet future demand or to create new or better products and to create future demand through investing in advertising and promotion. They also invest in inventories of raw materials, goods in process, finished goods and cash operating funds. The determinants of investment are the expected after tax rate of return on new investment, the current level of excess capacity, the after tax cost of funds to the firm, the terms under which credit is available, and the amount of current profits. Firms can raise funds in three ways: they can retain earning (i.e., not pay them out to shareholders), they can borrow or they can issue new shares.

Most large corporations raise a majority of their long-term funds through retained earnings; most of the rest comes from borrowing and a small portion comes from new issues of stock. New firms that are going public for the first time rely more heavenly on new issues. Firms borrow long term, i.e., they issue bonds, to finance long-term assets such as plant and equipment or land. Bonds may be mortgage bonds that are secured by real property, or collateral bonds that are secured by financial assets or unsecured bonds that are basically secured by the reputation of the company. Bonds are issued for terms of 10 years or more; usually 20 or 30 years, sometimes as long as 50 years. Can you imagine anyone holding a 50 year bond if there wasn't an active secondary market? Notes that can vary from 1–10 years finance intermediate-term assets. Very short-term assets, such as inventories, are financed by commercial paper that is usually under one year in maturity. Notes or commercial paper may be secured or unsecured.

## LIMITS ON THE ABILITY TO BORROW

Firms are limited in their ability to borrow by essentially the same things that households are. (Recall Chapter 4 above): First, net present assets (assets minus debt) plus any assets being acquired by the investment limit their ability to borrow. Assets provide collateral, either explicit or implicit (when debt is unsecured). Collateral is a plcdge by the firm that it intends to repay the debt. In the event of non-repayment the lender can take the assets pledged and sell them to attempt to get back its funds.

Second, the expected income stream limits the ability to borrow. For a new investment it is the new income to be created by the investment. Important are the expected growth of the income, the variability or uncertainty of the income and the amount of the income that will be available for debt service. To service its existing debt structure it is the net income stream of the firm that is important.

Third, the firm is limited by the terms under which credit is available. These include the interest rate paid, any fees or issue cost, the maturity of debt available, the collateral requirement imposed on the firm, the rate at which the debt can be amortized, and the term under which the debt is to be repaid.

Large corporations raise most of their debt through investment banking firms. These firms package the debt and sell it to investors usually indirectly through mutual funds, pension funds and insurance companies. For large issues they often parcel out part of the debt to other investment banking firms. New issues of equity are also issued through investment banking firms. Investment banking firms, unlike commercial banks, do not usually make loans. Instead they package the loans and sell them to the public making their money on a small margin between the issue price and the sale price of the loans. Credit rating companies rate the debt of large corporations and also the municipal debt of state and local governments. The companies or municipalities pay a fee to the rating company. The rating company then publishes the ratings so that they are available to potential investors,

Small businesses usually rely on bank loans or loans though mortgage companies or business finance companies. They also often rely on credit card debt even though it is very expensive. Proprietary firms and small family held corporations must save part of current income and invest it if they are to grow. With a large corporation the saving and investment decisions are separate. Shareholders are saving part of current income when they accept dividends that are only a portion of earnings. But the managers of the corporation need not forego current consumption for the firm to grow. They make the investment decisions, millions of individual shareholders or bondholders make the saving decisions.

## DERIVATIVE CONTRACTS

Other types of financial contracts that have grown greatly in recent years are called derivatives. They are called derivatives because they derive their value from some underlying asset, either real or financial. These include futures contracts, options, strips or swaps and many more. The purpose of most derivatives is to spread or diversifies risk. A farmer plants his corn in the spring and harvests it in the fall. But the price may rise or fall by fall. If he thinks it will fall he can lock in the present price by promising to deliver, say, 50,000 bushels in December for todays price of, say $4.00 per bushel. But who will buy such a contract? A cereal manufacturer may have to buy corn for production of corn flakes in the future but he doesn't want to risk a price increase. He can buy a 50,000 bushels contract at $4.00 per bushel for delivery in December. That way he has locked in the $4.00 price. So the farmer is betting against a price decrease: the cereal producer is betting against a price increase. By entering the futures market they can both hedge their bets.

The commodity exchanges trade these contracts for a small commission. In addition speculators buy or sell futures contracts in the hope that they bet the right way and make money. It is very similar to a loan contract. The borrower needs money today and promises to repay at a future date and at a given interest rate. The lender is offering the money today to be repaid at a future date at the agreed upon interest rate. With a futures contract you can trade without putting up the full amount of the money. Only about 10% down is required. If the contract increases in value your equity has increased. If it decreases in value your equity has decreased and you will be asked to either sell your contract or put up more cash. Buying on margin means you can leverage your gains but also leverage your losses. This makes investing in futures attractive to speculators. If they make money over and above the interest on the borrowed portion, it all accrues to the small initial investment. Thus if they are lucky you can make a very high rate of return on the initial investment. However if they are unlucky all the losses accrue to the original investment and they can make a very low or negative return on the original investment.

Futures contracts have also been extended to financial assets including government bonds, stock indexes, foreign exchange and many others. All work essentially to allow hedging of risk, but also allow a place for high-risk investors to invest and to carry some of the risk. The ability to invest with relatively high leverage adds to the attraction for high-risk investors. In addition to all types of futures markets we also have markers for stock options. Stock options give the investor an option to buy a stock at a future date at a predetermined price. If the price of the stock rises above this price the option is in the money and can be sold for a profit. On the other side an investor may be willing to buy an option to sell a stock at a predetermined price for delivery at a future date. If the price of the stock falls he can buy it at the lower price and deliver it at a profit. Again options only require a small down payment so investors can operate with relatively high leverage. In the 1990s with a rising stock market, stock options became an important way to reward executives. We discussed this earlier in chapter 14.

## FINANCIAL INNOVATION

Financial innovation is an important aspect of economic development. Secondary markets in stocks and bonds developed in the 19th Century in the US. This greatly reduced the cost of long-term funds to investors and helped finance the rapid industrial development of the later half of the 19th Century. Out of the Great Depression after World War II came the development of the amortized mortgage and later the development of a well functioning secondary market in home mortgages. This made cheap mortgages available to the bulk of the population and financed the movement out of the cities to the suburbs that has occurred over the past 50 years. Futures markets allowed hedging against risk first in agricultural markets and in the last 30 years the same type of markets have developed in all kinds of financial markets. These make markets more efficient and reduce the cost of doing business.

## COMPETITION IN FINANCIAL MARKETS

Competitive financial markets mean that financial services will be provided at least cost. This means that the gains of innovation are passed on to consumers in the form of lower costs of funds or better terms of credit. 50 years ago a typical homebuyer would be required to put down 30 or 35% to get a mortgage. The mortgage would probably not exceed 20 years. Now you can buy a home for as little as 5% down and even that you can usually borrow. Maturities now go up to 30 years. This has made mortgage credit available to many more people. And a well functioning secondary market has insured that mortgage rates are very reasonable.

In the last few years' financial institutions have been pushing interest only mortgages. With these the borrower pays only interest for several years then his/her payments increase dramatically as he/she starts paying principle plus interest. These types of loans are very risky for most borrowers and for financial institutions. The borrower does not accumulate equity in the early years of the loan. If home prices fall the borrower has a loan exceeding the value of the home. And when payments rise the borrower may no longer be able to service the loan. The amortized loan was one of the important innovations to come out of the Great Depression. Interest only loans are likely to lead to disaster if long-term interest rates rise and real estate values fall. The same is true of balloon mortgages. Here the borrower pays a modest payment for several years then the balance of the loan is due. He must either refinance the loan or pay it in full. Either case may be an untenable situation if interest rates have risen or if real estate values have fallen.

Credit card debt is the main area where cost of credit is still very expensive. This results from the fact that credit card companies find it easier to issue credit cards to practically all comers and let the good customers subsidize the bad customers. And they allow minimum payments that cover little more than interest. Credit card debt should be amortized just like mortgage debt is but over a much shorter maturity, say three or four years. Giving unsecured credit with almost infinite maturity is a recipe for disaster for many consumers and also for many small businesses that use credit card debt. Unfortunately it will take a financial crisis in the credit card market to bring reform to the system.

Credit markets for large corporations are well organized with active secondary markets. Most corporations that need funds can get them as long as they maintain a good credit rating. Small businesses face more serious limits on credit availability. Partly it's because small businesses have very uncertain income streams and are often not very profitable; partly it is because small businesses often do not have good bookkeeping and thus are unable to provide accurate records to financial institutions; partly it is because they often rely on credit card debt that is very expensive.

## SUMMARY

Financial markets serve to allocate funds from savers to borrower. Well functioning financial markets are crucial for the functioning of a modern economy. In general the developed economies of Western Europe, the US, Canada, Japan and Australia have well functioning financial markets. As we shall see in Chapter 24, many developing countries do not have well functioning financial markets. Well functioning financial markets include well developed secondary markets. In the absence of secondary markets long-term funds will be very expensive and this will be a deterrent to development. In order to have well functioning secondary markets you need relatively stable exchange rates and relatively low and stable inflation. In the US most firms and households have access to relatively low cost funds. There are exceptions. Credit card debt for households is expensive and the system encourages overuse of credit card debt by those people that can least afford it. Also for some small businesses, debt is expensive and hard to obtain. This is partly because of the uncertainty of income for many small businesses. Many small businesses end up financing much of their short-term debt on credit cards. This is very expensive and very risky.

## REVIEW QUESTIONS

Multiple Choice: Select the correct answer:

1. When the market price of bonds fall, current yields on bonds:
   a. Fall
   b. Rise
   c. Remain same
2. When interest rates rise bond prices will normally:
   a. Fall
   b. Rise
   c. Remain same
3. When stock prices rise, dividend yields normally:
   a. Rise
   b. Fall
   c. Remain same
4. When market interest rates rise or fall, the longer the maturity of a bond:
   a. The greater will be the volatility of its price
   b. The less the volatility of its price
   c. The will be no effect on price volatility
5. When the return on assets exceeds the cost of debt, increases in leverage can:
   a. Decrease the return on equity
   b. Increase the return on equity.
   c. Have no affect on the return on equity

### Essays

1. List and explain the main factors that limit availability of credit to firms.
2. Distinguish between primary markets and secondary markets. Why are secondary markets important? Explain.
3. The price of a stock represents the present value of its expected income stream. What makes up the expected income stream? Explain.
4. What do we mean when we say that a bond is selling at a premium or selling at a discount.

## SUGGESTED READINGS

Auerbach, Paul, *Competition: The Economics of Industrial Change*, Paperback Edition, Oxford: Blackwell, 1989, 148–201.

Burton, Maureen and Raymond Lombra, *The Financial System and the Economy, Principles of Money and Banking*, 3rd ed. Mason, Oh: Thompson-Southwest, 2003: Chapters 17, 18, 19.

Herendeen, James B. "The Role of Credit in the Theory of the Household, *Journal of Consumer Affairs*," 8, no. 2 (Winter 1974): 157–181.

Herendeen, James B. *The Economics of The Corporate Economy*, New York: Dunellen Publishing Company, 1975, 93–107.

Keown, Arthur J., David F. Scott Jr., John D. Martin, and J. William Petty. *Foundations of Finance: The Logic and Practice of Financial Management*, Englewood Cliffs: Prentice Hall, 1–25; 150–231.

Schumpeter, Joseph A. *Business Cycles, A Theoretic, Historic and Statistical Analysis of the Capitalist Process*, Abridged, New York: McGraw-Hill, 1939, 83–104.

## *Chapter Twenty-Two*

# Banking and Financial Services: Regulation and Deregulation

## INTRODUCTION

To understand the current structure of regulation of the banking industry we need to look at how the industry and its regulatory structure have evolved over the last 70 years. The current regulatory structure has evolved primarily from the regulations that came out of the Great Depression.

## THE GREAT DEPRESSION AND BANK REGULATION

During the Great Depression some 9000 banks, out of a total of about 25,000, became insolvent between 1930 and 1933. When President Roosevelt took office in 1933, many banks were already closed. He declared a Bank Holiday, closing all banks until they could be examined by the Treasury Department. Those that were solvent reopened; those that were insolvent closed. There was no deposit insurance then and millions of depositors lost part or all of their deposited funds. The President and Congress moved quickly to pass emergency bank legislation in 1933. The act passed was known as the Glass-Steagall Act. This act established the Federal Deposit Insurance Corporation (FDIC) that was to insure deposits of the banking system up to $2500 per account (later increased to $5000 per account). After World War II it was increased several more times until in 1980, it became $100,000 per account where it has remained since.

Second, the act separated investment banking from commercial banking. Commercial banks could not do investment banking and investment banks could not do commercial banking. Commercial banks could make loans and issue both checkable and non-checkable deposits. Other depository institutions were not allowed to issue checkable deposits. Investment banks had three primary functions: they could underwrite securities, (both debt and equity), they could trade securities, and they could sell securities at retail. The rational for the separation was to separate the more risky activities of investment banking from the supposedly less risky activities of commercial banking. It was thought at the time that the underwriting and trading activities had contributed to the failure of many banks. In hindsight this appears not to have been the case. Third, the act established deposit rate ceilings on non-checkable deposits and prohibited interest payments on checkable deposits. Also, even before the Great Depression there were branching laws both within states and between states that restricted branching either within a state or between states. The Mc Fadden Act prohibited interstate branching in 1927. This meant that banks were not allowed to branch across stare lines. The purpose of these branching laws was to protect small local and regional banks from competition from large city banks. Each state established its own within state branching laws.

The regulations of the 1930s must be understood in the context of the times. The nation was in the depth of the Great Depression and the banking industry was broke. The regulatory structure was designed to support the banking industry and to protect depositors. The US was still a nation of many small country banks, often family owned. In a sense the legislation was designed to save the family bank (as farm legislation at the time was designed to save the family farm). Zero interest on checking accounts and regulated interest of savings accounts were designed to keep the cost of funds to banks low. Deposit insurance for the public ensured that they would accept the low yields on their funds. But also it was decided that the FED could not be relied on to contain a run on banks with out the help deposit insurance. The branching laws were intended to protect small banks from the competition of the large money center banks. For forty years the system seemed to work well. Bank regulation and deposit insurance was considered one of the success stories of the New Deal Legislation of the 1930s. The banking industry recovered after World War II and there were no major bank failures until the 1980s.

## INFLATION: RISING INTEREST RATES AND FINANCIAL INNOVATION IN THE 70s

The 1970s brought rising inflation and rising interest rates. The system that had worked so well for forty years suddenly became a burden to the banking industry and to other depository institutions. With market rates increasing and much above the regulated rates of banks, thrifts and credit unions and with banks not allowed to pay interest on checking accounts, the industry found it difficult to raise funds. Banks innovated around the regulations by issuing large negotiable certificates of deposit that were unregulated. Brokerage firms developed money market funds that offered much higher rates to the small investor. Banks and other depository institutions borrow short-term and lend long term. With short-term rates rising relative to long rates, profitability of banks and thrifts was quickly eroded.

## 1980: DEREGULATION

By 1980 pressure from the industry and the regulatory agencies induced Congress to act. The result was the Depository Institution Deregulation and Monetary Control Act (DIDMCA) of 1980. This act was the first major bank legislation since the 1930s. It did several things. First it allowed all depository institutions (Commercial Banks, Thrifts, and Credit Unions) to issue interest bearing NOW (Negotiable Order of Withdrawal) accounts, which were in affect checking accounts on which interest could be paid. Gone were checking accounts that were not allowed to pay interest and gone was the bank monopoly in issuing them. Second, it ended regulation of interest paid on noncheckable deposits. Third, it standardized reserve requirements for all depository institutions. Now all were required to hold reserves at the FED and all had the same percentage reserve requirements. Third it allowed thrift institutions to enter new loan markets. Before they had been restricted to mortgage loans or government securities. Last it increased deposit insurance to $100,000 per account.

## THE THRIFT CRISIS

The Thrift Crisis was from 1981 to 1989. The basic cause of the problem was that in the early 1980s short-term interest rates rose relative to long-term rates. Thrifts basically borrow short term and lend long term. When short rates rise relative to long rates it means their cost of funds have risen relative to their yield on funds. This eliminated the profits of many thrifts and also of some banks. Banks were hit less severely during this period because they were much less reliant on real estate mortgages as their major use of funds. Even though thrifts were allowed to enter new markets with the 1980 Act, they still relied mainly on mortgages. When they did enter new markets it was often high-risk markets where they had little expertise. In 1981 and 1982 there was a recession that also severely eroded the profits of banks and thrifts. As a result by the middle eighties about one third of the thrift industry was insolvent. The Federal Savings and Loan Deposit Insurance Corporation did not have enough money to close them down. Regulations were relaxed to allow them to continue to operate in hopes that the problems would go away.

A secondary market in insured deposits was allowed to develop. This allowed thrifts and banks to sell insured deposits to brokerage firms in units of $100,000. The brokerage firms could resell them to the public in smaller units. Because they were government insured the brokerage firms and the public were glad to buy them, irrespective of the financial condition of the issuing thrifts or banks. This allowed many thrifts to continue to operate even though they were technically insolvent. Another policy that aided troubled banks was called the "Too Big to Fail Policy." This policy said in effect that some banks were too big to fail and that if they got in trouble the FED and the FDIC would intervene to prevent failure. This doctrine, in affect, guaranteed the deposits of non-insured depositors. Both brokered insured deposits and the "Too Big to Fail Policy" gave banks and thrifts, especially those who had little or no capital left, an incentive to take high risks. The government was in effect taking over the downside risk. If a bank or thrift gambled and won it got to keep the money; if it gambled and lost, the government picked up the losses.

## PARTIAL RE-REGULATION: 1989

Finally in 1989 Congress was forced to act. The result was the Financial Institutions and Recovery, Reform and Enforcement Act (FIRREA). It did several things. First it authorized the bailout of the Thrift Industry. It did this by creating the Resolution Trust Corporation that was empowered to take over and dispose of the assets of the insolvent Thrifts. The FSLIC was abolished and a new agency, the Saving Association Insurance Fund (SAIF) was established in the FDIC. Also established in the FDIC was the Bank Insurance Fund (BIF) for Commercial Banks. The Office of Thrift Regulation was established in the Treasury Department. Also thrifts were again restricted in the type of assets that could be held. 70 percent of their assets had to be mortgages or mortgage backed securities. They had to divest themselves of high-risk bonds (often called junk bonds) and were limited in the amount of real estate development loans they could make. The total cost to taxpayer of cleaning up the Thrift Crisis has been estimated to be $150–200 billion.

## THE BANKING CRISIS: 1989–91

In the late eighties and early nineties there was a banking crisis, very similar to the thrift crisis of a few years earlier. It came later in part because banks had a shorter maturity structure of loans than thrifts and thus were better able to weather the high short-term interest rates of the early eighties. However, in the late eighties several things contributed to problems for many banks. First, the end of the Cold War led to cut backs of defense expenditures. This hit New England and Southern California especially hard. In 1986, the oil market collapsed and this hit Texas very hard. In 1989 the collapse of the junk (high risk) bond market also had its effect. Banks could not buy junk bonds but they made loans to Investment Bankers and Corporate Raiders that were using junk bonds to finance mergers and takeovers. Added to all of this, the FED started raising interest rates to slow the expansion. Many banks were in trouble and a few were taken over by the FDIC. Banks had the same incentives to take high risk as thrifts because of deposit insurance, brokered deposits and the "Too Big to Fail Policy." The banking crisis might have been much worse but the FED lowered interest rates sharply as the economy entered the 1990–91 recession. The Federal funds rate came down from 8.5% in 1989 to 3% in 1992. Long-term rates fell much less and the spread between short rates and long rates on government securities was about four percentage points. Banks borrow short and lend long and many banks that were in trouble in 1990 were suddenly profitable again in 1992. The FED was not lowering interest rates to save the banks but rather to bring the economy out of recession, but it had the effect of saving the banks anyway.

## 1991: DEPOSIT INSURANCE REFORM

Partially as a result of the banking crisis, Congress passed, in 1991, the Federal Deposit Insurance Corporation Act (FDICA). This act did several things. First it abolished the "Too Big to Fail Policy." Second it restricted brokered deposits to only those institutions that had strong balance sheets. Third it established new capital adequacy requirements for banks and thrifts. Capital adequacy requirements are imposed by the FDIC and are a way of protecting the Insurance Fund. They vary with the type of assets held but usually are about 6%-8% of assets. Capital is the value of the firms stock. Secondary capital also includes long-term debt. Third it gave the FDIC the power to borrow from the Treasury if insurance funds were inadequate (as they were in the eighties). Fourth, it established risk based insurance premiums. Before, all banks and thrifts had paid the same insurance premium rates. Now institutions with high-risk balance sheets would pay higher premiums rates.

## CAUSES OF THE PROBLEMS FOR DEPOSITORY INSTITUTIONS

During the late seventies and early eighties trucking, airlines and depository institutions were all de-regulated. However, only with depository institutions did serious problems occur. What was different about the banking industry? The difference was that in airlines and trucking there was no government guarantee of the liabilities of the firms in the industry. Several airlines went broke in the eighties as did several trucking companies, but the government was not obligated to bail them out. In the banking and thrift industries the government guaranteed the major liabilities of the industry with deposit insurance and the "Too Big to Fail Doctrine." This gave banks and thrifts an incentive to take high risk, especially when their capital was depleted, and required that the government come to their rescue if their high-risk investments failed. Allowing brokered deposits to develop only made the problem worse.

## THE 1990S: DEREGULATION AND THE BANK MERGER MOVEMENT

From 1993 through 2000 we had a booming economy and a booming banking industry. Most states had removed their interstate branching laws in the 1970s and 1980s. Pressure had been building for years to repeal the interstate branching laws. During the late eighties and early 1990s the FED and the Office of the Comptroller of Currency (OCC) had granted many exceptions allowing many Bank Holding Companies to branch across state lines. In 1994 Congress passed the Interstate Banking and Branching Efficiency Act (IBBEA). This act repealed the McFadden Act of 1927 that had prohibited interstate branching. This act, plus high profits in the banking industry, drove the merger movement of the 1990s. Many of the nations largest banks moved quickly though mergers and acquisitions to become national in scope. Most were already international. Included were such banks as Bank of America, City Bank (later City Group), Chase, Wells Fargo and Bank One.

The argument was that mergers would lead to economies of scale and lower cost and provide better service to customers. It did lead to a relatively small number of large national and international banks. Whether it led to lower cost or better service for customers is still debatable. The main complaint against the large banks is that they are not much interested in small customers. Small deposits are relatively unprofitable. Small loans are both unprofitable and relatively high risk. Fortunately in most markets there are credit unions, thrifts, finance companies, small local banks and the Small Business Administration that service many of the smaller customers. The exception is the credit card business. The big banks have made a major drive to get credit cards to any one that will take them, good credit or bad. The reason is that the credit card business is very profitable. Interest rates run around 18%, late fees are very high and the retailer also must pay a fee of 2% or 3% of the value of the sale to the credit card company. The customer can avoid the high costs if he pays off his balance monthly but still usually pays an annual fee. In today's world most people need credit cards, the problem is that the minimum payments include little more than interest and people often get in over their head. The companies take these high risks because the high interest rates and fees allow the good customers and the retailers to subsidize the bad customers.

In 1999 came further deregulation. After years of debate, Congress eliminated the separation of commercial banking and investment banking that had existed under the Glass-Steagall Act since 1933. The new law allowed bank holding companies to own investment banks and insurance companies as well as banks and other related firms. The investment banks and insurance companies were to be run as separate subsidiaries in order to safeguard the Deposit Insurance System. The question is, are the separations of investment banks, commercial banks and insurance companies complete enough to avoid another banking crisis similar to the one of the late eighties and early nineties? Even if they are, are the large banks immune from the temptation of using insured deposits to finance high-risk loans as they and the thrifts did in the late eighties and early-nineties?

With the current low interest rates, banks have been pushing real estate loans and real estate refinancing. This is contributing to a boom in the real estate industry. As the FED starts raising rates as the economy continues to expand, will we get a collapse in the real estate market and financial difficulties for some banks and perhaps also for Fanny Mae and Ginny Mae the two main buyers of real estate mortgages? The government is not obligated to bail out Fanny Mae and Ginny Mae if they get in trouble, but most observers feel that they will have to if a crisis develops. The same is true of uninsured deposits of the large banks. The "Too Big to Fail Policy" was eliminated, but the Fed has never said that it would not come to the aid of a large bank should there be a crisis. Only time will tell if the current system can weather a serious financial crisis.

## THE "NARROW BANKING" CONCEPT

During the late eighties and early nineties there was considerable discussion of the concept known as "narrow banking". It was a revival of the idea of 100% reserves that had been discussed in the 1930s. 100% reserves was a plan for banks to back all deposits with either reserves (vault cash or deposits at the FED) or with government securities. Loans would have to be made by separate institutions that would raise their funds by borrowing, issuing debt securities or issuing capital. They would not be allowed to issue checkable deposits or saving accounts. The idea was to separate the money creation function of banks from the loan function. During the thirties and again in the eighties the collapse of loans had led to the collapse of deposits and thus the money supply. Once deposit insurance was passed in 1933, interest in the 100% reserves plan declined, as it was no longer viewed as necessary.

The crisis of the eighties and early nineties led to a revival of the idea in a somewhat different form. A leading proponent of the idea was James Pierce of the University of California-Berkeley. The idea was that banks should be divided into separate and independent subsidiaries. In the narrow bank subsidiary all funds would be raised as insured deposits, both checkable and non-checkable, and bank capital. The assets the narrow bank could hold would be bank reserves, government securities and prime commercial paper (short term debt of highly rated corporations). The loan subsidiary of the bank would make loans and could also hold government securities and probably even corporate securities. However its funds would have to be raised by non-insured deposits, by borrowing, by issuing securities or by issuing capital. It would not be allowed to issue checkable or non-checkable insured deposits. The loan subsidiaries would be similar to finance companies except that they could also issue uninsured deposits.

The main criticism of the idea was that the narrow banks would never be completely separate from the loan subsidiaries and other lenders. The reason is that loan proceeds have to be deposited to a checking account before they can be spent. And loans that are paid off have to be paid off by writing a check on a checking account (unless they are simply refinanced.). This means that the assets and liabilities of the narrow bank would fluctuate with the lending process. The main difference is that they would be better protected from insolvency because of their holdings of safe assets. And the narrow bank could always buy government securities to offset losses of deposits and to replenish reserves.

If we have another banking crisis in the future the narrow banking concept may see another revival. Policy makers and regulators lost interest in the early nineties when the FED lowered interest rates and the banking industry recovered.

## SUMMARY

In this chapter we have looked at the history of bank regulation from the early thirties up to the present (2006). The regulations of the thirties were in response to the Great Depression. Congress had to act both to help the banking system recover but also to revive confidence in the system by the public. The system that came out of the thirties worked well until it was hit with high interest rates, inflation and financial innovation in the seventies. This led to deregulation in 1980. Unfortunately deregulation on the asset side while the liabilities were guaranteed by the government gave perverse incentives that contributed to the thrift crisis and later the banking crisis. This led to a certain amount of re-regulation in 1989 and 1992. This re-regulation was designed primarily to protect the deposit insurance system. In the nineties we saw further deregulation of banking and financial services. This de-regulation may again make the system vulnerable to the type of excesses that developed in the eighties.

## REVIEW QUESTIONS

Multiple Choice: Select the correct answer:

1. State chartered banks:
   a. May choose be members of the FED
   b. Must be members of the FED
   c. Are not members of the FED
2. Deposit Insurance encourages banks to:
   a. Hold riskier assets
   b. Hold safer assets
   c. Neither of the above
3. Large numbers of banks in the US reflect mainly:
   a. The competitive nature of the industry
   b. The past regulatory structure of the industry
   c. Neither of the above

### Essays

1. What are the primary policy tools of the FED? How does each work? Explain
2. What is the "Narrow Banking Concept?" How would narrow banking separate the money creation function of banks from the credit creation function of banks?

3. During the late 70s and early 80s banking, trucking and airlines were all deregulated. The banking industry developed problems and was partially re-regulated in 1989 and 92. Why did the banking industry develop problems while the others did not? What was different about banking deregulation?

## SUGGESTED READINGS

Black, William, "Reexamining the Law-and-Economics Theory of Corporate Governance," *Challenge, The Magazine of Economic Affairs*, 46, no. 2 (March/April, 2003): 22–40.

Burton, Maureen and Ray Lombra, *The Financial System and the Economy*, 3rd Edition, Mason, Ohio: Thomson-Southwestern, 2003, Chapters 12, 13, 14, 15.

Kane, Edward J., *The Gathering Crisis*, Cambridge: The MIT Press, 1985.

Kane, Edward, *The S&L Crisis, How Did It Happen?* Washington, DC: The Urban Institute Press, 1989.

Litan, Robert, "Remedy for the S&Ls: Operation Clean Sweep," *Challenge: The Magazine of Economic Affairs*, 33, no. 6 (November/December, 1990): 26–32.

Phillips, Ronnie J. *The Chicago Plan and New Deal Banking Reform*, Armonk, N.Y.: M. E. Shape, Inc., 1995.

Pierce, James L. *The Future of Banking*, New Haven: Yale University Press, 1991.

Williams, William McFetridge, *The Politics of Boom and Bust in Twentieth Century America: A Macroeconomic History*, (Minneapolis, MN, West Publishing Company, 1994): 153–191; 415–465

# *Chapter Twenty-Three*

# Social Security: Is the System Going Broke?

## HOW THE SYSTEM WORKS

The Social Security System faces many problems, but none as serious as the Health Care System. This is primarily because it does not face the third party payer problem that we have in health care and to a lesser extent in public and private education. The government pays Social Security to eligible recipients. These are mainly the elderly, the disabled and dependents of Social Security recipients. These recipients get to spend the money as they see fit; there are no third party payers. Working people pay social security withholding over their working lifetime. Their employer pays in an equal amount. This is currently about 7.5 % of the salary for each. (Part of this is for Medicare.) For the employer, it is a tax-deductible expense; for the employee it is not. Social Security is withheld only from wage and salary income. It is not withheld from interest income, rental income or net profit. The self-employed do have to pay on their wage and salary income at the full rate. Also social security is withheld only up to a maximum income level, currently about $90,000. Recipients get benefits based on how much they have paid in and at what age they retire. You can retire at 62 and receive a reduced benefit. You can retire at 65 and get the standard benefit. This is currently at a maximum of about $16,000 per year. You can wait until 70 and get a higher benefit. But realize if you wait until 70, you will likely have fewer years to draw benefits. Social Security also pays benefits to disabled people if they have paid into the system long enough to be eligible or if they are a dependent of a recipient. And they pay reduced benefits to surviving spouses of recipients.

Social Security is a transfer program not a true pension system. The reason is that today's recipients are paid out of current contributions from today's payers. This means that it is a transfer from the working to the non-working. Except that some recipients are still working, because if you are over 65 you can earn income and still draw social security. In a true pension plan, members of the plan pay in over their lifetime and the money is invested in securities or real estate and earns interest or profits that are re-invested and accumulate over the years of contributions. This money is then used to pay retirees when they retire. Often with private plans, the company contributes part, or all of the contribution. But the employee can only draw on the company contribution if they work enough years to be vested.

Currently the social security system is running a small surplus of about 250 billion dollars. This is partly because the generation drawing benefits is the pre-baby boom generation, which was a relatively small cohort. The primary payers into the system are the baby boom generation, a relatively large cohort. But that will all change in another five years or so as the baby boom generation will start retiring and the primary generation paying in will be the post baby boom generation, another small cohort. The estimates are that the system will be running large deficits in another 10 or 15 years unless the system is reformed. There are several other reasons that the system is getting expensive. One is that we have an aging population. When Social security was adopted in 1935 the average life expectancy of men was about 65 years. This meant that you only had a 50% chance that you would live long enough to collect. Now the average life expectancy of men is about 78 years and for women about 81 years. We now have about three workers for every retired person. 50 years ago the ratio was about seven workers for each retired person. Also part of the Medicare program is paid for out of social security contributions. And Medicare expenditure have been increasing rapidly both because of rising cost of health care and because of the aging population.

## POSSIBLE REFORMS

The best way to reduce cost in the long run is to convert it to a mandatory government run pension system. This would reduce cost because the funds contributed would be invested and earn income that would be reinvested into the system. Private pension plans with similar withholding rates pay much higher benefits. The reason is that they earn and reinvest interest, dividends and capital gain on the invested funds over the working life of the beneficiary. If this is so why do we not convert to a pension (prepaid) system for Social Security? The primary reason is the transition costs. While converting, existing retirees and future retirees would still have to be paid their benefits until the transition was complete. This would mean that costs would have to rise for several years during the transition. The other primary reason is that Social Security contributions also fund much of Medicare. To have the system work well would require that we also convert to a prepaid system for Medicare that would also have high transition costs. (See Chapter 12.) Congress is strictly short run in its policy views. It is unlikely to increase current costs for future savings that may be years getting here. Other countries have gone to the prepaid system with very good results. Chile in South America is the most prominent example.

Much more likely is that Congress will make small changes to the present system. One option that is already being implemented is to increase the retirement age to 70. People could still retire earlier but at reduced benefits. With the increase in life expectancy, it makes sense to increase the retirement age. Under current law it will gradually increase over several years.

Another possibility is to reduce the indexing to the consumer price index. Under current law benefits are indexed to the Consumer Price Index. This means that if, for any given year, the CPI increases by 6% per year that benefits the following year will increase by 6%. Many economists believe that the CPI overstates the true rate of inflation, mainly because it does not adequately account for quality changes in products and services that are used to construct the index. It has been proposed that the indexing be reduced by one percentage point. If the index increased by 6%, then benefits would increase by 5%. With inflation rates being low in recent years this has reduced the political pressure to change the indexing.

If inflation should again rise, the issue will return. The main argument against this correction is that the CPI may not accurately reflect the cost of living of the elderly. This is because the prices of some services have been increasing much faster than the CPI. These services include health care, prescription drugs and legal services. These hit the elderly much harder than the rest of the population.

Another option that has been recommended by the Bush Administration is to put a portion of each person's contribution into mutual funds where the person would have some choice of how to invest the funds. The idea being that these funds would earn more than funds invested in government securities. The problem is that now only the surplus is invested in government securities and even that is a misnomer as Congress treats the surplus as part of current revenues and spends it. So the surplus is actually just a promissory note from Congress. Anyway with the stock market down, there is little chance that the proposal will pass Congress. Another option would be to increase the withholding limit. It has gradually increased over time anyway. In fact why have a limit. Why not allow social security to be deducted from all wage and salary income? The main argument against this is that benefits are limited so therefore withholding should be to. But if the system is going to be run as a transfer program why not make it less regressive.

Currently low income working people pay more in social security withholding than they do in income tax because there are no exemptions for the social security tax. The only exemption is for high-income people whose income is above the current limit. That portion of their income is exempt from Social Security withholding. And their non-wage income is completely exempt. The point is that there are lots of adjustments that could be made to make the current system solvent. If the system is going to be run as a transfer system, it makes little difference how the surplus is invested, since there isn't much surplus and if there are not soon some changes made, the surplus will disappear anyway. If we convert to a true pension system then of course it makes a lot of difference how the money is invested. If this option were to be chosen then Congress would need to set up an independent agency, similar to the Federal Reserve, to be in charge of managing the funds. But more likely Congress will continue to tinker with the existing system.

## DOUBLE TAXATION OF SOCIAL SECURITY WITHHOLDING

Another issue is the double taxation of social security withholding. We make a big deal out of the double taxation of dividends, but most people don't even realize that Social Security withholdings are also double taxed. The Social Security withholding is a tax on wage and salary income. But the Federal income tax does not allow us to deduct this tax in calculating our taxable income. If we want to give a tax cut that would help low and middle income working families, the best way to do it would be to allow tax exemption of Social Security withholding on the Federal Income Tax. It should be a tax deduction from gross income not an itemized deduction so that it would apply to all taxpayers not just those who itemize deductions.

There are counter arguments to allowing tax deductibility of Social Security withholding. The first is that the standard exemption for people who do not itemize and exemptions for number of family members already gives taxpayers exemptions that partially take care of this problem. The problem is that these standard exemptions are not designed for this purpose. It is intended as a way to simplify the tax return and still allow people to get the itemized exemptions without having to fill out the long form. And the exemption based on the size of the household is intended to recognize that larger families have higher living costs. Neither has any direct relationship to social security withholding.

Most private pensions do get tax exemption (either for the company or the individual depending on who puts the money in) and then you pay taxes on the money when it is withdrawn. IRAs (Investment Retirement Accounts) allow a person to invest additional funds and are tax exempt. You pay tax when the money is withdrawn. With an IRA (Investment Retirement Account) you must start withdrawing at 70.5 years and pay tax on the withdrawals. With a Roth IRA you can pay the tax when the money is invested but then withdraw during retirement tax-free. As long as the Social Security System is run as a transfer system and Congress considers Social Security withholding as part of tax revenue, it seems reasonable to allow tax deductibility. Not only is social security withholding not tax deductible, depending on your income you have to pay tax on up to 85% of your Social Security benefits. A person with private pensions in addition to Social Security usually pays at this top rate. If Social Security was tax deductible then it might make sense to tax social security withdrawals.

The second argument is that it would cost the government too much to do this. The lost tax revenue would have to be made up. But Congress and the President have just given across the board tax cuts and cuts in taxes for both dividends and capital gains despite the fact that the Federal budget is in deficit. And the lost revenue could be made up by removing some of the exemptions that now go to households and to businesses.

## SUMMARY

The Social Security System can be reformed either by going to a true pension system or by making changes in the present system. These reforms are easier to achieve than with the health care system mainly because there is no third party payer problem. Most likely are adjustments of the present system because this is politically much easier to do

## REVIEW QUESTIONS

Multiple Choice: Select the correct answer:

1. The Social Security System is run as a:
   a. Pension system
   b. Transfer system
   c. Insurance system

2. Increasing the retirement age would:
    a. Reduce the cost of the Social Security System
    b. Increase the cost of the Social security System
    c. Not affect the cost of the Social Security System

### Essays

1. Why have the costs of the social Security System increased over time and why will they increase much more over the next 20 years or so?
2. Converting to a pension system rather than a transfer system for Social Security would reduce costs and increase returns in the long run but would increase costs in the short run. Explain why.

## SUGGESTED READINGS

Adler, Moshe, "Can Economic Growth Save Social Security," *Challenge: the Magazine of Economic Affairs*, 44, no. 5 (September–October 2001): 88–94.

Gramlich, Edward M. "Different Approaches for Dealing with Social Security," *American Economic Review: Papers and Proceedings*, 86, no. 2 (May 1996): 358–62.

Kotlikoff, Laurence J., "Privatizing Social Security at Home and Abroad," *American Economic Review: Papers and Proceedings*, 86, no. 2 (May, 1996): 368–73.

Michl, T. "Why We Should Fund Social Security Permanently, *Challenge: The Magazine of Economic Affairs*," 44, no 6 (November-December, 2001): 78–92.

Mitchell, Olivia S., "Social Security Privatization: A Structure for Analysis," *American Economic Review, Papers and Proceedings*, 86, no. 2 (May 1996): 363–67.

Palley, Thomas, "Social Security: Pre-funding is Not the Answer," *Challenge, The Magazine of Economic Affairs*, 45, no. 2 (March–April, 2002): 97–118.

# *Chapter Twenty-Four*

# Growth and Development: Why Some Countries Grow and Others Do Not

## GROWTH AND DEVELOPMENT

What do we mean by growth? In economics growth normally refers to growth of aggregate income, growth in per capita income, or growth in income per worker. Which measure we use depends primarily on the purpose of the analysis. For our purposes growth in per capita income or growth in income per worker will be most useful. Normally the two will move together. In order to have per capita income grow, aggregate income must grow faster than the population. In order to have per worker income grown, aggregate income must grow faster than the employed work force. If population growth exceeds aggregate growth, then per capita income will decline. If the number of workers grows faster than the aggregate income then income per worker must decline. As we pointed out in Chapter 16, average income per worker can only grow if average output per worker grows. The problem is; how does average income per worker grow over time? We will discuss this below.

What do we mean by development. Usually when we talk about development, we also talk about growth. But development is broader than growth. Development usually means development of the institutions that make growth possible. These institutions include a stable government that encourages growth, a system of markets that allows capital accumulation, a system of property rights that allows individuals to keep a portion of the output they produce, an exchange rate system that avoids wide swings in the value of a countries currency, a monetary system that stabilizes domestic inflation, a financial system that allows financing of both the production process and the consumption process, an educational system that allows broad access to education, a political system that allows broad participation in the political process.

## WHY ARE SOME COUNTRIES RICH AND OTHER COUNTRIES POOR?

If we go back 250 years the developed countries of today were poor countries. Development, as we know it today, started with the industrial revolution. The industrial revolution occurred first in England (in the latter half of the 1700s), then spread to Western Europe, then the United States, then Canada and Australia. In the last 50 years it has spread to Japan, Korea, Malaysia, Indonesia, Hong Kong, Singapore, Mexico, China and India. Rich countries are rich because they have high output and income per worker. Poor countries are poor because they have low output and income per worker. But that doesn't tell us why this is the case. How did the rich countries become rich? Why have the poor countries remained poor?

The rich countries became rich through a long process of economic and institutional change. Prior to the industrial revolution, any surplus created by producers was taxed away to finance armies, to build cathedrals, and to be consumed by the very small ruling elite. Poor countries tax the many to support the few. The industrial revolution in England in the last half of the 18th Century allowed large increases in output per worker though the application of machinery to the production process. The steam engine as a source of power was a driving force in this revolution. Suddenly England was rich enough to fight its wars and still have a surplus left in the hands of entrepreneurs to reinvest in future increases in output.

But this probably wouldn't have happened without the political revolution of the previous Century that gave political power to the middle class. And along with the industrial revolution came the development of the banking system and the development of the corporate form of enterprise that allowed the organization and financing of the production process. In addition there was the legal revolution that defined property rights, enforced and defined contracts and defined the legal structure of the corporation. In other words, economic development came along with the development of a whole set of supporting institutions.

Some countries are rich because they have governments that have fostered and promoted institutions that are conducive to economic development. Some countries are poor because these institutions have failed to develop. The late economist Mancur Olson once said, "Poor countries are typically misgoverned, or are anarchies with no government at all, which is worse." By misgoverned he meant governments that ruled for the benefit of a narrow elite and taxed the many to the point where they had no chance of accumulating capital and no chance of developing a middle class society.

Although the majority of the world is still poor, great progress has been made over the last 50 years. Western Europe had per capita incomes of maybe half those of the US in 1950. Today their incomes are roughly comparable to the U.S. This is because for forty years after WWII their per capita incomes grew at a 5–6% annual rate, while ours grew at a 2–3% annual rate. For them growth was relatively easy because they had most of the institutions in place. Once they were relieved of the burden of large war and defense expenditures, their economies grew rapidly. This spurt of growth has now ended and for the last 15 years or so U.S. growth has been considerably faster than that of Western Europe. Much of Southeast Asia has also grown rapidly over the past 20 or 30 years.

Whereas if we look at much of South and Central America, at sub-Sahara Africa, and at the Middle East we see that per-capita income have grown very little. In South America only Chile, and perhaps Brazil, have made substantial progress. In Argentina per capita incomes are less today than they were 50 years ago. Mexico has made substantial progress in the last 15 years.

## THE ROLE OF SOCIAL OVERHEAD CAPITAL

A necessary condition for development is investment in what economists call social overhead capital. This includes such things as public education, highway systems, canals, ports, airports, railroads, water and sewer systems, public health care and many more. In the US, free public education started soon after the adoption of the Constitution. Much of this was done at the local level. As land was opened up for development, land was set aside for elementary schools within walking distance for the students. These country schools continued to be important up until the 1940s and 1950s when Central Schools, where students were bussed to school, gradually replaced them.

Public support for higher education came first at the state level with the establishment of State Teachers Colleges. Federal support for higher education came with the Morrill Act during the Civil War. This act provided grants of public land to the States that could be sold and the proceeds used to set up State Universities to teach "Agriculture and the Mechanic Sciences." The Mechanic Sciences became Engineering. Every state has at least one Land Grant University and over the years they have expanded their curriculum to become all-purpose Universities. Many of our great public universities are land grant universities: Berkeley, Wisconsin, Cornell (part public and part private), Texas A&M, Iowa State, Penn State, Minnesota, Purdue and many more.

In the early 19th century state governments subsidized the building of canals. In the later part of the 19th century both the state and federal governments subsidized the construction of the railroad system. State, local and the federal government have subsidized water and sewer systems for our cities. In the 20th century state and federal government have subsidized the construction of highway systems. Primarily the federal government, with state governments putting up some matching funds, built the Interstate Highway System. This greatly reduced the cost of transportation by allowing larger carriers and much faster travel and spurred whole new industries along the Interstate System: motels, hotels, restaurants, gas stations, truck stops, vacation travel, travel trailers, automobiles and many more.

The point is that development requires investment in all kinds of social overhead capital. In the absence of this kind of investment, development is very difficult. Many poor countries do not have the money to make these investments. The World Bank as well as other private and public international lenders has furnished money for these types of projects. Unfortunately, in many cases the money has not led to development. Many of the countries that have received World Bank loans are no better off now than they were 40 years ago. The reasons are many: often the money has been siphoned off by corrupt government officials; often it has been invested in projects that benefit the ruling elite but does little for the majority of the people; often the loans have had to be renewed and sometimes written off. The countries that have relied least on help from the World Bank have been the most successful.

Most developing countries have governments that represent tiny ruling elites. If these ruling elites are willing to let a middle class develop and eventually share political power with that middle class then development may follow. This appears to have been the case in Southeast Asia, in some of the Eastern European Countries, in Chile, in Mexico, and more recently in India and perhaps China. In most of Sub-Sahara Africa, in the Middle East (except for Israel), and in much of South and Central America, this has not been the case.

In other words the most important condition for development, is having a government that is willing to promote development by allowing and promoting the institutions that are necessary for development to occur: A well functioning banking system, enforceable property rights, enforceable rights of contract, a well functioning transportation system, a stable currency and stable exchange rates (in terms of purchasing power), a well functioning system of secondary financial markets, an economic system that is basically competitive; an education system that allows broad access to education and an open political system.

## THE ROLE OF MARKETS

Markets by themselves do not guarantee development. Markets have been around for thousands of years. Development, as we think of it, has only been around about 250 years. Development requires a government that can guarantee property rights, guarantee contracts, provide the necessary social overhead capital and not tax away the entire surplus that production creates. Without a surplus to invest growth and development are impossible. Markets are only one of the many things necessary for development.

## GLOBALIZATION: PROBLEMS AND PROSPECTS

Globalization means different things to different people. For most it means the spread of western values and culture to the rest of the world. Theses values include democratic political institutions, market oriented economic systems, the rule of law, secure property rights, a protected and sustainable environment, access to education, access to jobs and free trade. Not everyone agrees on all of these points. Many believe in democratic political institutions, but are highly hostile to free trade and market-oriented economies. They believe that high growth is destructive of the environment, and that free trade ends up exporting our high paying jobs to other countries where wage rates are much lower. The problem is that the only way that poor countries can become better off is through growth in income and output per worker. Slower growth in the west not only makes the developed countries worse off; it will also make the poor countries worse off. The poor countries become rich countries by producing goods and services to sell to the west.

However markets for goods and services, markets for funds and markets for money (foreign exchange) all need rules and often regulations, in order to work properly. If people perceive markets as primarily benefiting the rich countries and hurting the poor countries, then they will look for alternative ways to organize the international economic process. If rich countries do not use some of the benefits of growth to protect the environment and help poor countries to also protect the environment, then the arguments for slower growth may become accepted.

Growth and development are not inevitable. We had globalization during the period from about 1870 until World War I. After World War I, with, first the breakdown if the International Monetary System based on the Gold Standard; then the great Depression, which brought international trade to a near halt; and then the devastation of World War II; globalization came almost to a halt for a period of about 40 years. It gradually started again in the mid 1950s, partly as a result of the Marshall plan to help rebuild Europe, partly as a result of new international agencies such as the World Bank and the International Monetary Fund. Globalization really took off in the last 16 years after the collapse of the Soviet Union at the end of the 1980s.

The point is that the move to globalization may not continue. There is opposition from environmentalists (misguided in the author's view), there is opposition from the unions who see loss of jobs to cheaper foreign labor, there is opposition from many firms who see their industry moving overseas for cheaper labor, there is opposition from anti-immigrant groups who see immigrants as taking jobs from domestic workers. Most economists believe that the gains from globalization are much greater than the costs, both for the developed countries and for the developing countries. However, the political process responds to the pressures of well-organized interests. These interests may be able to bring to a halt the globalization process. The best way to prevent this is to reform the globalization process so that it is fairer in terms of stability, growth and distribution of income and fairer in terms of adjustment to financial crisis when countries are forced to devalue their currencies.

## SUMMARY

Some countries are rich because they have developed institutions that have promoted economic development. In the west these institutions have developed over the last 250 years or more. A country can only become rich if it has sustained growth in output and income per worker over a relatively long period of time. These institutions include secure property rights, a stable monetary system with relatively stable exchange rates and inflation, an open political system, a legal system that protects and enforces contracts, the development of secondary markets to ensure access to long term capital funds, a system of taxation that allows workers and business owners to keep a share of the surplus they create and a system of public education that allows easy access to education. Most important a country must allow the development of a middle class if development is to continue.

## REVIEW QUESTIONS

Multiple Choice: Select the correct answer:

1. For the aggregate economy growth in real income per worker requires:
   a. Growth of the price level.
   b. Growth of the work force.
   c. Growth of output per worker.

2. Trend growth in real GDP will rise if:
   a. Trend money growth rises
   b. Trend output per worker rises
   c. Trend inflation rises
   d. None of the above
3. The primary way that poor countries can become rich countries is by:
   a. Government ownership of the means of production
   b. Redistribution of the wealth of the wealthy
   c. Sustained growth in output per worker.
4. Sustained growth in per capita income of a country requires
   a. Growth of the capital stock
   b. Growth of the work force
   c. Growth of output per worker

### Essays

1. List and explain some of the main institutions that a country must develop if it is to achieve sustained in per capita income.
2. Distinguish between economic growth and development.
3. Over the past 50 years some formerly poor countries have had sustained growth in per capita income and have become developed or developing countries. Other countries have remained poor with no appreciable growth in per capita incomes. Why do some countries succeed and others fail?

## SUGGESTED READINGS

Bauer, P. T., *Reality and Rhetoric: Studies in the Economics of Development*, Cambridge: Harvard University Press, 1984.

De Soto, Hernando, *The Mystery of Capital: Why Capitalism Triumphs in the West and Fails Everywhere Else*, New York: Basic Books, 2000.

Diamond, Jared, *Guns Germs and Steel: The Fate of Human Societies*, New York: W. W. Norton, Paperback ed. 1999.

Diamond, Jared, *Collapse: How Societies Choose to Fail or Succeed*, New York: Viking, The Penguin Group, 2005.

Easterly, William, *The Elusive Quest for Growth: Economists': Adventures and Misadventures in the Tropics*, Paperback ed, Cambridge: The MIT Press, 2002.

Mokyr, Joel, *The Lever of Riches: Technological Creativity and Economic Progress*, (Oxford: Oxford University Press, 1990: 3–16.

Olson, Mancur, *The Rise and Decline of Nations*, New Haven, Conn., Yale University Press, 1982.

Olson, Mancur, "Distinguished Lecture on Economics in Government: Big Bills Left On the Sidewalk, Why Some Nations are Rich and Other's are Poor," *The Journal of Economic Perspectives*, 10, no. 2 (Spring, 1996): 3–24.

Olson, Mancur, "The Case For Liberalization of Markets" An Interview with Mancur Olson, Jr., *Challenge: The Magazine of Economic Affairs*, 11, no. 2 (September/October, 1997): 59–76.

Roderik, Dani, "Has Globalization Gone Too Far," Interview with Dani Rodrik, *Challenge: The Magazine of Economic Affairs*, 41, no. 2 (March/April, 1998): 81–94.

Zakiria, Fareed, *The Future of Freedom, Illiberal Democracy at Home and Abroad*, New York: W.W. Norton, 2002.

# Index

# About the Author

**James B. Herendeen** grew up in Farmington, New York (near Rochester). He received his BS from Cornell University, Ithaca, New York, his MS from Iowa State University, Ames, Iowa, and his PhD from the Pennsylvania State University, University Park, Pennsylvania. He joined the Faculty of Economics at Penn State in 1963 and retired from there in 1992 as Professor Emeritus. From 1992–2003 he served first as Visiting Professor then Senior Lecturer at the University of Texas-El Paso.

He has served as Visiting Professor at New Mexico State University, Las Cruces, New Mexico (Winter 1972 and Spring 1986), at the Naval Post Graduate School, Monterey, California (1978–79 academic year), Bond University, Gold Coast, Queensland, Australia (Summer 1990), and The Helsinki School of Economics and Business, Helsinki, Finland (March, 2002).

His publications include *Modern Political Economy: Ideas and Issues*, Editor, (Prentice Hall, 1968), *The Economics of the Corporate Economy*, (New York: Dunellen Publishing Company, 1975) and (with Raymond Lombra and Raymond Torto), *Money and the Financial System*, (New York, McGraw-Hill, 1980).In addition he has published numerous articles in professional journals and periodicals. His research interests have included financial models of the firm and the household, bank regulation, history and evolution of the corporate enterprise, and agricultural policy. His teaching interests have included Micro and Macro Economic Theory (graduate and undergraduate), Money and Banking, Principles of Economics, Issues in Economics and Economics of Corporate Enterprise.